THE INDONESIAN NATIONAL REVOLUTION

STUDIES IN CONTEMPORARY SOUTHEAST ASIA

THE INDONESIAN NATIONAL REVOLUTION 1945–1950

ANTHONY REID

LONGMAN

Longman Australia Pty Limited
Hawthorn Victoria Australia

Associated companies, branches, and representatives
throughout the world.

First published 1974

ISBN 0 582 71046 4 (Cased)
ISBN 0 582 71047 2 (Limp)

Typeset by Dudley E. King Pty Ltd
Printed in Hong Kong by Dai Nippon Printing Co., (Hong Kong) Ltd

for
Helen

CONTENTS

CONTENTS

APOLOGIA

The Indonesian revolution demands attention *as* revolution, and as an important chapter in the collapse of Western colonialism. In the first place, however, it is the watershed of modern Indonesian history, and must be understood in terms of that history.

Twenty turbulent years have passed since the masterly pioneering study of the subject by George Kahin. The decisiveness of the revolution is as obvious now as it was then, though not for all of the same reasons. Twenty years ago its primary claim seemed to be the achievement of independence itself, and the balance of political parties it had produced; ten years ago it was the impetus given to communism, to militant nationalism, and to political Islam. Now the historian of the revolution is forced to devote more attention to the origins of the army, the powerful undercurrent of centralism, and the changes which the revolution brought, and failed to bring, to the lower levels of Indonesian society. This at least was how it appeared to me on an extended visit to Indonesia in 1972, during which much of this book was written.

The case for a reassessment was not only the change in post-revolutionary Indonesia, but also the many Indonesian and foreign studies which have appeared in the past two decades. This book was not intended as a work of research in itself, and footnotes were therefore kept to a minimum. Yet even with such modest ambitions it proved impossible to be satisfied with existing literature in many areas (see bibliography). Primary sources—interviews and newspapers—have had to carry much of the narrative not only for the area of my own research interest in northern Sumatra, but also for most other developments outside Java and for the 1947–8 build-up to Madiun. Much more research is needed before even some basic problems can be answered from secondary literature.

It is not possible to list the many Indonesians whose information, advice, patience, and hospitality made this book possible. A few, whose help surpassed the requirements even of Indonesian hospitality, must stand for the many: Soebadio Sastrosatomo; Mochammad Tauchid; Prof. Riekerk; T. Luckman Sinar; Nip Xarim; Prof. Madjid Ibrahim. To my colleagues—John Smail, Masri Singarimbun, Soebardi, Lance Castles, Christine Dobbin—whose friendly criticism improved parts of the draft, and to Rita Mathews, who uncomplainingly typed it, I am also profoundly grateful.

Canberra
May 1973

INDONESIAN SPELLINGS

The official Indonesian spelling system, initially derived from Dutch orthography, underwent a minor revision in 1950 and a more fundamental one on 17 August 1972. Indonesian words and place-names are spelt below in accordance with the newest system, now used in both Indonesia and Malaysia. Although strange to old Indonesia hands, this has the advantage of similarity to English spelling. The only important differences from English practice are the use of **c** for the English sound **ch**, and **sy** for the English sound **sh**.

In personal names, however, I have had to follow the usage of the person concerned, which in most cases was Dutch usage, viz: **j** for English **y**; **dj** for **j**; **tj** for **ch**; **sj** for **sh**; and sometimes **oe** for **u**.

Dutch-derived names for some Indonesian cities were changed to Indonesian ones in 1942 (Batavia to Jakarta; Fort de Kock to Bukittinggi). Although the Netherlands did not accept these changes until 1949, I have used the Indonesian names for the whole period to avoid confusion.

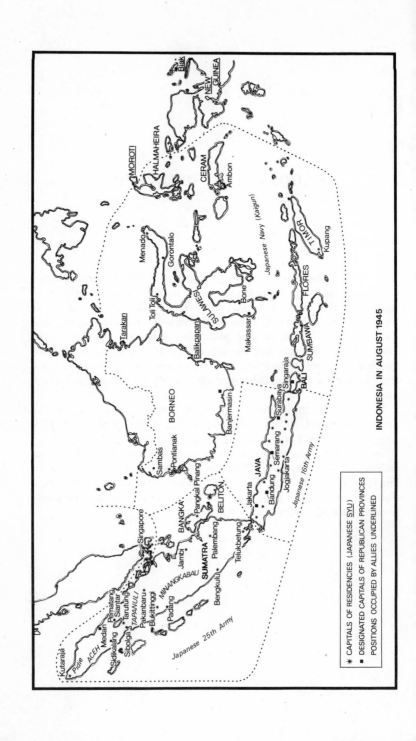

INDONESIA IN AUGUST 1945

* CAPITALS OF RESIDENCIES (JAPANESE SYU)
■ DESIGNATED CAPITALS OF REPUBLICAN PROVINCES
····· POSITIONS OCCUPIED BY ALLIES UNDERLINED

Chapter One

PRELUDE TO REVOLUTION

*'Ah, my son, we are not only divided in this
world, but we shall never meet again in the next.
Our Gods are different, and our worlds hereafter
will be different'*
Lament of Takdir Alisjahbana's father, about 1931[1]

The Making of an Indonesian Society, 1900–42
Modernity came suddenly to Indonesia. The great nineteenth
century wave of imperial self-confidence, which extended European
capitalism and administration throughout Africa and Asia, was
delayed in the Netherlands by domestic politics and the effects of a
crippling colonial war in Sumatra. In the first decade and a half of
this century, however, several stages were telescoped. That period
saw Dutch troops sweep through the remotest corners of Sumatra,
Borneo, Celebes, and the Lesser Sunda Islands. In some cases they
overcame the heroic resistance of ancient and colourful dynasties in a
terrible bloodbath. In others the very appearance for the first time of
troops from faraway Batavia (Jakarta) was enough to change the
power balance between local ruler and Dutch administrator. Rulers
remained, often with vastly increased wealth and splendour, but
there was no longer to be any doubt that it was the Dutch *controleur*
who was in command. During the same period the first Dutch-
controlled inter-island steam line, the KPM (established only in 1888)
tied the strings of island commerce to Batavia, rather than to
Singapore as hitherto. A Netherlands Indian state effectively came
into being with its own bureaucracy, currency, financial and legal
institutions, and languages (Dutch and Malay).

The knots tying this new state together were the burgeoning
cities, of which there were seventeen by 1930 with populations
over 50,000. Their combined population comprised 1·87m ethnic

1

Indonesians, 0·29m Chinese, and 0·14m Europeans, with social and economic status in inverse proportion to their numbers. The city became 'a scene of conflict', as a late colonial report put it, where these three distinct ethnic groups 'make use of the others and attempt to fathom them, but . . . carry on the struggle with quite diverse weapons and basically different rules, and with divergent life goals and ideals in view'.[2] Only in these competitive cities could the Indonesian bottom layer see itself as a whole, rather than as a number of unrelated cultural groups—Javanese, Sundanese, Balinese, Minangkabau, Batak, and so forth. It was assisted to this view by the cultural nationalism which transformed its rivals during the first two decades of this century. Both the Chinese and the Dutch-Eurasian communities were forced by political and social pressures emanating from their respective homelands, to abandon the leisurely 'Indisch' life they had shared with the Indonesian aristocracy. A reaction was not slow to follow among Indonesians, directed first against the Chinese with whom they came into more direct contact, but increasingly against the real colonial masters, the comfortable European top layer.

In comparison with even India or China, independent commercial activity among these urban Indonesians was pitifully weak. It was strongest in such declining traditional crafts as silverware and *batik* cloth manufacture. Most urban Indonesians were either salaried employees in government or Dutch and Chinese business, or part of a *lumpenproletariat* of hawkers, labourers, and menials. The key to status and success in such a milieu was a Dutch education.

In 1899 there were only thirteen Indonesian secondary school pupils, providing a tiny first generation of political and cultural pioneers. The colonial government belatedly accepted its responsibilities in this regard only in the first decade of this century. Opportunities for a modern Dutch education were expanded steadily thereafter until about 1925, when the government shifted its emphasis to the widespread provision of elementary three-year vernacular education. Over two million children were attending such 'popular' schools in 1940, which must have raised the literacy rate a little above the appalling 6·4 per cent established in the 1930 census.

It was Dutch-medium education, however, which opened new worlds, and which was in desperate demand by Indonesians. In the last fifteen years of Dutch rule the number of Indonesians enjoying a Dutch primary education in government and government-supported schools was between 65,000 and 80,000—considerably less than 1 per cent of the relevant age group. Higher up the educational pyramid the numbers declined sharply. At the end of the Dutch regime there were still fewer than 7,000 Indonesians enjoying any form of Dutch-medium secondary education, the great majority of them being in the intermediate 'MULO' schools. The university-level institutions set up for engineering (1919), law (1924), and medicine (1926), had graduated a total of 230 Indonesians by the time of the Japanese occupation.[3]

If this Western educational system was narrow, it was also rigorous, and of an extremely high standard. From the 1920s the new schools and universities began to produce what amounted to a new élite defined by education: fluent in Dutch, open to other European cultures, moving confidently in the modern technocratic world of the Indonesian cities, though less sure how to put their knowledge to the service of the traditional societies they had left. It was this new class which gradually built a new literature, a political style, and a change in religious attitudes, to name only a few points. It challenged the leadership of the traditional aristocracy and the legitimacy of feudal ceremonies and values on the basis of its own source of authority: technical expertise, foreign ideas, and leadership in a host of new urban-based organizations and associations.

Within this favoured group generational differences assumed more than usual importance. The first substantial group to receive Dutch education, graduating from universities and high schools in the 1920s, provided most of the prominent politicians of the 1940s. In relation to such men, the larger group still at school into the 1930s was identified as youth, the *pemuda* of the revolution. Students had to travel to the larger towns for even a good primary education, and secondary education took them from all over the archipelago to the cities of Java. To this physical separation from family and village was added the enormous mental and spiritual distance resulting from a Western style of education. The young student thus felt himself temporarily of a race apart, with a distinct freedom and a special responsibility.[4] Youth organizations centred on the Dutch-medium schools but spreading beyond them through scouting, sporting, and cultural groups, provided the major constituency for the very circumscribed adult nationalist movement.

The experience of common schooling in the cities also made the youth movement impatient of the regional or ethnic identification of their elders. It was at the second unity congress organized by the major youth movements in 1928 that the famous *sumpah pemuda* (youth oath) was pronounced, declaring the unity of the Indonesian people, the Indonesian nation, and the Indonesian language (Malay).

If this Dutch-educated urban élite believed it held the key to Indonesia's future, older élites knew that their strength lay in continuity with her past. Many Indonesians in Aceh, East Sumatra, Surakarta and Jogjakarta (both in central Java), West and East Kalimantan (Borneo), Sulawesi (Celebes), the northern Moluccas, and the Lesser Sunda Islands, were still nominally ruled by a varied array of 'self-governing' rajas. Dutch indirect rule had made these monarchies rigid and isolated from their subjects, and at the same time transferred many government tasks from their hands to specialized arms of the central bureaucracy. Nevertheless the rajas retained great influence, especially in areas remote from the cities and the educated Indonesians who mocked their outmoded life-styles.

Centralizing pressures steadily reduced the distinction between these 'self-governments' (*kerajaan* or *swapraja*) and the directly ruled areas where the Indonesian aristocracy had been more fully transformed into a salaried bureaucracy (*pamong praja*). Java outside the kerajaan was governed by sixty-seven regents (*bupatis*), scions of the hereditary aristocracy mirroring the regal manners of Jogjakarta and Surakarta, who were nevertheless subject to occasional transfer and to bureaucratic supervision. Despite continual efforts by the government to reverse the trend, both rajas and pamong praja were losing credibility as autonomous actors, and coming to be seen by urban Indonesians as overprivileged servants of the colonial régime.

Islam

An alternative source of traditional leadership was the *ulama*, the Islamic teachers and interpreters of the law. Every time of upheaval in Indonesia demonstrated again their ability to inspire peasant resistance and heroism. Rule by alien Dutch unbelievers established Islam more firmly as the symbol of separate identity and ultimate refusal to accept the conquerors. It was therefore natural that the first anti-colonial mass movement in Indonesia, founded in 1912, should bear the name Sarekat Islam (Muslim Union) and rely on the ulama for most of its rural support. As the Dutch Governor–General remarked of it, Islam

> can be described as 'everything the native can identify as his own territory'. When a trading association rejoices in the predicate 'Islamijah', this does not mean that it stands on the basis of the Muslim faith, but that it is a national, native association.[5]

The very success of Sarekat Islam, however, frightened Muslim leaders away from it. By 1921 it had provoked a series of violent incidents in rural areas, while communists, nationalists, and reformist Muslims fought bitterly to control its central leadership. During the 1920s urban Islamic leaders turned away from its loose mixture of religion and radical politics to a concern for purifying and deepening Islamic faith itself. The pace-setter was the modernist educational association Muhammadiah, established in Jogjakarta in 1912 but

flourishing only from the 1920s. It attempted to answer the challenge
of Dutch education and Christian missionary activity in terms of the
reformist ideas of Muhammad Abduh and Rashid Rida in Egypt.
It was also the first and most successful of many Indonesian
associations to respond to the tremendous demand for modern
Dutch-medium education through its school system. By 1937
Muhammadiah had 913 branches throughout Indonesia, each operating at least an elementary school as well as women's, youth, and
scout groups.

Conservative Muslims criticized Muhammadiah for disregarding
the traditional adherence of Indonesians to the Shafi school of law,
for flirting with Ibn Saud's wahabbites, and for its westernizing
ways. In rural areas of Central and East Java, Muhammadiah
aroused opposition because it disrupted time-honoured compromises
between Islam and Javanism, demanding that syncretic practices
be reformed in a purer Islamic spirit. Despite its non-political professions, Muhammadiah's modern and urban basis also gave it an
anti-colonial character, which was perhaps most apparent in
indirectly-ruled areas where it was usually in conflict with the
traditional religious authority of the raja.

More conservative Islamic associations therefore arose in reaction
to Muhammadiah: Nahdatul Ulama based in rural East Java (1926);
Al Jamiatul Wasliyah in East Sumatra and Tapanuli (1930); PUSA
in Aceh (1939); and various minor groups. Even though traditional
pesantrens usually provided the early leadership for such groups,
they quickly came to imitate Muhammadiah's organizational and
even educational methods. Within a remarkably short period these
associations established their leadership of Indonesian Islam at the
expense of both the Muslim politicians of Sarekat Islam (from 1929
PSII) and the hierarchy of state-appointed religious officials. They
drew closer together in the last years of Dutch rule in defence of
Islamic interests against government and secular nationalists alike.
In 1937 they federated in the Majlisul Islamil a'laa Indonesia
(MIAI), to sponsor annual religious conferences.

The growth of these organizations defined for the first time the
limits of a *golongan agama* (religious grouping), with its own leadership, its own programme for the liberation of Indonesia, and the
most impressive indigenous organization in the country. The boundaries of this group raised special problems in the Javanese-speaking
area (Central and East Java). The Muslim organizations were
beginning to demonstrate a point which became clear in the 1940s,
that syncretic Javanism was not just a relative lack of religious
knowledge or commitment, but a distinct and increasingly self-
conscious cultural identity. Post-war sociologists have popularized
the terms *santri*, (the people of the pesantren, the true Muslims),

and *abangan* (lit. the red people, the syncretists) for these two cultural orientations of Java.

Marxism

The importance of Marxism for Indonesian nationalists is difficult to exaggerate. Not only was the Indonesian communist party the strongest in Asia until its suppression in 1927; Marxist ideas were influential through the whole spectrum of politically active intellectuals. Their appeal rested primarily on the analysis by Lenin and Bukharin of imperialism as the last stage of capitalism. This provided an intellectually satisfying rationale to deeply-rooted Indonesian hopes for an end to the seemingly impregnable colonial system. For the more westernized it also offered a non-racial basis for anti-colonialism, vividly demonstrated by the support and sympathy Indonesian nationalists found from Dutch Marxists in Indonesia (before 1926) and in Holland. Moreover, in the period up to about 1924, when the colonial government could be considered to be carrying out its relatively progressive 'ethical' policy, Marxism appeared to identify more surely than nationalism the real enemy—private Dutch commercial, planting, and capitalist interests. No philosophy of liberalism was likely to emerge from a people without a bourgeoisie. Indonesian conservatives themselves, especially from the Javanese tradition, were inclined rather to centralized state paternalism. Even those who found a clear philosophical basis for anti-Marxism in modernist Islam were inclined to argue that socialist ideals were prefigured in Islam. Marxism was the major ideological training for Indonesian politicians as a whole.

The communist party, the PKI (Partai Komunis Indonesia), carried on the tradition of mass action which was repudiated by the Sarekat Islam in 1921. It quickly became caught between government repression and the messianic expectations which it encouraged in the countryside. The revolt into which it blundered in 1926 was suppressed within a few hours in Batavia, though it threw parts of rural West Java and West Sumatra into uproar for weeks. This premature attempt ensured the elimination of the PKI, though not of Marxism, for the remainder of the colonial period. The memory of the revolt, however, gave the communists the reputation of super-revolutionaries, so dangerous to colonialism that the party had to be banned and its members exiled to Boven Digul (New Guinea).

Nationalism

The crushing of the communists and the withdrawal of organized Islam left the political arena by default to secular nationalists in the last decade and a half of Dutch rule. Moreover a sharp change of direction in Dutch policies during the 1920s had the effect of polarizing resident Dutch and Indonesian views, and making the colonial tie itself appear to most Indonesian intellectuals the principal barrier to progress.

The period of the First World War had seen rapid political progress in Indonesia, climaxed by the establishment, in 1918, of a partly-elected *Volksraad* (popular council) in which leading nationalists had been able to say their piece. The radical mood of its first session had been met by promises of more fundamental reforms, and the appointment of a commission to review the whole constitutional basis of Netherlands Indian Government. But by the time further changes were effected, in 1922, the liberal tone of the commission's report had been submerged by harsher voices. Unmistakably absent was any serious intention to transfer political responsibility to Indonesian hands. The Volksraad remained an ineffective sounding board. At the end of Dutch rule those Indonesians qualified to vote for its members numbered 1,457. Conservative governments succeeded one another in the Netherlands, while the reactionary Vaderlandse Club, founded in 1929 to preserve the imperial connection 'fast and indissoluble, now and for ever',[6] led a move to the Right among Europeans in Indonesia.

Influenced by the disappointments of the early 1920s, the Perhimpunan Indonesia (PI), an association of Indonesian students in Holland, adopted a policy of non co-operation with the government in pursuing its goal of independence. Especially under the chairmanship of Muhammad Hatta (1925–30) it did much to popularize nationalism; the unity of Indonesia (a synthetic term hitherto confined to ethnological circles); and the Marxist critique of imperialism. In Indonesia it was the young engineer Sukarno who became the popular spokesman of these views. Between 1927, when his PNI (Persatuan [later Partai] Nasional Indonesia) was founded, and his exile in 1933, Sukarno was the leading figure on the political scene. Most of the PI members returning from Holland joined his party, but none understood as well as he how to fashion modern political concepts according to the cut of the Javanese mind.

For Sukarno non co-operation became the weapon to widen the gulf between 'us' and 'them'; the *sini* and the *sana*; the Pendawas and Kurawas of the beloved Mahabharata cycle of the *wayang*.[7] Tirelessly Sukarno insisted on the need for unity within the camp of the Pendawas, to ensure their inevitable triumph, the 'golden bridge' of independence. Dahm aptly calls him a 'necromancer of unity', who insisted that the competing strains of nationalism, Islam, and Marxism were not only compatible, but essentially one. 'I am a convinced nationalist, a convinced Muslim, a convinced Marxist', he professed.[8] Not that he was equally acceptable to these three categories. It was above all secular nationalists rooted in

Javanese abangan culture who shared his desire for ideological synthesis; his denial of the claims of rival ideologies to their separate imperatives.

Nevertheless Sukarno's success was amazing. He not only united the majority of secular nationalists and Marxists in his PNI, but also drew all important Indonesian parties, both non co-operating and co-operating, into a federative body in December 1927. Even the older parties, Sarekat Islam and Budi Utomo, were obliged to shift their emphasis towards all-Indonesian nationalism and non co-operation.

A split of permanent importance appeared within secular nationalist ranks after Sukarno's imprisonment and the dissolution of the PNI in 1930. The majority of party supporters, including Sukarno after his release in 1931, joined the new PARTINDO. A minority led by Perhimpunan Indonesia leaders Muhammad Hatta and Sutan Sjahrir broke sharply with this mainstream in 1931. They formed the PNI-baru (new PNI), the initials now standing for *Pendidikan* (education) *Nasional Indonesia*. Hatta had been in Europe for ten years, and the youthful Sjahrir had married a Dutch Marxist there, before their return in 1931 and 1932 respectively. Both had thoroughly absorbed both democratic and Marxist strains in European thinking. Moreover both were Minangkabaus from West Sumatra, a people whose culture appears to have accepted the existence of internal contradiction to a much greater extent than the Javanese. Although exceptions are numerous, this cultural distinctiveness appears to have given the Minangkabau a disproportionate number of intellectual leaders receptive to a Western, dialectical manner of thought, whether in the Islamic or the Marxist-nationalist tradition. To European observers it appeared that men like Hatta and Sjahrir were the hard realists of the Indonesian national movement, in contrast to the demagogues and dreamers in Sukarno's camp. In the eyes of many Javanese, however, it was Sjahrir and Hatta who were unrealistic, alienated from the aspirations of the Indonesian people by their excessively Western thinking.

The difference was well indicated in the tactics of the PNI-baru. Departing from the mass mobilization and oratory of Sukarno's PNI/PARTINDO, it adopted a cell structure and emphasized political education, discussion, and self-reliance. Leadership was decentralized and democratic, in contrast to Sukarno's emphasis on the need for guidance and for consensus rather than majority decisions. It was the tradition established in these years which gave the 'socialists', as they were later known, an influence far greater than their numbers in independent Indonesia.

The PNI-baru had more Marxism in its programme, and considered itself genuinely revolutionary in contrast to the unstable opportunism of PARTINDO. Yet as Sjahrir perceptively remarked from prison, although Hatta was often considered 'the most outspoken representative of the non co-operators', nevertheless he 'recognized one very important common basis for cooperation with the Dutch: namely an internal faith in the humane, democratic, and reliable methods of a government that outwardly he called unreliable'.[9]

Indonesia in 1941

In its final years Netherlands India bore a superficial air of calm. Repressive government action had succeeded in curbing the activities of radical politicians to such an extent that they could no longer mobilize mass support. Many observers believed that the radical nationalists were a marginal element supported only by a few displaced intellectuals, and that the real leaders of Indonesian opinion were the pamong praja, the non-political leaders of social and educational groups, and the co-operating nationalists. The ranks of this last-named group had been swollen by Moscow's Dmitrov doctrine calling for a common front against fascism. In 1937 a group of younger Marxists led by Mr Amir Sjarifuddin and Dr A. K. Gani established GERINDO as a radical co-operating party on the grounds that international facism was the first enemy. The largest co-operating party, however, was PARINDRA, led by M. H. Thamrin (died 1941), which was conservative in socio-economic matters and looked with sympathy towards Japan. These parties and others were concerting their efforts in the years before the Pacific war for such moderate goals as a full Indonesian legislature.

Stern government repression of all political radicalism, all talk of independence, had driven most Indonesian activists into social and especially educational endeavours. The national movement laid great stress on self-reliance and 'auto-activity', the social equivalent of non co-operation. In the late 1930s at least 130,000 pupils were attending so-called 'wild' schools of Western type,[10] twice as many as in government-supported schools. Apart from the Muslim organizations, the strongest Indonesian school system by far was Taman Siswa, led by the great educational philosopher Ki Hadjar Dewantoro. In its strong defence of indigenous value systems, its independence of government, and the nationalist background of its founder, Taman Siswa came to provide a similar educational base for secular nationalism to that which Islam had in Muhammadiah and other schools.

By the close of the Dutch régime a sizeable Indonesian constituency for national social and political issues had come into being in the cities. On the basis of approximately 50,000 members of political parties and associations, 20,000 members of Muhammadiah, and about 50,000 subscribers to major Indonesian newspapers, a Dutch estimate put the number in this group at approximately 200,000.[11] If school pupils are included, the pemudas of the 1940s, the number would be larger. In terms of the total Indonesian population (then perhaps 70m) it was a tiny élite, but it proved sufficient to bind the diverse cultures of the archipelago together through the turbulent decade to come.

Despite the outward calm, there was in reality a rapid alienation of this élite from Dutch rule in its closing years. Those who hoped for progress within the constitutional confines set by the Dutch were disillusioned by repeated rebuffs, even after Holland had been defeated in Europe and faced defeat in Asia. Despite the distaste with which the majority of influential politicians and intellectuals regarded Japanese militarism, there was a striking wave of popular enthusiasm for Japan in 1942. In Java an ancient prophecy of King Jayabaya was revived in a form which had the rule of white men replaced by a brief rule of yellow men, which in turn would give way to the millennial age of righteousness. In parts of the outer islands, where the memory of violent resistance to the Dutch conquerors had not died, the approaching Japanese inspired new outbursts. Dutch officials were killed or imprisoned in South Sulawesi, Gorontalo, and West Sumatra, while in Aceh a revolt eliminated the whole Dutch governing apparatus before the Japanese stepped ashore.

The Japanese Occupation

> Forward
> For you, my country
> Prepare the fire
> Chairil Anwar, 1943[12]

The Japanese conquest of Indonesia took barely two months. Java fell in a week ending on 8 March 1942. This shattering event marks a turning-point in Indonesian history at least as fundamental as the proclamation of independence three and a half years later.[13] Dutch rule, with all its vaunted solidity, practicality, and efficiency, evaporated in a moment. The fighting nationalists who had been exiled as dreamers and madmen were suddenly justified.

In a sense colonialism continued. Indonesia's economic resources were the principal prize of the war, and Japan fully intended to retain them without any concessions to Indonesian nationalism. But even the change in colonial masters brought some profound changes in Indonesian life. The Japanese were, for example, ignorant and contemptuous of the Dutch language. In contrast to Malaya and Burma the use of the old colonial language was banned in Indonesia, and the formerly Dutch-speaking élite had to learn to communicate in Indonesian. This gave a tremendous boost to the national language, whose status was never questioned after the war. Japanese ignorance about Indonesia forced them to place greater day-to-day responsibility in Indonesian hands. Where the Dutch had relied on superior technology and efficiency to justify and reinforce their sway, Japanese army methods were more crude, arbitrary, and theatrical. Whilst equally effective in ensuring control, these methods earned little respect from the Indonesian professional and technical officers who carried the burden of administration. They gained new confidence in their ability to do the job on their own.

However it was not just a case of changed colonial masters. The fundamental difference between Japanese imperialism and its Western forerunners was its provisional military character. For the Japanese military who ruled Indonesia, winning the war had to take priority over all purely colonial considerations. This is in marked contrast to the Dutch, who rejected the opportunity to mobilize the Indonesian population even when imminent defeat stared them in the face. The inhibitions of colonial tradition were too strong. But the Japanese military (the navy to a lesser extent than the army) were aware from the beginning that they were involved in a life-and-death struggle in which the peoples of Southeast Asia had to be involved, even though this might disrupt internal order. The problem of reconciling colonial control and wartime mobilization pervades the whole Japanese period, with control being increasingly sacrificed as the war turned against Japan. The passive, dispirited attitude of the average Indonesian, which had been the despair of the nationalists, received a full-scale assault at Japanese hands.

The Japanese attempted to make a complete symbolic break with the Dutch colonial past. The hereditary nature of 'self-governing' rajas was not accepted; Dutch treaty relationships with them were all abrogated; the symbols of sovereignty they displayed were reduced. After a new Japanese investiture, they were utilized as agents of the Japanese administration. Movements active in the Dutch period were also dissolved wherever possible, the most important exceptions being the powerful Islamic associations.

On the other hand one of the fundamental principles of the occupation was that 'existing governmental organizations shall be utilized as much as possible, with due respect for past organizational structure and native practice'.[14] Initially even Dutch administrators and technicians were retained, despite the difficulties this provided for Japanese anti-Western propaganda. Most were interned at the end of 1942, though a few specialists were retained in service a year longer. Naturally this maintenance of the status quo brought bitter disappointment from those groups which had most energetically welcomed the Japanese arrival. In some areas where the traditional rulers or pamong praja had strong enemies, of which Aceh was an extreme case, the latter had rallied to the Japanese in the hope of being rewarded with the overthrow of the pro-Dutch aristocracy. Such minor concessions as were initially made in this direction, however, endured only for a few months. In general the Japanese found, like the Dutch, that traditional aristocracies were the most efficient means of controlling and administering the population, and that despite their pro-Dutch past and orientation they remained too dependent on the ruling power to constitute any sort of threat.

The Japanese military had even less sympathy with political parties and pseudo parliamentary institutions in Indonesia than they had in Japan. All political organizations were suppressed at the beginning of the occupation. Despite the use made of the symbols of Indonesian nationalism by Japanese propaganda immediately before the occupation, the national flag (the *merah-putih*: red and white) and anthem were quickly banned. Political censorship was much harsher than under the Dutch. Nevertheless an important role was reserved for popular nationalist politicians and religious leaders, to arouse the population to greater efforts in the war against the Western powers.

The Japanese left nobody in any doubt that criticism or active opposition would not be tolerated. Indonesian politicians were given the choice between co-operation and remaining as 'neutral observers'.[15] The only prominent politician to organize active resistance was Mr Amir Sjarifuddin, who was given 25,000 guilders by the Dutch in 1942, to organize an underground through his Marxist and nationalist connections. Amir was arrested early in 1943. He escaped execution only through the forceful intervention of Sukarno. With the exception of his Surabaya-based group, the most active pro-Allied activities appear to have been among Chinese, Ambonese, and Menadonese.

In the category of neutral observers were most former members of the PNI-baru. Now led by Sjahrir, they maintained a network of 'underground' contacts in occupied Java. Sjahrir believed in the certainty of eventual Allied victory in the Pacific, and prepared for that eventuality by disseminating precious information from outside and fostering a spirit of scepticism about the Japanese. Numerous small groups existed outside Java with similar objectives, but only Sjahrir's had sufficient coherence to become a national force after 1945.

The great majority of politicians and religious leaders were prepared to work in the new organizations formed by the Japanese. The consideration and status the Japanese gave these activists contrasted so markedly with their experience under the Dutch that the non co-operation principle seemed no longer appropriate. Sukarno was one of many who believed that the occupation provided

'a magnificent opportunity to educate and ready our people'.[16]
Released from detention in July 1942, Sukarno quickly became the
most prominent Indonesian propagandist. Although he always
justified his co-operation in terms of the opportunity for advancing
independence, Sukarno undoubtedly found much to appreciate in
the Japanese military style. The emphasis on mass mobilization and
unity, the heroic rhetoric of struggle towards final victory, and the
dramatic public ritual of the Japanese regime all found echoes in
Sukarno's own style.[17] The same cannot be said for Hatta, yet he
too decided that more was to be gained by taking a very prominent
place within the Japanese régime than by remaining aloof.

Japanese Attitudes to 'Independence'
In considering the relationship between the Japanese and the
national movement, a distinction must be made between three
different regions treated entirely differently by the Japanese. Already
before Pearl Harbour the future conquests in Southeast Asia had
been divided between the Army and the Navy. The latter was
allotted the islands of Indonesia outside Java and Sumatra, on the
grounds that these were 'sparsely populated primitive areas, which
shall be retained in future for the benefit of the [Japanese] Empire'.[18]
The Navy in due course established a central administration for
these islands in Makassar, and until the last few months of the war
administered them as conquered territories—in at least one case
(West Borneo) by means of rank terror. In further contrast to Java,
Japanese were much more numerous and ubiquitous in these islands
than the Dutch had been, so that there was no wholesale promotion
of the Indonesian bureaucracy. There was absolutely no discussion
of independence, nor preparation for it, until the last few weeks of
the occupation.

Sumatra was administered initially by the Japanese 25th Army
in Singapore, together with Malaya, as 'the nuclear zone of the
[Japanese] Empire's plans for the Southern Area'.[19] Because of the
strategic location and resources of these areas, they too were not
initially considered for independence. Even after the 25th Army
moved to Sumatra in 1943 and its link with Malaya was broken,
nationalists in Sumatra were given little opportunity to organize
together, and none to meet their more advanced colleagues in Java.

Only unproductive Java was left politically undecided in the
original Japanese plan. The Japanese had been particularly well
received there. The first Java commander, Imamura, quickly established a good relationship with Sukarno and other nationalists, and
he succeeded in governing without resort to the draconian measures
used elsewhere. Within a year he was pleading for a public commitment to self-government for the island, lest Japan be forced 'to

partake of the same bitter cup suffered by the former Dutch regime'.[20] Throughout the war Java was well ahead of Sumatra in political development, and still further ahead of the other islands. The political dissimilarity between the major islands was vastly strengthened by the Japanese experience.

Examples of this abound. In Java alone Muslim organizations were permitted and encouraged to federate in a Java-wide body—at first the pre-war MIAI, from 1943 reconstituted as MASJUMI. In Java, Sukarno was permitted as early as March 1943 (and even this four months after it had been promised) to form an association known as PUTERA, intended to use the anti-Western content of nationalism to mobilize the urban élite throughout Java behind the war. Elsewhere such bodies were never allowed to extend beyond the level of the residency. Indonesian Advisory Councils for all Java and for each of its residencies were established in August 1943. In Sumatra comparable Councils were set up at the residency level the following November, but at the all-Sumatra level only in June 1945. In the Navy area these bodies were set up at the local level in 1944, though not in all areas, and were very strictly controlled. In Java, Bali, and Sumatra the Army administration began training, in late 1943, an embryo volunteer Indonesian army with its own officer corps. This force, called *Gyugun* (volunteer) in Japanese, but more popularly known in Java as PETA (defenders of the fatherland), formed by the end of the war a disciplined and dedicated force up to 40,000 strong in Java and 30,000 in Sumatra. It had well-trained if youthful officers up to First Lieutenant rank. In Java alone, prominent older Indonesians were given the ranks of Company and Battalion commanders, although their functions were more political and propagandist than military. This force, or rather this series of autonomous military units in each *kabupaten* or district of Java and Sumatra, was to be the nucleus of the army of independent Indonesia. In the Navy-administered area, however, military training was limited to the *Heihos*, Indonesians recruited from 1942 to perform menial duties as auxiliaries of the Japanese army.

Communication and travel between the islands was almost impossible for Indonesians during the occupation. Although inhabitants of the outer islands could read about the gradual progress made in Java towards independence, they were not involved in it until the last weeks of the war, and treated it with some scepticism. For most of the inhabitants of the Navy-administered area, with the partial exception of youth, the Japanese occupation was a negative experience of hardship and occasional terror unallayed by meaningful concessions towards self-government.

This geographical separation, partly deliberate, partly the result of communications paralyzed by war, was by far the most important divisive effect of the Japanese occupation. By contrast the attempt to play rival élites against each other has been too much emphasized in existing literature.[21] To the extent that suspicions were heightened in some areas between pamong praja and *pergerakan* (the 'movement', Islamic as well as secular nationalist), this was the result of the violence and instability which war and a change of masters injected into existing conflict situations. The tendency of Japanese policy was quite the reverse. It attempted in Indonesia, even more than in Japan itself, to make diverse organizations answer to a common leadership, and to build unity movements to support the government in every locality. Under the Japanese, nationalist and reformist Muslim leaders for the first time formed working relationships with members of the older aristocratic élite. It was by no means in vain that the nationalist politicians who led PUTERA appealed to the Japanese to ensure that the pamong praja, 'with whom PUTERA will always work for consensus, will demonstrate their open-mindedness and their abandonment of the old attitudes produced by the atmosphere of the Dutch East Indies'.[22] The total effect of the occupation was to produce leaders, both at the level of all Java (Sukarno and Hatta) and in most residencies throughout the country, whose primacy was acknowledged by all the three élites.

The favour shown to leaders of different groups varied solely in accordance with Japanese needs at different times. During 1942–3 religious leaders as a group enjoyed the most privileged position. Their pre-war organizations and journals were allowed to continue. They were represented in the top leadership of unitary propaganda bodies like PUTERA, but in Java could also operate within a separate Islamic unity body. The pre-war MIAI federation, in which anti-colonial politicians of the former PSII played a major role, was not wound up by the Japanese in Java until late 1943. It was replaced by MASJUMI (Majlis Syuro Muslimin Indonesia—Consultative Council of Indonesian Muslims), more narrowly based on the two great Muslim educational associations of Java—Muhammadiah and Nahdatul Ulama. Muslim leaders were also given preference for top positions within PETA, the Indonesian volunteer army in Java. The Japanese saw the Islamic leadership as an excellent means of mobilizing the peasant mass without having to make the political concessions demanded by the nationalists. The spectre of a holy war preached by rural ulama, which had haunted the Dutch more profoundly than nationalism itself, seemed to the early Japanese planners more easy to divert against the West. During 1943 the 16th Army in Java reversed the most basic Dutch policy by deliberately politicizing rural ulama through a series of propagandist training sessions. The Japanese were fishing in more

dangerous waters than they appeared to realize. Passionate resentment was aroused by early Japanese attempts to equate Islam with
Shinto, and to insist upon public reverence for their divine Emperor.
Islam, rather than nationalism, Marxism, or pro-Allied sentiment,
inspired most of the rebellions against Japanese authority in Java
and Sumatra.

The position of nationalist politicians depended on the degree of
Japanese commitment to some eventual 'independence', in which
they would be able to play the role for which they had prepared.
The darkest days for Sukarno, Hatta, and the nationalists who
chose co-operation came between May 1943, when Tokyo ruled
against Imamura's appeal for independence for Java, and September
1944, when the 'Koiso statement' made a new commitment to
independence in view of Japan's perilous military situation. In the
eighteen months between these dates the nationalists gained nothing
to show for their co-operation. PUTERA, which they had hoped to
use to radicalize the masses along nationalist lines, was first curbed,
and then suppressed in early 1944. In its place the Japanese formed
Jawa Hokokai, an organization designed for total mobilization of
Java for purely Japanese purposes. A Japanese headed the new
structure. Sukarno and Hatta were balanced by the two main
MASJUMI leaders in its central executive. Nationalist, Islamic, and
pamong praja leaders were all brought into its branches, along with
representatives of Chinese and other minorities. However, the role
of the pamong praja became more dominant at lower levels. In rural
areas it was simply another means of bureaucratic control. Its base
was the *tonarigumi*, a neighbourhood organization patterned on
wartime Japan, which organized food distribution, sentry duty,
labour corvees, and the dissemination of information and propaganda.

The prominence of Sukarno as propagandist for such an organization was a grave disappointment to younger nationalists for whom
the moral dilemmas were less sharp. In particular they could not
forgive his support for recruiting *romushas* ('voluntary' labourers),
hundreds of thousands of whom never returned from working on
Japanese military projects under appalling conditions. The sense of
betrayal among pemuda members of the political élite became
intense during 1944.[23] On the other hand few political rivals were
sufficiently guiltless to cast a stone. Among the masses of Java the
facilities of Jawa Hokokai enabled Sukarno's name, and even his
broadcast voice, to become uniquely familiar and popular. It was
this last fact which was to make him indispensable in the years
to come.

Japanese determination to retain the outer islands permanently
was one of the factors restraining further political concessions in

Java. As the Allies counter-attacked through the Philippines, New Guinea, and the Marianas, however, it became apparent that either the Navy Area (from MacArthur's S. W. Pacific Command) or Sumatra (from Mountbatten's S. E. Asia Command) would become a battlefield before Java. The Koiso statement therefore promised independence not only to Java but to an 'East Indies' of uncertain boundaries. In Java and Sumatra, the Indonesian national flag and anthem were immediately permitted; nationalists could speak of independence to come; and some intellectuals and pamong praja were groomed to take over the higher administrative offices occupied by Japanese. The naval commanders continued to oppose the participation of their area in these preparations until April 1945, when belated efforts were made to catch up.

The most meaningful concessions again occurred in Java. In August 1944 the Jawa Hokokai was given a youth wing under direct nationalist control, the *Barisan Pelopor* (Vanguard Corps). Initially designed as a propagandist unit, it was quickly transformed into a para-military organization about 80,000 strong, trained in guerrilla warfare. Soon MASJUMI obtained a similar para-military youth corps of about 50,000 the *Hizbullah*.[24] At last the politicians in Java had some fighting teeth.

Even so progress was painfully slow and artificial in relation to the increasing physical suffering of the population, particularly in overpopulated Java. Practical moves to prepare the structure of a new state were delayed even in Java until 28 May. Only then, after the fall of Okinawa, did a committee of representatives from all groups in Java meet to discuss a constitution. The mobilization of youth for the final patriotic sacrifice grew ever more feverish, directed against the Allies, the European imperialists, the *sana* of Sukarno's polemic. Yet the positive attraction of alliance with Japan for the pemudas was strained to breaking point by the starvation and deprivation of the last year of the war. Some of the best educated turned towards Sjahrir. The majority prepared for action against the enemy without any real certainty how he was to be identified.

References
1 S. Takdir Alisjahbana, *Indonesia: Social and Cultural Revolution*, Kuala Lumpur, 1966, p. 33.
2 Official Memorandum, 'Town Development in the Indies', 1938, as translated in *The Indonesian Town. Studies in Urban Sociology*, The Hague/Bandung, 1958, pp. 66–7.
3 These figures regarding education are derived from S. L. van der Wal (ed.), *Het Onderwijsbeleid in Nederlands-Indië 1900–1942. Een bronnenpublikatie*, Groningen, 1963, pp. 693–700.
4 An interesting attempt to base the distinctiveness of the pemuda on traditional Indonesian attitudes is in B. R. O'G. Anderson, *Java, in a time of revolution, occupation, and resistance, 1944–1946*, Ithaca, 1972, pp. 1–10.

5 Idenberg to de Waal Malefijt 7 October, in Van der Wal, *Onderwijsbeleid*, p. 215.

6 As quoted in J. S. Furnivall, *Netherlands India*, Cambridge, Reprint 1967, p. 417.

7 *Sini* = here; *Sana* = there. In the Javanese *wayang* (drama), particularly the universally popular *wayang kulit* (shadow puppet play), this dichotomy is reinforced by the invariable introduction of the Pendawas, the representatives of virtue, from the right, and their evil enemies, the Kurawas, from the left.

8 Cited in Bernhard Dahm, *Sukarno and the Struggle for Indonesian Independence*, trans. Mary F. Somers Heidhues, Ithaca, 1969, p. 200. This important work convincingly demonstrates the traditional dimension to Sukarno's thought.

9 Soetan Sjahrir, *Out of Exile*, trans. Charles Wolf, New York, 1949, p. 204.

10 Van der Wal, *Onderwijsbeleid*, p. 585n.

11 S. L. van der Wal (ed.), *De Volksraad en de staatkundige ontwikkeling van Nederlands-Indië*, Part 2, The Hague, 1965, pp. 593–5.

12 'Diponegoro', in Burton Raffel (ed.), *The Complete Poetry and Prose of Chairil Anwar*, Albany, 1970, p. 114. My translation.

13 A. Teeuw, *Modern Indonesian Literature*, The Hague, 1967, pp. 105–8, makes a strong case for regarding 1942 rather than 1945 as the real revolutionary watershed, at least in language and literature.

14 Principles governing the administration of occupied southern areas, 20 November 1941, in Benda, Irikura, and Kishi (eds), *Japanese Military Administration in Indonesia: Selected Documents*, New Haven, 1965, p. 1.

15 Mitsuo Nakamura, 'General Imamura and the Early Period of Japanese Occupation', *Indonesia* 10, 1970, p. 20.

16 *Sukarno: An Autobiography. As told to Cindy Adams*, Hong Kong, 1966, p. 173.

17 This theme is very well explored in B. R. O'G. Anderson. 'Japan: "The light of Asia",' in Joseph Silverstein (ed.) *Southeast Asia in World War II: Four Essays*, Cambridge, Mass., 1966, pp. 21–5.

18 Benda, Irikura and Kishi, p. 7.

19 *Ibid.* p. 169.

20 *Ibid.* p. 239.

21 This pattern was set by the first satisfactory study of the Japanese occupation, A. J. Piekaar's, *Atjeh en de Oorlog met Japan*, The Hague, 1949, which examined an extreme case (Aceh) of pre-war tension. It underlies two other fine studies: H. J. Benda, *The crescent and the rising sun: Indonesian Islam under the Japanese occupation 1942–1945*, The Hague, 1958, and B. R. O'G. Anderson, *Some aspects of Indonesian politics under the Japanese occupation: 1944–1945*, Ithaca, 1961.

22 Report on first three months of PUTERA, 16 August 1943, in *The Putera reports: problems in Indonesia-Japanese wartime co-operation*, trans. W. H. Frederick, Ithaca, 1971, p. 34.

23 In the otherwise self-indulgent *Sukarno: An Autobiography* pp. 183–94, Sukarno strikingly testifies to the anguish of this period; the 'scars I will carry to the grave'.

24 These figures, provided by the 16th Army for the time of the Japanese capitulation, are in M. A. Aziz, *Japan's colonialism and Indonesia*, The Hague, 1955, p. 230n.

Chapter Two

PROCLAMATION OF THE REPUBLIC

> *. . . joyfully they took the news back*
> *to their respective villages : 'Now*
> *our raja is a Javanese raja, – a raja*
> *with a* pici [*black fez*]
> Pramoedya Ananta Toer[1]

Blueprint for a State

The opportunity, long awaited by nationalists, to come together to plan a future independent state, was realized at the hands of the Japanese on 28 May 1945. The sixty-two member *Badan Penyelidik Usaha Persiapan Kemerdekaan Indonesia* (Body to investigate measures for the preparation of Indonesian Independence) or BPKI, inaugurated on that day, was given considerable freedom by the Japanese to debate constitutional and ideological questions. Fortunately for the harmony of proceedings, its composition ensured the domination of Sukarno's secular nationalist mode of thinking. On the one hand inadequate representation was afforded the outer islands (half a dozen members had been born in the outer islands though long-term residents of Java); the Muslims (seven members); Youth (none); and Western-oriented Marxists (Hatta was the nearest). On the other hand most of the pamong praja representatives were sceptical about the operation and unprepared for detailed practical debate. For Sukarno and his fellow nationalists this was the chance to prove that the humiliations endured under the Japanese had not been in vain. It was, above all, Sukarno who provided the drive which pushed the committee to a conclusion with a speed which surprised the Japanese.

After three days mainly devoted to ideological manifestos, the BPKI formed a subcommittee of seven under Sukarno to resolve the knotty religious question. The full committee met again from

10–17 July in a more determined mood, and in that short time adopted a constitution of fifteen Articles. The most difficult minority had been the Muslim representatives, who had always argued the need for a Muslim state in which religious law would be enforceable. Sukarno's position, outlined in his famous *Pancasila* (five principles) speech of 1 June, was that the State should be based on 'belief in the One, Supreme God', whether worshipped in Muslim or Christian terms. If the Muslims wanted more than this they should strive for it through the democratic process.[2] Muslim representatives were far from satisfied, and Sukarno directed all the force of his personality to achieve a compromise. On 22 June the subcommittee produced a draft prologue to the constitution, which conceded 'the obligation for those who profess the Islamic faith to abide by Islamic Laws'.[3] The July session of the BPKI made the further concession that the president should be a Muslim. Although well short of Muslim hopes, this was to prove the highest point in their pursuit of an Islamic State.

Other issues provided less opposition to the long-held principles of the secular nationalist mainstream which was led by Sukarno and given legal precision by Professor Soepomo. By considerable margins the BPKI voted for a republic rather than a monarchy (55–6); and for a unitary rather than a federal state (17–2 in sub-committee).[4] The authoritarian element already evident in Sukarno's pre-war thinking was reinforced by the conditions of the war against the Western democracies. All the leading members felt obliged to reject 'Western' liberalism and individualism. It was predictably the few members born outside Java, notably the Minangkabaus Hatta and Yamin and the Ambonese Latuharhary, who provided what little ineffective defence there was for the rights of the region and the individual as against the centre.[5]

The draft '1945 Constitution' which the BPKI adopted placed few restrictions on the power of the president. Elected every five years by a supreme advisory council (MPR), he had full executive power including the appointment and dismissal of ministers, while he shared legislative power with a representative assembly (DPR) and could veto all legislation. As Sukarno informed a critic of this last provision: 'What embodies the sovereignty of the people is the president, not the representative assembly'.[6] About the composition of the MPR and DPR the constitution stated only that this would be fixed by law.

The Japanese had also allowed the BPKI the unusual privilege of debating the boundaries of the future Indonesian state. A substantial majority (45 to 19) opted for a 'Greater Indonesia', embracing Malaya, British Borneo, and Portuguese Timor as well as the former Netherlands India.[7]

The collapse of Japanese defences and communications during the middle months of 1945 caused a drastic change of pace in independence preparations. By mid-July Tokyo was planning for independence 'at the earliest possible moment'[8] and forcing local commanders to rush their plans accordingly. Hurried conferences during the ensuing three weeks produced a draft timetable in which independence, scheduled for 7 September, would be prepared by a *Panitia Persiapan Kemerdekaan Indonesia* (Committee for the Preparation of Indonesian Independence), or PPKI, which would meet from 18 August to complete the work of the BPKI. The 'Greater Indonesia' idea was rejected by the Japanese, presumably because the relatively few Malay radical nationalists who supported it were of limited use in mobilizing the mixed population of south and central Malaya (the overwhelmingly Malay northern Malayan states having already been consigned to Thailand). Nevertheless the whole of former Dutch territory was to be declared independent in September, including the unprepared Navy-administered area. Effective Indonesian control could come later. 'Those areas which have not completed preparations shall gradually be transferred to the jurisdiction of the new independent nation in accordance with the progress of independence preparations.'[9] The detailed execution of these measures would be left to the military commanders in Java, Sumatra, and the Navy Area, who were expected to retain an influential 'advisory' position in their respective areas after independence. Despite the strong unitary sentiment of the Java BPKI meeting, Japanese planning as well as the collapse of communications suggested that a highly autonomous federal structure was more likely to emerge. The Sumatra command and the Navy even began to organize separate independence preparation committees in their respective areas.

The announcement that independence would be rapidly prepared by a new committee was duly made on 7 August, after it had become certain that Russia would enter the war. Two days later Sukarno, Hatta, and the elderly BPKI chairman Radjiman flew to Dalat (South Vietnam), to be told formally by Marshal Terauchi, Commander of the Japanese Southern Army, that independence was in their hands. Only while in Vietnam did the Indonesian leaders learn about the atomic bomb on Hiroshima, though they could not know how close Japan was to surrender. They returned on 14 August to a Jakarta seething with rumour and unrest.

On the last stage of the return journey Sukarno and Hatta were accompanied by the Sumatran delegates to the PPKI, now rescheduled to begin its meetings on 16 August. Twenty-two members had been appointed to this body, including eight specifically representing the islands outside Java. Despite communications difficulties the Japanese managed to fly two prominent nationalists from Makassar (Sulawesi) as well as the three Sumatrans. These were the only areas outside Java where significant independence preparation had occurred. The PPKI was to meet, however, in circumstances wholly different from those of its conception.

The Revolutionary Situation and Youth
> *Smash whatever you've made*
> *End without inheritance, without family*
> *Ask no forgiveness for your sins*
> *Give no farewell to anyone*
> Chairil Anwar, 1946[10]

The final year of the Japanese occcupation was one of unprecedented hardship for the majority of Indonesians. The shipping of goods was impossible; such essentials as cloth were almost unobtainable; inflation was out of hand. Every district was expected to meet its own needs as well as those of the Japanese, who began stock-piling supplies against the threatened counter-attack. The 1944 rice crop was disastrous. In many districts Japanese rice requisitions made the difference between subsistence and starvation. In January 1945 an official report recorded of Java:[11]

> ... malnutrition has caused a serious decline in the people's health . . . [which] has been further accelerated by the shortage of medicines . . . [and] adequate clothing, and by the returning *romusha* [forced labourers] who usually bring back to their native villages all kinds of infections, particularly malaria and skin diseases . . . in general the death rate now exceeds the birth rate.

Starvation, beggary, and disease were visible as never before in the streets of the cities, particularly in Java.

Young men gained partial diversion from these pressures through the increasing tempo of Japanese propaganda and mass mobilization. In Java and Sumatra, Japanese strategy placed coastal defence in the hands of Indonesian militia, with the main Japanese and Gyugun/PETA forces holding centres further inland. Other Indonesians were hastily trained for guerilla operations behind future Allied lines. In addition to the more long-standing youth corps in Java such as Hizbullah and Barisan Pelopor, shadowy groups emerged throughout Indonesia with names reminiscent of Japanese ultra-nationalism—'Black Dragon', 'Black Fan', 'Death-defying Unit'. The mystique of such groups has been well described: 'Xenophobia, radicalism, strong comradely loyalty, authoritarianism, superb, if almost suicidal courage, and a belief in salvation through direct action'.[12] Drilling with wooden rifles and sharpened bamboo stakes was extended to as wide a group of youths as possible through neighbourhood *tonarigumi* and other associations.

This mixture of deprivation and high-pitched, theatrical propaganda was explosive. Despite the Japanese reputation for terrible and often arbitrary retaliation, peasant uprisings with varying degrees of religious inspiration had occurred since late 1943 on a scale unknown since the 1920s, though in traditionally volatile areas like Aceh, West Java, and Toli-Toli (north Sulawesi). In 1945 a Dayak revolt became widespread in West Borneo. Supernatural portents of disaster were seen all over Java. All these were sure signs of popular restiveness. However only the growing rebelliousness of educated youth in the last months of the war had serious potential for revolution.

Influential politicians, intellectuals, religious leaders, and pamong praja all enjoyed privileges from the Japanese which insulated them from the suffering. Elite status in a sense embracing all these groups therefore came to the perceived and resented to an unprecedented degree. 'The reputation of the leaders', said one of them, 'is ruined in the eyes of the people'.[13] The educated *pemuda* (youth) themselves constituted an élite, especially those whose personal connections with leading politicians gave them a prominence in the whole pemuda movement. Nevertheless their youth freed them from direct responsibility to the Japanese. As a group they stood apart from the older élite, and increasingly saw themselves as representing the aspirations of 'the people' as against the compromised leaders. Last-minute Japanese attempts to court pemuda leaders as potential anti-Allied activists gave them a new sense of solidarity and power as the occupation regime began to crumble. Typically, however, they attempted to force the older leaders to return to more heroic traditions of the 1930s, rather than abandoning these leaders altogether.

To the Japanese the most alarming demonstration of pemuda discontent came from the Gyugun/PETA soldiers—theoretically among the most Japanized. On 14 February 1945 the battalion at Blitar, led by 22-year-old officers, left its barracks in armed revolt against the Japanese. In July a similar, if smaller, affair took place in Pematang Siantar, Sumatra. Though easily crushed, these revolts provided an inspiring incentive to other youths.

The unarmed revolt of the educated urban pemudas was of greater long-term significance because it was allowed to succeed. In June 1945 youth rallies were held all over Java, some of which gave rise to uncontrollable anti-Japanese outbursts. It was increasingly necessary both for the nationalist leadership and for the Japanese in these critical days to control and harness the youth movement. Their efforts however had the opposite effect. The turning point came in Jakarta on 6 July, at the founding session of a 'New People's Movement', the GRB (Gerakan Rakyat Baru). This movement was to be the first to bring pemudas into its leadership, and they came prepared to force a tougher line on their elders. When they were outvoted on a proposal to include the premature title 'Republic of Indonesia' in the GRB charter they began to attack the whole basis of the meeting. Eventually several of them walked out, causing the collapse of the movement. The Japanese regime was no longer sufficiently sure of its direction to bring them to heel. The pemuda leaders in Jakarta from this point saw their task as one of preparing for revolution.

The pemudas in question were capable of very little on their own. Directly involved were only about two hundred well-connected youths in Jakarta, most of them either students at the Medical Faculty (the only tertiary institution still open), or ex-students grouped around one of the Japanese-sponsored propaganda bodies. Some of the medical students in particular had never had much respect for the Japanese and therefore came into the orbit of Sjahrir as the chief exemplar of non co-operation. The other principal foci in the capital for educated young nationalists were two *asrama* (hostels) established under Japanese patronage to attempt to channel the nationalist zeal of youth in directions potentially useful to the Japanese. One of these, at Menteng 31, included young nationalists like Sukarni, Adam Malik, and Chaerul Saleh, who had been prominent in pre-war nationalist youth groups and in Japanese propaganda offices.

The other, the *Asrama Indonesia Merdeka* (Free Indonesia hostel), was under the patronage of Admiral Maeda, head of the Navy's liaison office in Army-administered Java. Like many Japanese naval officers Maeda had a relatively liberal approach to politics, and in addition he was free to take a frequently critical view of army administration policies. For these reasons his asrama enjoyed considerable freedom under the direction of the veteran nationalist Mr Subardjo and the left-wing pemuda leader Wikana. From November 1944 about a hundred élite pemudas attended courses there given by the leading nationalists in Jakarta, even including Sjahrir. The 'Kaigun (Navy) group', as these young students and the older nationalists close to Subardjo were collectively called, enjoyed precious immunity for their revolutionary activity of August through Maeda's protection.[14]

During July and August the ideological differences between these various pemuda centres were submerged by the rising tide of anti-Japanese militance. Sjahrir's prestige rose rapidly in the eyes of all these pemudas as the most prominent focus of opposition to the Japanese. As an experienced politician Sjahrir's calculations were largely tactical. He had never believed the Japanese could win the war, and during late July and August he knew from Allied broadcasts that they were near collapse. He believed that an essential precondition of subsequent Allied recognition was that independence should be seen to come in opposition to the Japanese rather than as their gift. These calculations suited the pemuda demand for action. Consequently they gained currency among the widening group of Jakarta youths who knew that Japanese surrender was near.

17 August 1945: the Proclamation[15]

The return of Sukarno and Hatta to Jakarta on 14 August brought to a head the confrontation between two generations. The older leaders, Hatta as well as Sukarno, knew that an orderly transfer of Government from Japanese to Indonesian hands was virtually certain provided that war continued as expected for at least a few more weeks. Whatever happened thereafter the Indonesian Government would be in a strong position to bargain with all comers. The rumours of surrender on the 14th, confirmed with virtual certainty the following day, came as a severe shock to their plans. The only way left open to them appeared to be to speed up the plans for independence with tacit Japanese approval. To act provocatively against the Japanese seemed to spell inevitable disaster to the structure built up thus far—a disaster in which Sukarno and Hatta themselves would be the first casualties.

Pemuda thinking was by no means as clear about the way forward. For the representative pemuda leaders in Jakarta the manner in which independence was obtained was crucial. Above all it must not be a *hadiah* (gift) of the Japanese, but a revolutionary, sacrificial act of the Indonesian people. Here the educated pemuda leaders were in tune with a large section of their age group throughout Java, in whom Javanese millenarianism, the nationalist tradition of revolution and mass action, Japanese propaganda, and economic hardship had fused to form a chiliastic, desperate mood difficult to satisfy with diplomacy alone.[16]

However, strategy was woefully dependent on the older leaders. They turned to Sjahrir, the only leader of status to share their demand for confrontation with the Japanese. But Sjahrir knew that a revolutionary move would have no effect made in his own name—a Sumatran known only to a tiny political élite in Java. 'Whether he liked it or not, in the initial stage the situation forced him to work together with those leaders branded by the Allies as "collaborators"'.[17] Although he encouraged his pemuda contacts to prepare a coup to seize the Jakarta radio station and other points, he appeared to acknowledge that such action would be suicidal if the 'collaborating' nationalists opposed it. In discussions with Hatta and Sukarno on 14 and 15 August, Sjahrir stressed that the proclamation must be made by the two leaders alone rather than by the PPKI as they had planned. The Allies would never recognize a Republic which sprang from this Japanese-instituted machinery. Yet as Hatta pointed out, the Allies could be expected to have even less time for a Republic proclaimed by the 'arch-collaborator' Sukarno. It was this dilemma which took the initiative away from Sjahrir during this crisis.

The conflict came to a head on 15 August, when the Japanese Emperor's noon broadcast made clear to Japanese officers and a few of their Indonesian confidants that the war was really over. Sjahrir was planning a strike against the Jakarta radio station for that evening in the hope that Sukarno would agree to a 'revolutionary' independence declaration. Sukarno, and after some initial hesitation also Hatta, insisted on first establishing from the Japanese command both that Japan had officially surrendered and that it would not oppose a speeding up of the already agreed progression to independence. If this assurance could be obtained they planned to put the issue of independence before a hastily summoned special session of the PPKI at 10 a.m. on the 16th. On the afternoon of the 15th the two leaders and Subardjo learned unofficially from Admiral Maeda that the surrender was a fact, but little more.

Later that afternoon some of Sjahrir's pemudas failed to persuade Hatta to back their revolutionary programme, and left in disgust to report back to Sjahrir. Whatever plans had been made for revolution were called off. Leading pemudas from all the main groups gathered the same evening in a tense mood to decide how to deal with what they regarded as the pusillanimous attitude of their leaders. They resolved to ask Sukarno and Hatta 'for the last time, to proclaim independence at once and break all ties and connections with the promise of *Kemerdekaan Hadiah* (independence on a platter) a la Japan'.[18]

Wikana and Darwis, the pemudas delegated to present this 'ultimatum', had a dramatic confrontation with Sukarno in the presence of Hatta, Subardjo, and a number of other leaders who had gathered to plan their moves. When the pemudas threatened violence on the morrow if their demands were not met, Sukarno and Hatta angrily challenged them to carry out their threat, and see what they could do on their own. Everybody present was tense and unsure. By reacting angrily to the pemuda taunts Sukarno and Hatta lost what chance they had to reach a comprise satisfactory to pemuda pride by including them in the following days' discussions. Instead Wikana and Darwis were humiliated and challenged. They left Sukarno's house 'overwhelmed with mixed feelings of anger and dejection',[19] to report back to the wider pemuda group.

Meeting again at midnight, the pemudas still stuck on the indispensability of Sukarno and Hatta. Chiefly on the initiative of Sukarni and Chaerul Saleh, it was decided to remove Sukarno and

Hatta outside Jakarta to the PETA garrison in Rengasdengklok, while preparations for anti-Japanese defiance continued in the city. The first part of the plan was carried out efficiently in the small hours of 16 August, both Sukarno and Hatta accepting the story they were given about the danger of remaining in the city. The pemudas evidently hoped the two leaders could now be persuaded to make the independence proclamation at Rengasdengklok, though no radio or other facilities were provided for the purpose. At least there the Japanese could not force them to condemn a pemuda revolt. But the revolt itself was patently unplanned. Scarcely any of the armed PETA garrisons were informed, and no anti-Japanese action whatever developed on the 16th. The Sjahrir group which was best prepared for action was not in full agreement with the Sukarni group which organized the kidnapping, and it is probably the latter acted without making any serious plans for revolt.

Meanwhile in Jakarta the PPKI delegates gathered and eventually dispersed again when Sukarno and Hatta failed to appear. Subardjo, who was responsible for organizing the PPKI, spent the morning checking with his Japanese Navy patrons on the one hand, and his pemuda assistant Wikana on the other, to try to find Sukarno and Hatta. Admiral Maeda here played a central role. He appears to have been genuinely concerned to see Sukarno and Hatta resume the initiative from the more dangerous pemudas, and carry through the independence that the Japanese had promised them. As a bargaining point with the pemudas he therefore pledged the weight of his own influence and protection for an independence proclamation as soon as Sukarno and Hatta returned to Jakarta.

This was sufficient to allow Sukarni and the other pemudas at Rengasdengklok to retreat gracefully from an impossible situation. Sukarni, Subardjo, and one of Maeda's aides brought Sukarno and Hatta back to Jakarta late on the night of the 16th, and preparations began immediately for a declaration of independence in the security of Maeda's house (the pre-war British Consulate). The members of the PPKI began to gather there about midnight, and were joined by selected youth leaders.

However Maeda, Sukarno, and Hatta had first to establish Japanese army approval for the proclamation. General Yamamoto, chief of the military administration, had already received instructions at noon on the 16th that he was responsible to the victorious Allies for the preservation of the status quo in Java. Although earlier prepared to let an independence move go ahead, he now refused even to see the Indonesians. Instead they negotiated with his deputy Nishimura in the small hours of the 17th. Although equally unwilling to acknowledge Indonesian independence openly in any way, Nishimura eventually conceded that the Japanese might not act against a spontaneous movement from the Indonesian side. Maeda's emphasis on the danger of bloodshed from unruly pemuda outbursts evidently carried much weight with Nishimura, who naturally preferred to see the initiative remain with the 'constittutional' leaders. Like Maeda and many other Japanese, Nishimura probably also felt a genuine moral obligation to the Indonesians to whom independence had been promised.

The final confrontation of this proclamation drama came at Maeda's residence between 3 a.m. and dawn on 17 August. The pemudas present had obviously lost their struggle to have independence proclaimed in defiance of the Japanese. Nevertheless as a final flourish they made their bid to alter the text of the independence proclamation carefully worked out by Sukarno, Hatta, and Subardjo in consultation with the Japanese Maeda, Nishijima, and Miyoshi. This read:

> We the Indonesian people hereby declare Indonesia's Independence. Matters concerning the transfer of power and other matters will be executed in an orderly manner and in the shortest possible time.

Sukarni on behalf of the pemudas objected to the caution of the second sentence, and demanded its replacement by the words:

> All existing government organs must be seized by the people from the foreigners who still occupy them.[20]

Not surprisingly, this change was rejected by the PPKI majority. Finally the pemudas absurdly demanded that they rather than the PPKI delegates should sign the proclamation, since they represented the people and the PPKI represented only the Japanese. As a compromise Sukarno and Hatta alone signed it as 'representatives of the Indonesian people' at about 5 a.m. Later in the morning Sukarno read the proclamation formally to a few hundred people gathered outside his own house. The Republic was symbolically launched with the raising of the red-white flag.

To whom should go the credit for the proclamation of Indonesian independence—the heroic pemudas or the cautious leaders? *perjuangan* (struggle) or *diplomasi*? The issue was close to the heart of Indonesian political debate, for it represented in microcosm the conflict which endured throughout the revolutionary process. Pemuda spokesmen claimed that it was only their pressure, especially through the Rengasdengklok affair, which forced the leaders to declare independence. The kidnapping of Sukarno and Hatta became a model for pemudas throughout the country, who frequently felt the need to force a more spirited approach on their compromising leaders. The older generation have replied that Rengasdengklok achieved nothing but a day's delay in proceedings, that pemuda plans for a revolution in Jakarta were farcical, and that only the leaders' ability to negotiate with the Japanese allowed the Republic to get off the ground.

The weakest part of the pemuda case was the inadequacy of their revolutionary plans. The threat of violence in August was still very limited. When challenged Sukarni and Wikana talked pathetically in terms of killing Ambonese or burning Chinese homes.[21] Without the support of the PETA and Heiho units (most of which refused to move without authorization from Sukarno and Hatta), and without any mass organization, this was about all they could do. Thus they were only too ready to retreat from their high posture given some concession to their pride. Sjahrir's planning was more serious, but he was quick to admit the necessity of Sukarno's support. Undoubtedly the threat of violence was a factor predisposing the Japanese to treat the proclamation leniently, but this was the threat less of a pemuda revolution than of a general descent into anarchy.

On the other hand, had Sukarno and Hatta really acted speedily to declare independence on 15 August it seems probable by hindsight that the Japanese would have allowed them to get away with it. The anxiety of the older politicians to seek assurances which the Japanese could not give suggests that pemuda pressure was necessary to impress the real urgency upon them. The cautious movements of Sukarno and Hatta before their kidnapping give reason to doubt whether they alone would have carried the PPKI to an independence proclamation on the 16th or for some time thereafter.

First Steps

General Yamamoto and his staff evidently were disagreeably surprised to find Maeda involved with the independence proclamation, and continued to state their formal opposition to it—yet they did nothing to prevent the establishment of a republican constitution and government. As in the proclamation crisis, this forbearance arose partly from a sense of commitment to promises already given, and partly from anxiety that Sukarno and Hatta should remain in a position to hold the anti-Japanese youths in check. The two leaders were allowed to proceed along the lines more or less fixed before the Japanese surrender in return for their tacit undertaking to prevent any violent outbreak against Japanese authority.

The first steps toward statehood were taken on 18 August by the PPKI. Sukarno attempted to give it broader authority by adding nine members, six of whom were older nationalists holding key government positions in Jakarta, while the other three were the pemuda leaders Chaerul Saleh, Sukarni, and Wikana. The latter however chose to boycott the 'Japanese-made' assembly, and thus a challenge to the Sukarno-Hatta policy within the committee was temporarily averted. Hatta's alleged reply to the pemudas sheds interesting light on the nature of these first weeks after the proclamation:

> Bung Hatta explained that for them (Sukarno-Hatta) it was difficult to separate their *responsibility* to the Japanese from their *duty* to the people. For this reason, said Hatta, . . . we follow two paths, telling the Japanese that this is a meeting of the PPKI, while we guarantee to the people that this is the first meeting of the Indonesian National Committee.[22]

Despite the fact that the PPKI included a good percentage of outer island delegates and faced a very different situation from the BPKI, very few changes were made to the constitution worked out in July. The most important change resulted from the urgings of a Japanese Navy spokesman, who impressed upon Hatta the dissatisfaction of important Christian minorities within the Navy-administered area over the concessions to Islam. Hatta was able to persuade the principal Islamic spokesmen in the PPKI to accept the elimination of all references to the special place of Islam, on the plea of not alienating any minorities at such a critical moment for the republic. The other major changes related to the transitional period before the representative bodies, allowed for in the constitution, could be elected. Until then, 'their competences shall be exercised by the President assisted by a National Committee'. In case presidential powers were not yet adequate it was added that for six months following the end of the war the President 'shall regulate and prepare everything stipulated by the constitution'.[23] Sukarno and Hatta were elected President and Vice-President by the PPKI. This great stress on the transitional powers of the presidency can only be understood by the delicacy of the relationship with the Japanese. Members felt that 'at that time it was only Sukarno and Hatta who could induce the *Gunseikan* (head of the military administration) gradually to transfer power from the hands of the Japanese army'.[24] Similar reasons explain the ease with which Hatta pushed through the secular state ideals which the nationalists had previously been forced to compromise after bitter debate.

The PPKI met formally again on 19 and 22 August. During these sessions satisfaction was given to the outer island delegates who had pressed for a high degree of regional autonomy. Indonesia was divided into seven provinces: West Java, Central Java, East Java, Sumatra, Kalimantan (Borneo), Sulawesi (Celebes), Maluku (Moluccas and New Guinea), and Sunda Kecil (Lesser Sunda Islands from Bali to Timor). Governors were named for each province, in most cases from among PPKI members themselves. Below the province level was the residency (*Shu*), the key unit of Japanese administration, under a resident. At both residency and province level there would be a national committee to advise and assist the executive. In practice the beginning of the revolution was clearly going to provide ample scope for regional autonomy, as the centre could provide little assistance in the matter of wresting power from local Japanese commanders.

The PPKI entrusted Sukarno and Hatta with the appointment of a Central Indonesian National Committee (Komite Nasional Indonesia Pusat or KNIP), as the provisional representative advisory body. Twelve ministries were decided on. The President was to establish a national armed force to replace the disbanded PETA/Gyugun and Heiho, but initially this would be disguised as a section of a war victims aid society in order not to provoke Japanese retaliation. This section would be called *Badan Keamanan Rakyat* (Peoples' Security Body) or BKR. Finally it was decided to establish a state party headed by the President and Vice-President, to mobilize all forces for the love and defence of the homeland. It would be known as the *Partij Nasional Indonesia* (PNI) in deliberate evocation of Sukarno's pre-war party. The state party was intended to continue the work of the Jawa Hokokai and comparable bodies outside Java. The central leadership announced was basically Hokokai, some of the 'Kaigun group' of Subardjo and some pemudas.

On 22 August the PPKI completed its work. The delegates from Sumatra and Sulawesi flew home in Japanese aircraft the following day. A theoretical basis had been laid for an élitist, authoritarian state, embodying the dislike of liberal democracy which was a common feature of Javanese and Japanese nationalist thinking. The hope was that the progress made in Jakarta could be repeated throughout Indonesia, with leaders trusted by the Japanese using the threat of pemuda violence to gain ever larger concessions from sympathetic or disinterested local commanders.

The Extension of Republican Authority in Java:
August-September 1945
News of the independence proclamation was transmitted throughout Java within hours by young Indonesians in Japanese news and telegraphic agencies. Bandung pemudas succeeded in broadcasting it over the local radio. In each major centre of the island there was a nucleus of the élite and a larger group of pemudas who, through their respective connections with the capital, knew and understood the independence proclamation within a few days. Outside these small groups the proclamation was either disbelieved or regarded as just another act in the play being stage-managed by the Japanese. The public announcement of the Japanese surrender, made only on 22 August following a meeting of Japanese commanders in Singapore, made a much more profound impression on most Indonesians.

An era indisputably had ended. Nobody could be sure what would come in its place.

The 'revolutionary' pemuda élite and the pragmatic older nationalists each attempted to provide direction in their own way. For the latter the primary stress was on gaining control of the administrative apparatus in Java. Most of the the members of the first Republican ministry announced on 4 September[25] were 'collaborating' nationalists who had already been appointed heads or advisers of the departments concerned by the Japanese. The major exceptions in the seventeen-member Cabinet were Foreign Minister Subardjo, who had been attached to Maeda's Navy office, and the Information Minister Amir Sjarifuddin, still languishing in prison as the leader of the anti-Japanese underground of 1942–3. Although the Japanese could not officially recognize any Republican cabinet, they could continue to recognize the remaining individuals within it as Indonesian heads of their respective departments. As the Indonesian employees of government departments proved increasingly unresponsive to instructions from their Japanese superiors, the latter yielded effective control fairly readily to the republican ministers.

A similar process occurred at the local level, with the promotion of Japanese-appointed vice-residents to Republican residents. Special efforts were made to ensure the support of the four Javanese princes for the Republic. Despite strong anti-monarchic traditions in the nationalist movement the PPKI had recommended no change in their status. On 19 August a ministerial mission was appointed to the princely lands. It rapidly secured agreements that the four states formed *daerah istimewa* (special regions) of the Indonesian Republic. Finally the Republican leadership gave priority to winning over the top echelons of the pamong praja at an all-Java conference convened on 30 August. There Sukarno explained the 'gentleman's agreement' with the Japanese for the transfer of administrative functions to Indonesians. He promised to maintain the status and position of the administrative hierarchy.[26]

Hatta lucidly explained the strategy adopted in these first weeks as 'the seizure of power from within'. The alternative of creating a wholly new government in defiance of the Japanese, he argued,

> would have caused a violent struggle and the victory would not certainly have been ours. It would have created two different government administrations side by side.
> . . . the administrative structure capable of working effectively would have been allowed to fall into the hands of the Japanese to be handed over to the Allies.[27]

Cogent as this reasoning was, it did not reconcile pemuda enthusiasts to the other side of Sukarno's 'gentleman's agreement'—his undertaking to curb violent confrontations with the Japanese. Insofar as the pemudas can be said to have had a policy it was one of action, mass mobilization, and intimidation. A few of the Jakarta pemuda élite associated with Sukarno were strongly influenced by Tan Malaka's 'mass action' strategies. This veteran revolutionary, still incognito, had taken lodgings in Sukarni's house on the night of 14 August. But the pemudas were short on organization—indeed most of them came to distrust large scale organization of any kind. The leaders in the capital owed their eminence to their pre-war political role and their links with Sukarno, Hatta, Subardjo, and Sjahrir. But more typical pemuda leaders were those in charge of semi-militarized groups during the Japanese occupation, or who for other reasons were able to persuade and inspire a group of followers to join them in the streets. The relationship between pemuda groups was one of example rather than command.

Up to the second week of September pemuda action was mainly directed towards raising red and white flags on public buildings, distributing information and exhortation, and taking over some facilities. By mid-September, however, pemuda militants in the cities had gained both the ability and the determination to organize mass rallies. These had been expressly forbidden by the Japanese because of the danger of violence. For that reason Republican officials also tried to discourage them, though they could not refuse to address them if held. Surabaya was the first city where mass meetings were organized, on 11 and 17 September. It remained the most extreme case in Java where pemudas held the initiative from a rather unimpressive older group. Because of the influence of the Republican leadership Jakarta had no such rally until 19 September, and then only because Sukarno and Hatta were presented with a virtual fait accompli. It was however a massive one. Up to 200,000 people filled the vast central square now called Medan Merdeka. Japanese tanks and guns threatened from every corner of the square. In the briefest of speeches Sukarno pleaded that everyone should trust their leaders and at once go home quietly. The crowd obeyed. Violence was avoided, and Sukarno demonstrated in compelling terms his indispensability to the Japanese or anyone who wished to take their place in Java.

For the population at large, these mass rallies in mid-September were the first opportunity for participation in the new independence movement. As Anderson puts it, they represented 'a psychological emergence from the cocoon created by the Japanese aura of omnipotence'.[28] Pressure mounted on senior government officials to ignore their Japanese superiors, whose attendance in office was made increasingly disagreeable. By 25 September the transfer of effective power had gone far enough for the government to call an end to the system of dual responsibility. All officials were finally declared to be officials of the Republic. Only token resistance to these moves came from the Japanese.

The PPKI decisions of 22 August had established three government organs alongside the administration itself: the Komité Nasional Indonesia (KNI); the PNI State Party; and the para-military BKR. Each of these was to be duplicated at province, residency, and lower levels. The state party, however, was suspended at the end of August, leaving the KNI in each region as the representative body linking the administration and popular forces at each level, and the BKR as the teeth of the government. KNIs were set up quickly in the regions, generally as extensions of wartime Jawa Hokokai branches with a few prominent additions. They were therefore very much the organs of the older nationalist élite. In some areas, such as Bandung, they seem to have retained the initiative vis a vis militant pemuda groups until the outbreak of major fighting. In other centres, notably Surabaya, the KNI was never a very effective mediator. For their part the pemudas were much less homogeneous. Although in early September the leftish intellectuals among them formed youth groups such as API in Jakarta, PRI in Surabaya, and AMRI in Semarang, these could not for long control the increasing number of young men flocking to wherever the action was.

The BKR could have been a very effective weapon for the government had it succeeded in smoothly absorbing the Japanese-trained PETA/Gyugun and Heiho units. Nasution estimated there were 150,000 Indonesians in Java and Sumatra with military training.[29] But on this point the Japanese were firm, in the interests of their own self-preservation as well as their responsibility to the Allies. In the period 18–22 August all PETA and Gyugun units in Java, Bali, and Sumatra were disarmed and asked to return to their homes. In most cases this manoeuvre preceded news of the Japanese surrender, and where necessary it was camouflaged by suggestions that the Indonesian soldiers would be rearmed with heavier weapons. The soldiers were too stunned and confused to attempt resistance, and their political leaders gave them no encouragement to do so. Only near Jakarta did a few PETA men desert with their arms. The Heiho soldiers throughout the Achipelago were even easier to demobilize because of their completely subordinate position.

Continuity within the army was therefore lost. In any case the autonomy of local PETA/Gyugun units gave little opportunity for military leadership above the company level. The BKR had to begin almost from scratch, on a footing not very different from the *badan perjuangan* ('struggle bodies') which began to form at about the same time from among educated anti-Japanese pemudas,

Japanese-sponsored youth organizations, and various religious, ethnic, or other pemuda groups. The strength of the BKR in each area depended on the initiative the local ex-Gyugun officers showed in re-assembling and guiding their men. In general they were more disciplined than other pemudas and more prepared to accept the authority of local officials. Unless they took a positive lead in confronting the Japanese, however, they quickly found themselves surpassed by 'civilian' units in the area. Initiative remained entirely local. The Republican cabinet showed extreme caution in moving to co-ordinate BKR activities or provide it with arms. No appointment was even made to the defence portfolio until 5 October, when it was entrusted symbolically to Lieutenant Suprijadi, leader of the Blitar revolt and generally assumed dead.

Nevertheless arms flowed swiftly from Japanese to Indonesian hands, especially in regions where there was co-operation between the 'diplomatic' leaders trusted by the local Japanese officers, and the pemudas. Japanese commanders in Java and Sumatra quickly came to accept a standard formula, typified by the response of the *Shuchokan* (Resident) of Madiun in early September 1945:

> The demoralized *Shuchokan* explained that he was unable to surrender his arms just like that, because it would be contrary to the instructions he had received; but if the people attacked, he would be forced to surrender his arms on the grounds of preventing bloodshed. He therefore suggested a mock attack by the people. In accordance with this pretence, on a certain day thousands of people and pemudas carrying sharpened bamboos, knives, and machetes surrounded the barracks of the Japanese unit, which finally surrendered all its arms without resistance.[30]

Sometimes the pretence turned into reality, one side or the other did not keep to the rules, and blood was shed. But large quantities of arms did pass into the hands of the bolder pemuda leaders at very little cost, strengthening the romantic view that heroism and *perjuangan* (struggle) alone was the key to victory.

By the end of September there was throughout Java a government machinery in Indonesian hands, an increasingly violent and well-armed 'revolutionary' pemuda movement, and a top political leadership accepted as legitimate by the great majority of inhabitants. What was lacking was co-ordination between the three. The caution required by Sukarno and Hatta's 'revolution from within' strategy inhibited the political leaders from effectively mediating between the revolutionary movement and the administration. There was, therefore, a general devolution of authority and initiative to the residency or kabupaten level. At each level pemuda enthusiasts and administrators established their own uneasy relationship. A revolutionary process was beginning spontaneously in numerous centres throughout Java.

The Republic Outside Java

Before the war all the important Indonesian political and social organizations had headquarters in Java and branches throughout the archipelago. All sizeable Indonesian towns were cosmopolitan in population and national in political orientation. In normal times one would have expected developments in Java to be repeated on a smaller scale throughout the archipelago. But the cleavages the Japanese occupation had created between Java, Sumatra, and the Navy-occupied territories, were not easy to bridge. The objective of isolating the outer islands from the relatively advanced political atmosphere of Java, which had been pursued ineffectively and ambiguously by the Dutch, was achieved almost unwittingly by the Japanese.

Given the separate paths followed by Java, Sumatra, and the Navy-administered area under the Japanese, the factors impeding a vigorous independence movement in the latter two areas could be summarized as follows:

1 Their less concentrated and urbanized population.
2 The strength of traditional monarchies in many areas, allowing the Dutch ample scope for manipulating and intimidating semi-autonomous rulers. The threat of deposition on the grounds of having collaborated with the Japanese was an effective Dutch weapon against many rajas.
3 The more politically repressive and intensive Japanese administration in these areas, showing the pre-war Dutch régime in a better light by contrast.
4 The extremely belated and inadequate Japanese preparations for independence.
5 The substantially greater Japanese troop strength (especially in relation to population) in the outer islands. At the surrender there were over 125,000 Japanese troops in the Navy area, as against about 71,000 in Sumatra and about 50,000 in Java.[31] Not surprisingly, Japanese co-operation with the independence movement after the surrender seemed to be in inverse proportion to Japanese numbers.[32]
6 The earlier Allied presence. General MacArthur's Southwest Pacific Command already occupied Tarakan and Balikpapan (Borneo), Morotai, and parts of New Guinea before the surrender, and Dutch Civil Affairs units were established in all these centres. Admiral Mountbatten's Southeast Asia Command parachuted

several units into northern Sumatra in July 1945, as part of the preparation for the invasion of Malaya planned for 7 September. By contrast there had been no Allied preparations for any operations in Java.

In all these respects Sumatra occupied a middle position between Java and the islands under the Japanese Navy. Although anxious to keep Sumatra completely autonomous, the Japanese 25th Army in Sumatra was much more influenced by developments in Java than was the Navy. Most concessions in Java towards Indonesian participation at the residency level were followed in Sumatra within a few months: advisory councils, *gyugun* (equivalent of PETA), and some propaganda organizations for the nationalists in 1943; permission to use the Indonesian flag and anthem in late 1944; the appointment of Indonesians as deputy residents and assistant residents in 1945. Within each residency nationalist leaders were permitted to extend their popular following considerably. But neither Sukarno and Hatta from Jakarta nor anybody within Sumatra was permitted to build a pan-Sumatran organization or following.

Only in the last three months of the occupation did the Japanese 25th Army take any effective measures to counteract this deficiency. Probably they realized that only by doing so could they expect to retain influence over Sumatra within the coming 'independent' Indonesia. An all-Sumatra Central Advisory Council met once, from 27 June to 2 July 1945. At the last minute the 25th Army attempted to build around it in Bukittinggi some permanent co-ordinating organs under the leadership of Muhammad Sjafei, a respected Minangkabau educationist. However, the Sumatran delegation to the PPKI did not include any of those being groomed for leadership in Bukittinggi; nor did it include the only national-level politician in Sumatra, Dr A. K. Gani, soon to become the successful Republican Resident of Palembang. Two of the three PPKI delegates were intellectuals from Medan. Not surprisingly the PPKI chose one of them, the Acehnese lawer Mr Teuku Hasan, as Republican Governor of Sumatra, and Medan rather than Bukittinggi was his capital.

Although the potential for anti-colonial militance was at least as great in Sumatra as in Java, the three PPKI delegates who returned to Sumatra on 23 August were in a poor position to co-ordinate this enthusiasm. Until about the middle of September the independence proclamation was known and understood by only a handful of leaders in each major city. The appointed republican capital was a city notoriously rent by hostility between the 'indigenous' Malay aristocracy and the 'immigrant' Indonesians who comprised most of the nationalist intelligentsia. Moreover Medan was the first city in Java or Sumatra where British and Dutch officers attempted to establish authority of their own, as soon as the first of Mountbatten's parachute units made its way to the city on 1 September. Not until Medan pemudas became mobilized at the end of September as a result of news from Java and southern Sumatra did Hasan publicly announce the decisions of the PPKI. On 3 October he began to act officially as Republican governor, and to appoint residents for every part of Sumatra.

Up to this point, with the notable exception of Dr Gani in Palembang, nationalist leaders in most Sumatran residencies were inhibited by lack of any clear mandate. The initiative fell to the militant pemuda organizations which had formed in all the towns during September, usually led by former gyugun officers. The result, to a greater extent even than in Java, was that pemudas came to see themselves as the vanguard of the revolution, not necessarily answerable to any of the older leaders.

The administration of all the important residencies was in Republican hands by the middle of October. But Mr Hasan, an administrator previously unknown in southern and central Sumatra, was never able to establish his authority over all the diverse regions and cultures of the island. It was a godsend for eventual Indonesian unity that the 25th Army had made no better use of its opportunity to build a separate Sumatran leadership.

In most of the area controlled by the Japanese Navy there was little opportunity for a viable Republican movement to develop at all. The Navy had belatedly made public its commitment to Indonesian independence only on 29 April, 1945—the Emperor's birthday. On that auspicious date Sukarno, Subardjo, Admiral Maeda, and others came from Jakarta to address a rally in Makassar, where for the first time the red and white flag was flown. Maeda appears to have been responsible for ensuring that Jakarta-based leaders played a part in independence preparations in the Navy area, unlike Sumatra. In June, Sukarno and Subardjo also visited Bali, while Hatta visited Banjermasin. But although well received by youth, these critical visitors encountered some resistance among the more aristocratically-oriented politicians of the Navy area.

In late June 1945 the Navy for the first time sanctioned a nationalist mass movement, abbreviated as SUDARA, initially in South Sulawesi and later in Banjermasin and Bali. Only in South Sulawesi was it allowed to become effective. Its chairman there was the Raja of Bone, the most influential and anti-Dutch of the South Sulawesi rulers. Its effective organizer was the veteran Menadonese (North Sulawesi Christian) nationalist Dr G. S. S. J. Ratulangie, who had been brought from Jakarta to Makassar a year earlier as a mainly decorative 'adviser' to the administration. Ratulangie was able to build through SUDARA the basis of his future Republican staff.

After the surrender the Navy transferred most civilian functions to the local rajas or officials, some of whom had been prepared beforehand. But there was no opportunity to transform these diverse local authorities into a Republican government. Of the four governors appointed by the PPKI to the Navy area, Ir Pangeran Mohamad Noor never reached Borneo, nor Mr Latuharhary the Moluccas. Mr Pudja, Governor of the Lesser Sunda Islands, made his way to Bali and established a government there, but his influence never extended beyond that island. Dr Ratulangie, on the other hand, was flown back to Makassar and told by the Japanese that he would be responsible for civil government in South Sulawesi. Elsewhere everything depended on the disposition of a few local leaders. In Sumbawa, for example, an individual raja was sympathetic to the Republic. However, it was easy for the incoming Allies to eliminate such a movement by arresting or intimidating the raja concerned.

South Sulawesi was a special case not only because Navy preparations for independence had been almost wholly concentrated there, but also because of the relatively independent attitude of its half-dozen major rulers. These had been brought under effective Dutch control only forty years earlier, and some, such as the Raja of Bone, had fought as young men against that control. The Bugis and Makassarese people had not adapted as willingly to colonial education and administration as some of their Christian neighbours, and found the Dutch administration in Celebes heavily staffed by Ambonese and Menadonese. This tendency was reversed to a significant extent under the Japanese, creating further reluctance on the part of Bugis and Makassarese to see a restoration of Dutch rule. Although Ratulangie was never able to control Makassar town, where pro-Dutch elements were strong, he did succeed in the course of October in obtaining the support of all the major rajas of South Sulawesi.

The situation confronting the Allies in October might be summarized as follows: in Java a functioning government apparatus accepting the authority of Sukarno's Republican cabinet, though strongly challenged in many areas by pemuda activists; in Sumatra a series of functioning Republican governments in the major residencies, though with little co-ordination between them; in South Sulawesi and Bali Republican governors more or less supported by the local aristocracy; elsewhere no broadly-based Republican movement, although there was a militant anti-Dutch pemuda movement in every sizeable town.

References

1 Pramoedya Ananta Toer, 'Dia yang menyerah', in *Tjerita dari Blora*, Jakarta, 1952, p. 277.

2 The relevant sections of the *Pancasila* speech are translated in H. Feith and L. Castles, *Indonesian Political Thinking 1945–1965*, Ithaca, 1970, pp. 44–8. Like many Javanese intellectuals Sukarno developed a belief in the equivalence of the great religions, particularly after his contact with Catholic missionaries while in exile in Flores. M. P. M. Muskens, *Indonesië: Een strijd om nationale identiteit*, Bussum, 1969, pp. 141–2. *Sukarno, An Autobiography as told to Cindy Adams*, Hong Kong, 1966, p. 114.

3 This prologue became known as the 'Jakarta charter' of 22 June 1945. It is in Muhammad Yamin, *Naskah-Persiapan Undang-Undang Dasar 1945*, Jakarta, 1954, Vol. I, p. 154.

4 *Ibid.*, Vol. 1, pp. 184 and 259.

5 *Sukarno, An Autobiography*, p. 195, gives Hatta's belief in federalism as one of the reasons for this, though the incomplete record of BPKI debates in Yamin identifies by name only Latuharhary as a spokesman for federalism; p. 258. For the concern of Hatta and Yamin about checks upon executive power see Yamin Vol. I, p.p. 299–300, 230–9 and 330–6 respectively.

6 Yamin Vol. I, p. 263.

7 *Ibid.* Vol. I, p. 214.

8 Proposal of the Cabinet, 12 July 1945, in Benda, Irikura, and Kishi (eds), *Japanese Military Administration in Indonesia: Selected Documents*, Yale Southeast Asia Studies, 1965, p. 272.

9 Decision of the Supreme War Guidance Council 17 July 1945, in *ibid.*, p. 274.

10 'Kepada Kawan', in Burton Raffel (ed.), *The Complete Poetry and Prose of Chairil Anwar*, p. 114. I have slightly altered Raffel's translation.

11 Notes of Sanyo Kaigi (Council of Advisers) 8 January 1945, translated by B. Anderson in *Indonesia* 2, 1966, p. 93.

12 B. R. O'G. Anderson, *Some Aspects of Indonesian Politics under the Japanese Occupation: 1944–1945*, Ithaca, 1961, p. 48.

13 Ki Hadjar Dewantoro, in *Asia Raya* 19 June 1945, as cited in Dahm, p. 304.

14 There has been some unnecessary speculation about the motives behind Maeda's sponsorship for allegedly 'communist' indoctrination at this school; G. McT. Kahin, *Nationalism and Revolution in Indonesia*, Ithaca, 1952, pp. 115–21. Although one of Maeda's principal assistants Yoshizumi appears to have come by the surrender to share the nationalist and vaguely Marxist orientation of many Indonesian intellectuals, and to have fought subsequently for the Republic, no evidence has emerged for specifically communist flavour at the asrama. Many Indonesians who either before or after the war considered themselves communists did work for the Japanese, but nobody known to be active in the cause of Moscow was left at liberty. On this point see Anderson, *Java*, pp. 44–7; and Subardjo in the *Djakarta Times* 15 and 30 July 1945.

15 The importance, both symbolic and real, of this episode has ensured a relative abundance of accounts by the principal Indonesian participants. These are discussed below, pp. 175–83, in the review of literature.

16 It is difficult to establish at what point the influence became important of Tan Malaka, the most consistent and able Indonesian exponent of mass action. Tan Malaka had returned clandestinely to Indonesia in 1942 after 20 years exile, and on the night of 14 August he came to lodge with Sukarni, a prominent leader of the Menteng 31 asrama. Although he evidently

argued for mass revolution, his influence was probably limited until his real identity became known in September.

17 Adam Malik, *Riwajat dan perdjuangan sekitar proklamasi kemerdekaan Indonesia 17 Agustus 1945*, revised ed., Jakarta, 1970, p. 69.

18 *Ibid*. p. 35.

19 *Ibid*. p. 37.

20 *Ibid*. p. 54.

21 Hatta, *Sekitar Proklamasi 17 Agustus 1945*, Jakarta, 1970, pp. 35 and 49–50.

22 Malik, p. 63. My translation closely follows that of Anderson, *Some Aspects*, p. 108. Malik is, of course, a hostile source.

23 The official English translation in Yamin Vol. I, p. 56.

24 Iwa Kusuma Sumantri, *Sedjarah Revolusi Indonesia*, II, Jakarta, n.d., p. 31.

25 This is the date usually given, though the generally reliable Koesnodiprodjo, *Himpunan Undang 2, Peraturan 2, Penetapan 2, Pemerintah Republik Indonesia 1945*, Jakarta, 1951, pp. 87–8, reproduces an announcement of the cabinet on 19 August. Possibly nominations to ministries, as to governorships, were made by PPKI committees but not presidentially confirmed or publicized until September.

26 Anderson, *Java*, pp. 113–14. An earlier reference by Sukarno to the 'gentleman's agreement' on 29 August is in Koesnodiprodjo, p. 122.

27 Anderson, *Java*, p. 112, quoting Hatta, 'Isi Proklamsi'.

28 *Ibid*. p. 124.

29 A. H. Nasution, *Fundamentals of Guerrilla Warfare*, Singapore, 1965, p. 31.

30 Susanto Tirtoprodjo, *Sedjarah Revolusi Nasional Indonesia*, Jakarta, 1966, p. 31.

31 Details of Japanese troop concentrations are in the official Indian and Australian war histories, viz. Rajendra Singh, *Post-war Occupation Forces: Japan and Southeast Asia*, Kanpur, 1954, pp. 253–6; Gavin Long, *The Final Campaigns*, Canberra, 1963, p. 555.

32 'In all [Navy] areas the Japanese strove to behave with meticulous correctness'; Long, *op. cit*. p. 568.

Chapter Three

THE ALLIED COUNTERREVOLUTION

*Java drifts towards anarchy. The British
seem unable to send enough troops there.
The Dutch seem unwilling to make any move
politically. The Indonesian nationalist
leaders seem powerless to direct the movement
of which they are supposed to be the head*
The Times special correspondent, 15 October 1945

Allied Planning for Post-war Indonesia

The Japanese surrender caught the Allies totally unprepared to assume authority in Indonesia. Not only was there a woeful lack of men, transport, intelligence information, and logistic planning to occupy this vast country rapidly; even the principles on which the post-war government of Indonesia should be built had not been clearly settled by the powers concerned. As one of the belligerents, Holland was secure in Allied recognition of her legal sovereignty over all her pre-war territory. Allied governments had continued to deal with a Netherlands Indies Government functioning provisionally at Brisbane under a relatively progressive Lieutenant Governor-General, Hubertus van Mook. Dutch Civil Administration teams and even token Dutch fighting units were attached where possible to Allied invasion forces on Indonesian territory. Yet the view was taken seriously by the more powerful Allies that the war must result in 'liberation for all peoples',[1] which could hardly mean the simple restoration of pre-war colonial regimes. During the war there was little serious questioning of vaguely-worded Dutch pronouncements about a new post-war order. Differences came quickly into the open after the surrender.

Detailed arrangements for the post-war administration of Indonesia were complicated by the transfer of responsibility for the Indonesian area on 15 August from MacArthur's Southwest Pacific

Command, based first in Australia and then in Manila, to Mount-batten's Southeast Asia Command (SEAC), based in Ceylon. Prior to this only Sumatra had been within Mountbatten's sphere, and the Admiral had resisted any further responsibilities until he had a Southeast Asian base in Singapore. The principal Dutch liaison effort had been with the Southwest Pacific Command. Van Mook had less than two months' notice of the transfer, and then only in the vaguest terms.

It was only on 24 August 1945 that a formal Anglo-Dutch Civil Affairs Agreement was concluded to cover the new situation. This posited a transitional phase of Allied military administration in which full *de facto* authority (but not *de jure* sovereignty) would reside with the Allied (British) Commander. Administration of civilians would as far as possible be entrusted to the Dutch personnel of the Netherlands Indies Civil Administration (NICA) who would enforce pre-war laws. NICA would therefore form part of the Military Administration under overall British control, until the British considered the military situation allowed them to transfer all powers to the Netherlands Indies Government.

These plans assumed a readiness on the part of the Indonesian populace to accept a return of the pre-war régime, with gradual modifications. Very little was known by the Allies about the development of the nationalist movement under the Japanese. The independence proclamation was dismissed as a Japanese manoeuvre, and Sukarno as an unprincipled collaborator who would be condemned by his own people. Until the first British party reached Jakarta on 15 September SEAC had to make do with the sparse and one-sided intelligence provided by NICA. The propaganda, broadcast or air-dropped under Allied auspices, continued to stress that the 'legal' régime would be restored and that collaborators would be punished. Such propaganda only strengthened the determination of pemudas with any Japanese training to resist an Allied occupation.

The Dutch Position
In comparing the rigidity of Dutch colonial policy in 1945 with that of Britain or even France, it is necessary to emphasize the enormous economic stake which Holland had in Indonesia. The wartime Prime Minister of the Netherlands pleaded,[2]

> if the bonds which attach the Netherlands to the Indies are severed there will be a permanent reduction in the national income of the Netherlands which will lead to the country's pauperization.

However much Holland's post-war performance has made nonsense of this gloomy prediction, it was widely held before 1950. Moreover the conservative trend of immediate pre-war Dutch policy had so successfully pushed Indonesian nationalist leaders to the periphery of public life that few Dutchmen had any conception how deep and strong the nationalist current ran. Sukarno and his colleagues in the infant Republic were regarded by most Dutchmen as unrepresentative extremists whose rapid rise during the Japanese regime was further evidence of their treachery. Those who had suffered most from the Japanese (the Dutch prisoners-of-war and internees) regarded Sukarno with special hatred as the supreme anti-Dutch spokesman and symbol. To them it was inconceivable that he would go unpunished, let alone be honoured as a President.

Even in the depths of its wartime weakness, the Netherlands Government-in-exile made no concessions to ultimate Indonesian independence. Its principal statement was the Queen's speech to the 'Netherlands Indies' on the anniversary of Pearl Harbour, 6 December 1942. The then Prime Minister later emphasized that although the statement was drawn up partly to satisfy American anti-colonial sentiment, it 'was based on the indivisibility of the Kingdom within the framework of the established Constitution'.[3] Its only firm promise was to summon a post-war conference of the various parts of the Kingdom to consider their relationship to one another. The speech indicated, however, that an acceptable result of such a conference would be 'complete self-reliance and freedom of conduct for each part [of the Kingdom] regarding its internal affairs, but with the readiness to render mutual assistance'.[4] There was no reference to democratization or the transfer of responsibilities to Indonesians. The promises held out were, if anything, more restricted than those of 1918.

The first break in the thirty year succession of conservative Dutch cabinets came in June 1945, when a new post-liberation, extra-parliamentary ministry gave the Dutch Labour Party its long-denied voice in the government. Catholic-Labour coalitions predominated for the following five years. The first Colonial Minister of the new government, Professor Logemann, had, like Van Mook, been a member of the small pre-war *Stuw* group of progressive intellectuals in Indonesia, who recognized the reality of Indonesian nationalism and the need to accommodate it by a gradual progression towards independence. The Governor-General of Netherlands India, Tjarda van Starkenborgh Stachouwer, released from Japanese imprisonment in Manchuria on 19 August, resigned his post on 16 October because he could not agree to co-operate with Indonesian nationalism. Van Mook therefore continued to be the senior Dutch representative in Indonesia.

This significant shift in official Dutch policy was hardly noticed initially in Indonesia. The great majority of Dutchmen in the East continued to talk and act in terms of the traditional policy. This was pre-eminently true of the chief military spokesmen, Admiral Helfrich and General van Oyen, and of most officials confirmed in their pre-war positions as they emerged from Japanese camps. As one Dutch officer noted,[5] the reappointment of pre-war officials

> made the population suspicious, because they thought they saw in this a return to pre-war colonial conditions, instead of their expectations of important political and social reforms . . .
> Indeed the tactless behaviour of some colonial officials gave reason to strengthen them in that opinion.

During October 'roving patrols of trigger-happy Dutch and Ambonese soldiers', armed by the Allies, attempted to terrorize or provoke Republican pemudas in a manner strikingly at variance with Van Mook's policy.[6] Whether this resulted from vengeful individuals or from a military attempt to sabotage any Dutch agreement with the Republic the effect on Indonesian opinion was the same. In short, the gulf between Republican and Dutch opinion in 1945 was so wide that differences within each camp were of minor importance. However they differed about long-term aims, Dutch officials were united in seeking an initial restoration of Dutch authority. The Republic, which manifestly and increasingly spoke for the great majority of articulate Indonesians, was equally united in commitment to its own continued existence.

The Australians in Former Navy Territory

It soon became apparent to the British military commanders in Indonesia that the Anglo-Dutch agreement of 24 August left the most difficult question unanswered. Given the fact that the Republic was the only effective government over most of the Indonesian population, were the Allies committed to destroying that government and imposing Dutch rule by force on a largely unwilling people? No clear official answer was ever given to this question. The Allies in the event reacted pragmatically to the situation before them and the limited force at their disposal, and their policy varied widely from one area to another.

It was in the area previously under Japanese Navy control that 'the fullest and smoothest implementation of the plans drawn up' by the Allies occurred.[7] Although this area, like Java, was technically transferred to SEAC on 15 August, Mountbatten had far too few men to cope even with Sumatra and Java. Until sufficient British or Dutch troops could be mobilized, therefore, the Australian Army, released from the now dissolved Southwest Pacific Command, was requested to take responsibility for Borneo, Sulawesi, and all the eastern islands except Bali and Lombok.

The Australians already had substantial strength in British and Dutch Borneo, in New Guinea, and in their forward headquarters at Morotai. After the Japanese surrender they were able to move with much greater speed than the British to occupy the main cities in their sphere: Kupang (Timor) on 11 September; Banjermasin on 17 September; Makassar on 21 September; Ambon on 22 September; Menado on 2 October; Pontianak on 16 October. Because the Australians with their associated NICA units reached most of these centres well before any organized Republican movement, they had relatively little difficulty carrying out the original plan to prepare a Dutch takeover of the administration. When anti-Dutch demonstrations occurred in the cities of Borneo and Sulawesi the Australians had no hesitation in suppressing them. A working Republican government in Gorontalo was dismantled by a Dutch/Australian force on 29 November, and its leader, Nani Wartabone, arrested. Although both the overall Allied commander, Mountbatten, and the Australian Labor Government supported a negotiated solution to the Dutch–Indonesian conflict, the Australian military was able to act on different presumptions.[8]

The biggest test for Australian policy was in South Sulawesi where the rajas, with obvious popular support, backed Ratulangie and refused any dealings with the Dutch. To impose Dutch rule by force in these areas, as Indonesians were not slow to point out, would gravely disturb the law and order the Allies were there to maintain. The Australian 'Makassar Force' was faced with two contradictory obligations: on the one hand to remain neutral in internal politics; on the other to regard NICA as an integral part of its military administration. The early commander, General Dougherty, placed primary emphasis on the first principle, to the point of restricting Dutch troops to barracks after they had provoked an ugly incident on 16 October. His successor from 19 October, General Chilton, was more concerned with the second. As he explained in a memo to local commanders:[9]

NICA is an integral part of the military administration and its orders and instructions have the authority of the Force Commander. . . It is our duty to assist in establishing the authority of NICA, and in the restoration of a more orderly civil administration. Some local chiefs and propagandists purport to dissociate NICA from the AMF [Australian Military Forces]. They say that they will obey the orders of the military commander, but will not recognize, obey or cooperate with NICA. It will be quite evident from the above that this attitude is entirely incorrect.

From 20 October the Australians began a policy of active patrols throughout South Sulawesi to provide protection for returning

NICA units, since 'it is not yet advisable for NICA ... officers to travel into the interior if not adequately escorted'.[10] Most of the rulers, led by the strong-minded Raja of Bone, continued to avoid all relations with the Dutch officials sent to their districts, though as long as the Australians were there they did not proceed to hostilities. By the end of November, however, the rajas began to feel that the tougher Australian line gave them no choice but to accept NICA at least temporarily.

Cooperation with NICA was forced on the local rulers in many ways, primarily by making them go to the NICA representative for rice, petrol, etc. This went a long way towards re-establishing the authority of NICA.[11]

Resistance to the Dutch went suddenly underground in December.

Although British troops continued to be unavailable for the islands outside Java and Sumatra, it proved possible for Dutch (KNIL) military units to relieve the Australians in most areas during December, and even in South Sulawesi a month later. On 2 February the Australians handed their remaining nominal authority to a British Indian Brigade in Makassar, but the effective Allied presence outside that single city was Dutch. The British did not interfere when the Dutch arrested Ratulangie and six of his assistants on 5 April. These republicans were exiled three months later to an island off New Guinea. The two most prominent politicians left at liberty in Sulawesi, Mr Tadjoeddin Noor and the mayor of Makassar Nadjamoedin, agreed to pursue their nationalist goals within the narrowing constraints set by the Dutch.

The remaining nominal authority of SEAC outside Java and Sumatra was surrendered on 13 July 1946, leaving the Dutch free to set about erecting a series of federal governments there with which to offset the Republic (see chapter 6).

The British in Java and Sumatra

The relationship between the Allied military administration and NICA in the Australian-occupied area was in Dutch eyes a simple fulfilment of the Anglo-Dutch agreements. They continually demanded similar treatment in Java and Sumatra. But Allied military forces reached these islands later than any other important part of Japanese-occupied Southeast Asia, and they found on arrival a vastly more difficult problem than the Australians.

The first landings of British Indian troops did not take place until 30 September in Jakarta; 20 and 25 October respectively in the two other major ports of Java—Semarang and Surabaya; 10 October in Medan and Padang; and 25 October in Palembang. Liaison teams operating earlier in various places, primarily in the interests of the internees, found that the only effective administration in most areas was Republican. From their reports Mountbatten learned before the landings that NICA would not be accepted without a severe fight. This he was unwilling to undertake with only three divisions of Indian troops, the most he could have available even by November.

On the eve of the first landing in Jakarta, therefore, Mountbatten drastically limited Allied objectives. Only two (later raised to four) key towns in Java, and two (later three) in Sumatra, would be occupied. Outside these areas the re-establishment of Netherlands authority was to be entirely a Dutch responsibility, with British troops assisting only in disarming Japanese and rescuing internees. Lieutenant General Sir Philip Christison, the hastily-appointed Allied Commander, Netherlands East Indies, made these general policies public at a momentous press conference in Singapore on 29 September. He was quoted on radio SEAC as having said that the Republican leaders would not be removed as collaborators. On the contrary he would 'ask the present Party leaders to treat him and his troops as guests', and to co-operate in assisting internees.[12]

The Dutch claimed with indignation, and the Indonesians with relief, that this remark constituted *de facto* recognition of the Republic. The British denied this. They had to profess that they recognized no authority in Indonesia save that of the Dutch. Yet it was already clear and becoming clearer that the British found NICA a liability in attempting to come to terms with the Indonesian population. Christison needed the Republic as the only authority which could be held responsible for Indonesian actions. His statement, especially in the exaggerated form it reached Indonesian newspapers, undoubtedly had the effect of legitimating the Republic in areas which had previously been undecided.

True to this British policy of avoiding where possible being drawn into any large-scale armed conflict in Indonesia, Christison curbed the provocative activities of Dutch and Ambonese troops in the occupied towns. In the face of strong Republican protest against the landing of 800 Dutch marines at Jakarta on 30 December he forbade further landings. Most Dutch troops were diverted to the Australian-occupied islands. In late October, the hated NICA was replaced in Java and Sumatra by AMACAB (Allied Military Administration—Civil Affairs Branch) under tighter British control. AMACAB was 'personal rather than territorial in character, controlling only Dutch, Indo–Europeans, and other minority communities. Indonesians were controlled, if at all, by the Republican administration'.[13]

Mountbatten believed the only solution to the unexpected difficulties in Java and Sumatra lay in Dutch concessions towards Sukarno, comparable to his own dealing with Aung San in Burma. With general support from London, he put pressure on Van Mook to reach an agreement with the Republic before March 1946. By this date he estimated political pressure in India would necessitate the withdrawal of his troops.

To the Netherlands this was anathema. When Van Mook began discussions with Republican leaders at the end of October the uproar in Holland forced his government to disavow him completely. Discussions with the 'arch-collaborator', Sukarno, were specifically ruled out by The Hague. Yet the Dutch could do little except bluster. Van Mook had calculated that a military strength of at least 75,000 men would be necessary to restore Dutch authority in Java and Sumatra. There was no chance of the Dutch having more than half this by the March 1946 deadline. Moreover the sympathy of the Australian Left for Indonesian political internees and seamen who had spent the war in Australia led on 28 September to a wharf labourers' ban on shipments for the Dutch in Indonesia.[14] Besides setting back Dutch attempts to move officials, stores, and troops from Australia to Indonesia, this gave warning of the sort of international action which might be expected on a bigger scale if systematic military operations against the Republic were attempted.

These factors made it impossible for the Dutch to reject out of hand British pressure to negotiate with the Republic. The formation of an 'anti-collaborationist' Sjahrir ministry on 14 November made the pill easier to swallow. Van Mook was authorized almost immediately to negotiate with Sjahrir, though not with Sukarno. Even so the Indonesian and Dutch positions were poles apart. In December Van Mook flew to Holland to try to persuade his government to adopt a more realistic position.

The Battle of Surabaya: October–November 1945
The achievement of gaining this degree of British and Dutch recognition for the infant Republic was by no means that of the sophisticated politicians in Jakarta alone. Militant pemuda action in Surabaya and elsewhere had conjured before European eyes the terrifying spectre of uncontrollable mass violence in the event of Allied action against the Republic.

The landing of Allied troops in Jakarta at the end of September raised the level of tension throughout Java by posing a latent threat to the gains already made by the Republic. During October relations between the *pasukan* (fighting bands) of the pemudas and pro-Dutch elements worsened markedly. The ethnic out-groups— Eurasians, Chinese, Ambonese, and Dutch internees—began to face intimidation, kidnap, robbery, and occasional murder, especially in cases where they appeared to be preparing an enthusiastic welcome for the Allies and NICA. As such minor incidents began to multiply there was a steady deterioration of order. The Indonesian police and BKR were inadequately prepared to fill the role abdicated by the Japanese.

The policy of the Republican leadership was steadfastly to avoid armed confrontation with the British or Japanese. Massive rejection of this policy on the part of pemudas began to occur only as the Republic suffered what was from their viewpoint one humiliating defeat after another.

The growing Allied presence and power in Jakarta was disturbing enough to pemuda sentiment, though the Republican Government was in a position to prevent major clashes there. The loss of Bandung on 10 October was of a quite different order. The city had been under effective Republican control since the end of September, and negotiations had placed the main stock of Japanese arms at least nominally in Indonesian hands. However as a result of either specific instructions through the Allied representative, Major Grey, or their own resentment against pemuda attacks on their installations, the strong Japanese force of the Bandung command struck back with unprecedented vigour. On 10 October they forced the leading pemuda spokesmen in Bandung at gunpoint to appeal for an end to attacks on the Japanese, while their troops seized all important buildings and captured or expelled armed pemudas. Military control of the city remained firmly in Japanese hands until the British arrived to take over a week later. For Bandung pemudas it was a drastic humiliation, symbolized by a present of lipstick from their more successful brethren in East Java.[15]

The Bandung affair increased the strain on verbal agreements between Japanese and Indonesian leaders in other parts of the island, whereby the Japanese had usually agreed to stick to their bases and provide a varying proportion of their arms in return for safety and food. In Semarang a state of open warfare began to develop by 14 October. In reprisal for pemuda attacks including the arrest of about 300 Japanese civilians, the Japanese began to clear the city of armed militants. The latter retaliated by massacring their Japanese prisoners, and this in turn provoked the Japanese troops to wholesale killing. By the time the British landed on 20 October the Japanese had clearly regained the initiative at a cost of about 2,000 Indonesian lives and hundreds of their own.

This episode in turn added fuel to the fires in Surabaya, where militant pemudas were much more strongly placed. They had been among the earliest to mobilize against the Japanese. By late September street fights with Dutch and Eurasian youths had become commonplace. Moreover Surabaya was the principal Indonesian base of the Japanese Navy, and Vice-Admiral Shibata was in effect if not in theory the leading Japanese figure in the town. His attitude, like Maeda's in Jakarta, was extremely favourable to the Republic, with the result that the bulk of the Navy's arms and ammunition, and much of the Army's, was in Indonesian hands by the first week of October. In subsequent fighting the Indonesians deployed twelve tanks, much heavy artillery including anti-aircraft guns, and enough arms to equip a regiment.

A further aggravation of tension in Surabaya was the exclusively Dutch composition of the first Allied representation in the city—a concession to the pride of the Dutch military. After a preliminary inspection on 22 September, Captain Huijer of the Dutch Navy was sent back to Surabaya with four Dutch assistants on 28 September to prepare for the later Allied landings. Not only was Huijer incapable of checking the steady drift towards anarchy in Surabaya; he exacerbated it by increasing pemuda suspicion of Allied intentions. No longer able even to communicate with Jakarta, he attempted to leave the city on 8 October but was stopped by a mob. With the other Allied Together with representatives, he remained thereafter under protective arrest by the Resident.

Much later, on 25 October, a brigade of Indian troops under Brigadier General A. W. S. Mallaby landed in Surabaya with very little idea of what to expect. Initially the British were welcomed cordially by the leaders of the TKR (formerly BKR), the most organized of the many forces in the city. This mood lasted hardly a day. Among the first British actions was the rescue of Huijer and his men, which was seen by Indonesians as a mockery of Mallaby's promises not to assist NICA. Worse, on the 27th the RAF dropped leaflets over Surabaya demanding the immediate surrender of all Indonesian arms. These leaflets were a complete surprise to Mallaby, who had already arranged his own much milder terms with the TKR leaders.

To the pemudas this was compelling proof of the uselessness of negotiating with the Allies. Clearly they were preparing for an imminent Dutch return. In the afternoon of 28 October a sudden attack was launched on the 6,000-odd Indian troops by an estimated 20,000 TKR soldiers and 120,000 other pemudas. The hunger for action which had been suppressed with difficulty for the past six months burst into a fury of destruction.

The city itself was pandemonium. There was bloody hand-to-hand fighting on every street corner. Bodies were strewn everywhere. Decapitated, dismembered trunks lay piled one on top of the other . . . Indonesians were shooting and stabbing and murdering wildly.[16]

It was clear that the British Brigade would have been wiped out if this had continued for many days, along with thousands of Dutch civilians. In desperation the British flew Sukarno, Hatta, and Amir Sjarifuddin to Surabaya, as the only Indonesians likely to be able to call a halt to the carnage. At a conference on 30 October the Presidential group browbeat the extremely reluctant pemuda leaders into accepting a cease-fire agreement. Fighting seemed to be over by mid-afternoon when Sukarno returned to Jakarta.

Had this cease-fire held, the fighting would have been an unqualified victory for the Republic and its leadership. But soon after the President left Surabaya there was renewed shooting by undisciplined pemudas. Brigadier Mallaby was shot and killed while trying to enforce the cease-fire.[17] It was a severe blow to Sukarno's standing, not only with the British but also with the pemudas to whom he was now obliged to appeal in more humiliating terms:

> In an organized state the people cannot take the law into their own hands. The events in Surabaya are weakening us in relation to the international community. . . .
> Once again, brothers, I hereby order that fighting against the Allies cease.[18]

The Surabaya militants were sufficiently stunned by the dramatic events and the urgency of Sukarno's appeal to allow the British to evacuate 6,000 Dutch detainees and land the 5th Indian Division on 9 October without opposition. Its commander, General Mansergh, was then in a strong enough position to declare war on Surabaya, with an ultimatum which was not intended to be met. 'Crimes against civilization' the ultimatum declared, 'cannot go unpunished'.

This tough British attitude had the remarkable effect of uniting the normally 'diplomatic' Republican establishment in Surabaya with the militant pemudas. The politicians' usual insistence on avoiding a clash with the Allies looked lame in the face of British demands for immediate and unconditional surrender of all arms in the city. Despite his earlier appeals, even Sukarno was now willing to say no more in response to urgent queries from East Java officials than 'we leave it to Surabaya'.[19] At 11 p.m. on 9 November the Governor of East Java, not the pemuda leaders as on 28 October, announced over Radio Surabaya that the city would resist to the last.

The British were staggered at the resistance which met their sweep into the city the following morning. Air strikes and naval bombardments were called for, devastating several parts of the city. The troops crept forward block by block, inflicting enormous casualties on the frenzied defenders. After three days they had taken two-thirds of the smouldering city, but only three weeks later did the fighting finally subside to sporadic exchanges along a fixed perimeter of the city.

The battle of Surabaya was far heavier than any later Republican stand, even against the Dutch. The Indonesians never again had such a concentration of armament in one place, nor did they recapture quite the same fanatic heroism. This defiant unity was rapidly diluted in the more complicated game of diplomacy. Similarly there was no better illustration of the dark uncontrollable forces which frightened European observers: the 'hysterical ferocity, fanaticism, self-sacrifice, and wasted effort'[20] which seemed to be the very antithesis of the urbane and convincing diplomacy of Republican leaders in Jakarta. Indonesian and British sources alike bear witness to the indiscriminate slaughter of Europeans and suspected 'NICA spies'; the dismemberment of bodies; the ritualistic drinking of the blood of victims, which marked the earliest stage of the Surabaya fighting.

From a military viewpoint a few staunch Republicans agreed with Wehl about the 'wasted effort' of Surabaya. Their heaviest arms and some of their best fighting men were left behind in a battle they could not win. Had this material been withdrawn strategically from Surabaya and other cities, an Indonesian commander was later to argue,[21] a well-equipped army superior to anything the Dutch possessed could have been organized in the interior. But this is idle speculation. It was the spirit of Surabaya, not its armament, which inspired Indonesia and startled Britain.

For the *perjuangan* (struggle) ideal Surabaya was the monument and the model. Posterity has continued to hallow 10 November as a public holiday—*hari pahlawan* (heroes' day)—not least because it was one of the few mass actions behind which all important sections of the Indonesian community were united: politicians, pemudas, Muslims, and peasants. There can be little doubt, moreover, that the defence of Surabaya enormously increased the pressure on the British, and through them the Dutch, to abandon thought of military solutions in favour of negotiation with the Republic.[22] In October the Dutch had been arguing strongly,

> and the ease with which the Japanese have re-established themselves in Bandung supports their theory—that a few whiffs of grapeshot will restore their authority.[23]

This theory was shattered irreparably by the battle of Surabaya. Independence was sealed in blood. There could be no going back.

Violence and the Bersiap Time

> *People were brave enough in the face of*
> *enemy cannons—but how terrified they were*
> *of enemy spies! This terrible spectre howled*
> *like a hurricane over the cities and inside*
> *the hearts of men, levelling everything in its*
> *path—courage and rationality alike. Everyone*
> *suspected everyone else, and to free themselves*
> *from the torment of this spectre they killed*
> *one another.*
>
> Idrus, 'Surabaya'[24]

The fighting in Surabaya galvanized the pemuda struggle throughout Indonesia. Even in the cities of Borneo and Sulawesi there were anti-Dutch demonstrations on 29 October. Throughout Java and Sumatra the attacks on Allied soldiers and allegedly pro-Dutch civilians were at a peak during the last two months of 1945. The pemudas of Bandung returned to the offensive.[25] This period became known as the *bersiap* time, when pemudas in the cities were constantly being summoned to meet some new crisis by the drawn out cry: *siaaap* (get ready). In rural areas where there were no obvious non-Indonesian enemies the same period is known as the *daulat* time, when Indonesians in positions of authority experienced 'the people's sovereignty (*kedaulatan*)' in the form of kidnap, intimidation, or murder. Nowhere was there fighting on a scale comparable to Surabaya, but the slogan *merdeka atau mati* (freedom or death) was a constant challenge to restless action. Fear of the impending arrival of the supernaturally cunning NICA produced suspicions approaching paranoia in some pemuda groups. It was somehow expected that NICA would mark its spies with a special sign. Many were killed for no better reason than an accidental arrangement of red, white, and blue clothing (the Dutch colours).

The prevalence of suspicions and allegations of this type facilitated both revolutionary levelling and simple plunder. Chinese and others with wealth were particularly likely to be labelled NICA agents after the initial commandeering of Japanese stores ceased to provide a source of revenue. For many young men the only way of ensuring a full stomach was to join a *badan perjuangan*, which made it difficult to prevent the dilution of patriotic heroism with more basic motives.

In other words a revolution was taking place. The established government had dissolved; the Republic was unable fully to take its place. Violence was necessary if the Republic was to survive, but violence produced its own type of leader and style. When the killing began in Surabaya and elsewhere the leadership of youth groups changed rapidly, as many original political leaders with education proved unsuited to the brutal work. A distinct style of pemuda leader emerged, with long flowing hair, military attire, a pistol—the badge of revolutionary authority—at the waist, and a sharp, decisive way of giving commands. The contrast with traditional Javanese wielders of authority was immense, emphasizing the sharp emotional break the revolution represented for those caught in it.

Many of the characteristics of violence and revolutionary upheaval in Indonesia were universal, parallelling for example the picture given of Algeria by Franz Fanon.[26] Frenzied moments like the battle of Surabaya, however, which involved thousands of people from every background including the most traditional, need also to be seen in terms of a distinctively Indonesian tradition, or set of traditions.

The common denominator of these traditions might be called the spiritual quality of power. Successful Javanese kings, like Javanese mythical heroes, possessed supernatural power deriving from their closeness to heaven and the own inner qualities. Similarly, successful warriors, rebels, and even bandits must necessarily possess magical powers making them invulnerable (*kebal*) to all bullets and blows except at one sensitive point. They could fly, be in two places at once, or move through fire. For ordinary men a limited degree of invulnerability could also be acquired in a variety of ways. One well-known manifestation of this is the trance temporarliy induced in the dances of many regions, notably the Balinese *barong* dance, during which the dancer's body appears to be able to withstand sharp knives. Such a state of invulnerability may be achieved by recitation (*dzikir, ratib*) of certain mystic formulae, either Islamic or pre-Islamic. Particular weapons too have their own power, and are treasured from generation to generation for this reason. Probably the most common means of acquiring invulnerability, and the simplest, is to obtain an amulet (*jimat*), usually a piece of white cloth with some koranic phrases on it, from a *kramat* (holy man) or *guru* (mystic teacher) with a reputation for this science of invulnerability. Each specialist in the art has his own unique ritual, and the most famous attract clients from hundreds of miles away.

Though such beliefs affect the normal lives of Indonesians hardly at all, they have re-emerged at each time of major upheaval when all men's fears and hopes are heightened. They help to explain scenes, in Surabaya and later also Bandung, of ranks of pemudas advancing upon British tanks armed only with bamboo spears or knives, perhaps chanting *Allahu Akbar* (God is great). When the enthusiasm of rural youths without military discipline was aroused, hundreds could be killed in heroic sacrifices of this kind. When the spirit began to falter and the invulnerability to fail, on the other hand, the resistance of the same untrained enthusiasts could simply melt away.

Within this general pattern there were a number of distinct elements of leadership which came to the fore during the bersiap time. In varying degrees they posed a temporary challenge to the authority of all the educated élites: not just the pamong praja and the politicians but also the more disciplined youth in the BKR/TKR and the urban badan perjuangan.

The Islamic schools (*pesantren*) provided one such source of leadership. The pupils lived at the school, often far from their own homes, and formed a close bond of loyalty to their teacher. In traditional pesantrens they often learned Indonesian forms of self-defence, *silat* or *pencak*, involving spiritual as well as physical discipline. Their teacher himself might understand the mysteries of invulnerability. Modern as well as traditional *ulama* were conscious of the sacrifice demanded by a holy war (*jihad*) and the rewards for those who fell in it (*mati syahid*). As the centre of the santri belt of Java's north coast, Surabaya was more than usually affected by this strain of thought. In November the ulama of the region declared that resistance was an obligation, to be fought under the scriptural conditions for a holy war. The call was echoed at gatherings of ulama throughout Java and Sumatra. But the 'holy war' character of the revolution quickly faded after November, in part because it was an embarrassment to the Republican leadership,[27] but more because the nature of the struggle did not evoke it. Apart from dramatic crises of self-defence like Surabaya, it became a matter of doubt for ulama whether a jihad was an appropriate form of struggle for a state which promised no stronger place for Islam than its Japanese and Dutch predecessors. Muslim fighting strength became gradually more organized, if more limited, in the Hizbullah and Sabillullah armies with their Japanese-trained core.

Many Indonesian rural cultures recognize the special place of the village fighter, for whom the term *jago* (lit. fighting cock) is the most general. Skilled in pencak and silat, the jago often had a reputation for invulnerability and other magic powers, related to his birthdate, nickname, and other distinguishing features. Often serving as protector of village officials or village property, he was not necessarily outside the law. His relative freedom from conventional social restraints, however, made him a potential recruit to banditry. In Indonesian rural areas banditry has traditionally been as difficult to distinguish from rebellion as has piracy on the seas. Unsuccessful rebels were forced to resort to banditry; successful bandits often achieved recognition through negotiation with the authorities. Alien rule gave the bandit added respect, and the breakdown of central authority gave him opportunity. The revolution gave power to many such figures. Because of their ability to attract armed followers and to provide protection at a time it was in great demand, bandit leaders in such traditional jago areas as West Java and Tapanuli were even confirmed by the Republic as regional officials or military officers.[28]

Finally a unique feature of leadership during the early revolution was the radio. The Japanese had used the radio as a primary means of politicizing the countryside, and each large village in Java (though not elsewhere) had been provided with a receiver. Radio Republik Indonesia was the main contact between the Republican leaders and the rural mass. But during the Surabaya fighting it was a private station, *Radio Pemberontakan* (Radio of Revolt), which provided immediate exhortation and leadership. It was set up on 12 October by 25 year old Sutomo, one of the early PRI leaders in Surabaya. As 'Bung Tomo'[29] of Radio Pemberontaken, he became the symbol of the pemuda movement in Surabaya. His promise not to cut his flowing hair nor touch a woman until Indonesia was free, as much as his passionate exhortations to ultimate sacrifice, provided a romantic style for pemuda-ism. A certain exotic fascination was added by English-language broadcasts over Radio Pemberontakan by one of the first Britishers to choose the Republican side—K'tut Tantri as she was known to Indonesians; 'Surabaya Sue' to the British troops. Bung Tomo's closest followers eventually formed an important *badan perjuangan*—the BPRI (Badan Pemberontakan Republik Indonesia). But his symbolic value was a challenge to all organization—the pure voice of perjuangan.

References

1 US Undersecretary of State Sumner Welles, 30 May 1942, quoted H. J. van Mook, *The Stakes of Democracy in South East Asia*, London, 1950, p. 167.
2 P. S. Gerbrandy, *Indonesia*, London, 1950, p. 27.
3 *Ibid.* p. 59.
4 The full text of the speech is in *ibid.* pp. 192–4.
5 Lt Brondgeest, referring to Medan, in *Enquêtecommissie Regeringsbeleid 1940–1945* Vol. 8, The Hague, 1956, p. 586.
6 Kahin, p. 143, quoting Major F. E. Crocket, the U.S. Military Adviser in Jakarta. Mountbatten was equally scathing about the 'most reprehensible' behaviour of the troops. S. L. van der Wal (ed.), *Officiele bescheiden betreffende de Nederlands-Indonesische betrekkingen 1945–1950*, Vol. I, The Hague, 1971, pp. 358 and 571.
7 F. S. V. Donnison, *British Military Administration in the Far East 1943–46*, London, 1956, p. 433.
8 Compare the military instructions cited in Gavin Long, *The Final Campaigns*, Canberra, 1963, pp. 567–8, with the discussion of political policy in Paul Hasluck, *The Government and the People, 1942–1945*, Canberra, 1970, pp. 604–7.
9 Instructions to all officers of Makforce, 21 November 1945, in *War Diary HQ 21 Infantry Brigade*, Australian War Memorial (henceforth abbreviated as AWM) 8/2/21.
10 Report on Political Affairs by CONICA, 24 October 1945, in AWM.

11 Report on the Operations of Makforce 22 September—20 December 1945, in *War Diary HQ 21 Infantry Brigade*, AWM 8/2/21.

12 Dutch anger at this broadcast was exacerbated by the inflammatory way it had been reported in a Dutch-language SEAC broadcast. The English and Dutch texts are in Van der Wal, *Nederlands-Indonesische betrekkingen*, Vol I, p. 316. For the bitter controversy surrounding the statement see also *ibid.* pp. 233–5 and 300–17; David Wehl, *The Birth of Indonesia*, London, 1948, pp. 31–46; Donnison, pp. 422–6; Van Mook, pp. 186–9; Anderson, *Java*, pp. 135–7.

13 Donnison, *op. cit.*, p. 430.

14 For a detailed study of the background to the strike see Rupert Lockwood, 'The Indonesian Exiles in Australia, 1942–47' in *Indonesia* 10, 1970, pp. 37–56.

15 The Bandung affair is very well described in John Smail, *Bandung in the Early Revolution, 1945–46. A Study in the Social History of the Indonesian Revolution* Cornell Modern Indonesia Project Monograph, 1964, pp. 58–67. For this sub-chapter I have also leaned heavily on Anderson, *Java*, pp. 139–66.

16 *Sukarno: An Autobiography*, p. 228.

17 Most Indonesian sources argue the likelihood that Mallaby was shot by his own men or Dutch *provocateurs*, while British accounts entertain no such doubts.

18 Sukarno broadcast of 31 October 1945, as reproduced in Osman Raliby, *Documenta Historica*, Jakarta, 1953, p. 522. Anderson, *Java*, pp. 163–4, translates from a different source. An ambivalent government appeal for 'solidarity with our brethren in Surabaya', is in Koesnodiprodjo, p. 77.

19 H. Roeslan Abdulgani, *Heroes Day and the Indonesian Revolution*, Jakarta, 1964, p. 71.

20 Wehl, *op. cit.*, p. 67.

21 A. H. Nasution, *Guerrilla Warfare*, pp. 21–2 and 28.

22 Even Wehl (a SEAC official), *loc. cit.*, a few lines after castigating the 'complete waste' of the defence of Surabaya, admitted the great influence it had on British policy.

23 *Times* special correspondent, 15 October 1945.

24 Translated S. U. Nababan and Ben Anderson, *Indonesia* 5, 1968, p. 10.

25 Smail, p. 108, accepts a figure of 1,500 Dutch, Eurasians, and Chinese killed in Bandung alone up to March 1946.

26 Franz Fanon, *The Wretched of the Earth*, trans. Constance Farrington, London, 1965.

27 Hatta issued a decree forbidding 'the proclamation of (holy) war by any individual', on 17 October 1945. Koesnodiprodjo, p. 60.

28 The *jago* phenomenon is discussed from a Dutch viewpoint in P. M. van Wulfften Palthe, *Psychological Aspect of the Indonesian Problem*, Leiden, 1949, pp. 27 ff, a translation of his pamphlet *Over het Bendewezen op Java*, Amsterdam, 1949. See also a review of the latter by D. H. Meijer, *Indonesië* III, 1949, pp. 178–89, and Smail. pp. 88–9 and 123–5. A good recent study of rural violence in Java is Sartono Kartodirdjo, 'Agrarian Radicalism in Java', in Claire Holt (ed.) *Culture and Politics in Indonesia*, Ithaca, 1971, pp. 71–125. Raymond ('Turk') Westerling, *Challenge to Terror*, London 1952, pp. 61–7 and *passim*, gives a fascinating picture of the attempt of this Dutch 'counter-insurgency' killer to develop the same sort of mystique as his *jago* opposite numbers.

29 *Bung* was adopted as a revolutionary title by all the leading figures in the Republic in 1945–6, but it stuck only to those most strongly identified with the romantic charisma of the period—Bung Karno and Bung Tomo.

Chapter Four

SOCIAL REVOLUTION

*Externally our revolution is a national revolution;
internally it develops according to the laws of a
democratic society and bears a social character. If
we do not fully comprehend this truth, and so, internally,
do no more than promote a national revolution . . . we
shall be in grave danger.*

Sjahrir, 1945[1]

*This revolution is like a flood, and now no-one
can control its course. Whatever we do, it follows
its own road, heedless of us who created it.*

Mochtar Lubis[2]

The dominant emotion of the early months of independence was unquestionably the desire for national freedom—'freedom or death' for the pemudas; the survival of the Republic for the politicans who had contributed to its birth; an end to racial humiliation for everybody. Beyond the goal of national freedom few had time or inclination to look in the difficult days of August, September, and October. Action was all-important and, had to be judged by its capacity to achieve or sustain national freedom in the constantly changing situation.

Yet at two different levels there were Indonesians who regarded the struggle from its inception as a *revolution*, and not simply an assertion of national independence. Among the nationalist politicians, firstly, there was a strong tradition which held that independence could only come by revolution, since imperialism and international capital would never voluntarily surrender their hold over Indonesia. Nurtured in the pre-war non co-operative movement, this revolutionary tradition had both Marxist and more popular messianic variants, frequently in combination. In the first months of independence Sukarno often spoke as if national and social revolution were inseparable.[3]

The leading pemuda intellectuals in Jakarta had demanded a 'revolutionary' proclamation of independence from the Japanese, and continued to demand 'revolutionary leadership', for somewhat different reasons. Their most important demand was for total *involvement*, of themselves and the whole people, in the events taking place. *Revolusi* became the political expression of this need, and the most compelling slogan for an articulate section of educated youth, even if *perjuangan* was a more widespread characterization of the pemuda task. *Revolusi* represented urgency, action, exhilaration, and impatience with legalistic or diplomatic fussiness.

One of the first indications that the demand for independence might in reality involve revolutionary demands within Indonesian society was the growing popularity of another slogan: *kedaulatan rakyat* (the sovereignty of the people). This had been mentioned in the preamble to the constitution, and was already more prominent in the oath taken by members of the KNIP (Komité Nasional Indonesia Pusat) on 29 August.[4] Its popularity in the months that followed, however, was primarily the work of pemudas demanding more active policies from appointed leaders. At first it was used to urge existing leaders and officials to heed the will of 'the people'; gradually it came to justify the removal of unpopular leaders by pressure from below. It was a major element in all the movements for democratic or social revolution within the independence struggle.

The revolutionary situation of minimum government control over an insurgent population was most fully realized between early October 1945 and about February 1946 in Java, and a couple of months later in Sumatra.

During this period the status of all those who had wielded authority under the Japanese was at its lowest ebb. At the village level, headmen were brought to account for their role in enforcing harsh Japanese demands for rice and manpower. At the national level, to take the opposite extreme, Sukarno was a disappointment to the leading advocates of *perjuangan*, and a liability to the adherents of *diplomasi*. At every level in between pemudas engaged in fighting the Japanese and, seizing their arms, turned against the local leaders for their policy of compromise and their association with the discredited régime. No alternative Republican power structure was yet established.

Neither political organization nor motivation existed, however, to utilize this revolutionary situation for fundamental democratization of the social structure. The most influential Marxist leaders in practice threw their weight against immediate social revolution. For the group of intellectuals best categorized as 'international' Marxists, whose priorities were those of European Marxism and the world power struggle, it was still orthodox to believe that a bourgeois democratic national revolution must necessarily precede a socialist one. The French revolution was considered a much more relevant model than the Soviet. Sjahrir even found it necessary to warn his fellow Marxists against too facile an identification with the French revolution, because of the international nature of both modern capitalism and its enemies.[5]

The pragmatic corollary of this theory was that internal upheaval, particularly if accompanied by violence, would alienate the great-power support Indonesia required to achieve independence. The needs of the national revolution must take precedence over those of the social revolution. The 'Dimitrov doctrine', which for years had urged communists to support a common front against fascism, had more-over created genuine trust in the potential of democratic forces in Europe to advance the cause of freedom in Asia.

Another reason has been suggested[6] for the failure of Indonesian politicians to grasp the opportunity for fundamental social revolution. According to this argument there existed an unspoken assumption among élite politicians, however verbally radical, that the fundamental differences between Indonesia's ethnic groups, religions, and *aliran* could only be bridged by the Dutch-educated urban élite; and that any attempt to arouse the masses *against* the élite or a large section of it could only lead to violence and anarchy, fatally weakening Indonesia in the independence struggle. The experience of the early revolution must have tended to confirm such an assumption. It may help to explain why even such an imaginative and committed revolutionary as Tan Malaka, long freed from the blinkers of Moscow, made little attempt to turn the spontaneous levelling movements of this period to permanent account.

For all these reasons the most profound social upheavals occurred despite the national leadership and in areas remote from national politics.

Upheaval in the Villages
Generally speaking the colonial order had isolated the village headman from the villagers among whom he lived by making him function primarily as an agent of government control. Japanese military rule had suddenly increased the harshness and arbitrariness of the impositions the headman had to enforce, whilst increasing his coercive powers through a new village police force. The crumbling of the Japanese régime and the revolutionary mobilization of youth therefore forced headmen to answer for the unpopularity of wartime measures.

The 'social revolutions' which affected north and central Sumatra in early 1946 (see p. 65) all had repercussions in the villages. Head-men in Aceh and East Sumatra who were identified with the higher authority of the raja were overthrown, and new men more identified with the village were elected. When the same principle was applied in the Batak homeland of Tapanuli, however, where headmen had previously been selected on the basis of a rigid kinship system, the long-term effect was to undermine village autonomy and coherence. Customary law and government authority no longer reinforced each other.

The Javanese village unit (*desa*) was larger (generally between two and twelve thousand people), more bureaucratically organized, and less coherent as a community than the Sumatran. Besides the *lurah* (headman) himself there was a considerable hierarchy of minor government officials, collectively known as the *pamong desa*. Instead of salary, however, the colonial order rewarded this village élite with the usufruct of land, in a systematization of older Javanese feudal practice. In addition to his personal property, the *tanah bengkok* (official land) of the lurah was sufficiently extensive to give him a lordly position far above that of the ordinary villagers. The lesser officials in colonial times generally received less than a tenth as much *bengkok*. Although the Dutch had introduced elections by landholders, these occurred only at the death of the incumbent lurah, and rarely did more than confirm the succession of his son.

In the months after Japan's defeat became known in rural Java, many lurahs were forced out of office. The way in which pressure was mobilized has been described in one case:

> Shortly after the fall of Japan, a Tamansari villager . . . refused to deliver his [rice] quota and was called before the lurah. The villager insisted that, since the Japanese government had fallen, there was no longer any obligation to deliver quotas. An argument developed and the lurah struck him. . . . The event immediately became a *cause celebre* and was converted by the lurah's opposition into an issue with which to force his dismissal. A mass meeting of the whole *kalurahan* [village] . . . unleashed the resentments of the preceeding few years, and the leaders at the meeting were in vigorous agreement that Hadji Daran should be dismissed. The district office in Modjokuto accepted the decision, Daran resigned, and a new election was held.[7]

Although duplicated all over Java, such actions implied no necessary structural change. Very frequently the unpopular *lurah* simply retired in favour of his son. Where there was sufficient upheaval to bring about a switch from one leading family to another, this was usually because a santri candidate used the opportunity to unseat an abangan incumbent, or vice-versa. In such cases the villagers sometimes successfully demanded a reduction of the lurah's bengkok, the source of his dominance in the village, and a distribution of the surplus among landless peasants. This represented reform of the system, not revolution; its significance lay in demonstrating the capacity for action of the generally quiescent Javanese peasant mass.

Since organized revolutionary politics had not yet reached the villages, utilization of this capacity for permanent change was dependent on the existing conservative bureaucracy. The maximum that could be achieved in these conditions is apparent in the special region of Jogjakarta, where the local prestige and power of Sultan Hamengkubuwono and his closeness to the national political élite made revolution from above possible. In April 1946 the Jogjakarta government announced that new elections would be held for lurah, pamong desa, and a legislative council in each desa. Three or four villages were grouped together to form a larger desa community thought capable of supporting a council, after which elections for the enlarged villages were held during 1947. A ceiling of 4 hectares irrigated or 6 hectares unirrigated land was placed on the new lurah's bengkok—an area still at least ten times the average peasant holding.[8] Bengkok above this limit was declared common village property (*kas desa*) whose product should be used on village projects.

These Jogjakarta reforms were the maximum achieved by the revolution in the Javanese village. The central government declined in November 1945 to extend its democratic reforms to the village level after a defence of traditional Javanese *adat* (customary law) by some KNIP members. Several residents and bupatis did order elections of new lurahs in order to head off the wave of actions from below. Viewed in perspective, however, the structural changes introduced into the village by the revolution were at most an updating of a powerful tradition. The disappearance of unquestioning acceptance of lurah authority, noted by Jay in 1953–4,[9] was a more fundamental product of revolutionary politics, but it has not proved to be permanent.

Regional 'Social Revolutions'
Higher officials were also affected by the discrediting of the Japanese régime and all its representatives. In towns and cities with educated and organized pemuda, upheaval was likely to be catalysed by the conflict between perjuangan and diplomasi; between the pemuda demand for heroic militance and the establishment's anxiety to arrange things with a minimum of violence and dislocation. Particularly explosive situations arose where negotiations with the Japanese or British had preceded (if not necessarily produced) bloodshed and humiliation for the pemudas. The Bandung humiliation of 10 October, for example, appears to have precipitated the fall of the leading officials of the town, and perhaps also the murder of West Java's most prominent nationalist, Oto Iskandar di Nata. Having

proposed Sukarno for president in the PPKI on August 22, Oto might be considered the first of the revolution's own sons to be devoured by it. The attempt of the Republican Resident of Pekalongan (north Central Java) to mediate in a nasty Japanese-pemuda clash began another wave of actions against the pamong praja Republican establishment, which became known as the *Peristiwa Tiga Daerah* (three regions affair). Although few were killed, virtually the whole official hierarchy of three kabupatens was swept from power for three turbulent months.

Behind the overt perjuangan-diplomasi clash there usually lurked a much older rivalry between the pamong praja and altern-ative élites—either Muslim or political. The most affected rural areas were santri strongholds such as Banten (West Java), Pekalongan, Aceh, and West Sumatra, where prominent Islamic teachers temporarily took the place of the ousted pamong praja. In larger towns leftish politicians relatively free from the Japanese taint were the most usual beneficiaries. Ethnic rivalry was a factor still further in the background. In East Sumatra and West Java the traditional Dutch-supported aristocracy was indigenous to the region while the national movement of the towns, including the pemuda movement, was an ethnic mixture in which Javanese or Batak leadership was most prominent. Action against the ruling class was therefore seen by the victims, though not the promoters, as ethnically-based. In reality, however, the absence of ethnic or aliran feeling was one of the remarkable features of the pemuda upsurge at the beginning of the revolution. The reappearance of both was one of the results, rather than causes, of the 'social revolutionary' wave.

Specifically egalitarian political ideology has not been stressed here for reasons already discussed. Marxist ideas and leadership were brought into the 'social revolutions' despite the leading Marxists. They served to legitimate and justify in national revolutionary terms the upheavals taking place at a local level. Because of this, individual communists who chose to identify with the 'social revolutions' had a brief influence in some areas out of all proportion to their following. If they supported and expressed in impressive revolutionary terminology the pressing pemuda demand for change, they could even move the social revolutionary process forward to some degree. But without solid grass-roots organization, and above all without support from their prominent communist colleagues in the capital, they could not turn this revolutionary situation to their permanent advantage.

In Indonesian memory the term 'social revolution' has come to apply particularly to the actions which achieved some permanent success—those which were directed against the remaining monarchs in Java and Sumatra. In Java the mantle of the ancient Mataram empire had descended in different degrees to four monarchs sharing two capitals: the Susuhunan and the Mangkunegara in Surakarta; the Sultan and the Pakualam in Jogjakarta. Although the nationalist movement had always opposed these as feudal anachronisms, the PPKI had sanctioned them on 19 August 1945 in the hope of bringing their considerable influence onto the Republican side. This succeeded so well in the case of the forceful young Sultan Hamengkubuwono that the Republican government moved to Jogjakarta on 4 January 1946 as his guest. The alliance between Republic and Sultan became essential to both, with the result that the Sultanate was the only monarchy to emerge unscathed from the revolution. In Surakarta, by contrast, a newly enthroned Susuhunan of twenty-two was no match for the revolutionary pressures beginning to overwhelm him in January 1946. Since Surakarta was caught up in national politics, however, this will be discussed below (p. 93).

The only other 'self-governing' traditional states within Republican territory were in northern Sumatra. Both the 107 *uleebalangs* of Aceh and the Malay, Karo, and Simelungun rajas of East Sumatra had been raised under Dutch rule to pinnacles of local power far beyond their pre-colonial means. They had thereby become isolated from popular movements. Both the Muslim reformist PUSA under Daud Beureu'eh in Aceh, and the secular nationalist movement in East Sumatra, tended to look upon the *kerajaan* (royal governments) as the primary enemy—even before the Dutch. The crisis of 1942 had brought these rivalries to a head. After assisting the Japanese by successfully rebelling against Dutch authority in Aceh, the PUSA group made clear that it expected to be rewarded by the abolition of uleebalang power. Some radicals within the national movement in East Sumatra made the same demand against the rajas. The Japanese response however was to accept this internal rivalry as a fact of Sumatran society, and to use both sides without satisfying either.

For almost a month following the Japanese surrender, the universal assumption in northern Sumatra was that the Dutch would return. The proclamation of the Republic was known to only a handful of leaders, for whom it seemed much less real than the Allied parachute teams and propaganda leaflets which were rapidly in evidence. The first break with the continuity of Japanese administration was not the Republican movement but the resumption of pre-war powers by rulers who believed their time of troubles was over.

The Pidië region of Aceh had been the centre of the pre-war and wartime conflict between uleebalangs and PUSA. It was in this region that the uleebalangs most recklessly showed their hand, by resuming pre-war powers and deriding the beginnings of pemuda republicanism in October 1945. When the Dutch failed to appear, and the influential ulama threw in their lot with the Republic, the most prominent uleebalangs were too late and too proud to back down. Positions rapidly polarized in December, with all the Pidië uleebalangs falling into line behind the haughty, stubbornly courageous Teuku Daud Cumbok out of fear of the growing hostility of the anti-Dutch movement under PUSA leadership. The 'Cumbok war' raged hot in the first two weeks of 1946, before all the uleebalang strongholds in Pidië were taken and the most prominent members of uleebalang families killed.[10]

Although this bloody affair had been limited to Pidië, its effects were felt throughout Aceh. Within a month a systematic movement had begun to arrest all the uleebalang in Aceh. They were imprisoned in Takengon and their places in the Republican administration were taken by ulama prominent in the pre-war PUSA. Only a handful of the best-educated aristocratic Acehnese were retained in key administrative posts, like the new resident, T. Daudsjah. But the thoroughness of the Acehnese 'social revolution', which was complete by March, produced a remarkable harmony between the ulama led by Daud Beureu'eh and the technocrats and educated pemudas whose responsibilities were rapidly expanded. Despite the unparalleled severity of the January fighting, Aceh for the remainder of the struggle for independence was a model of stability and of popular support for the local leadership. It was also the only residency the Dutch made no attempt to enter. As a popular movement to replace one social group in power by another, the Acehnese social revolution was the most complete and successful. For that very reason, however, Aceh could not fit easily into post-independence Indonesia. For all their unpopularity, the uleebalangs were much more able to speak the language of the educated nationalist elite of the Republic than were the new ulama class who replaced them.

If Marxism was peripheral to the Aceh social revolution,[11] it played a larger role in East Sumatra. This residency had been in the mainstream of the pre-war national movement. The contrast between its large plantation proletariat and the spectacular wealth some of its rajas derived from oil and plantation concessions ensured that Marxism predominated in its politics. Until April 1946, however, the moderate 'international' Marxist line was virtually unrepresented. The local Republican officials had little effective support in their policy of mediation between the mutually antagonistic pemudas and rajas.

The rajas of East Sumatra were on balance more conservative but less headstrong than those in Aceh. By February, when Dutch weakness was manifest, they realized their only hope was the government of the Republic, and entered serious negotiations with it for the 'democratization' of their autonomous states under

Republican auspices. This only intensified the suspicions of pemuda and radical leaders, who feared the artificial revival of the *kerajaan* from the position of virtual impotence to which revolutionary politics had reduced them.

On 3 March, immediately after the Acehnese movement had reached its climax with the removal of the first Republican resident, the East Sumatran social revolution was launched on instructions of the local Persatuan Perjuangan (Struggle Front), which had already assumed quasi-governmental powers because it effectively represented the armed pemudas. As Malay, Simelungun, and Karo rajas and their relations throughout East Sumatra were arrested, and new leftist officials elected in their place, the army and the acting Governor acquiesced with 'a feeling of gratitude to God'. The reaction came only on 13 March after the first of a series of killings and atrocities against the imprisoned aristocrats. A three-cornered struggle ensued among the army, the moderate older nationalists, and the ill-organized social revolutionaries. The two former were each trying to end the social revolution in their different ways, while among the latter it was a group of communists who were the most consistent in trying to use it to transform the structure of government fundamentally. The communists themselves, however, were far from disciplined or precise in their goals. Their party structure, with supporting badan perjuangan, was a child of the revolution like its rivals, and could not be expected to bring a new type of discipline to it. A communist-led economic body briefly obtained official sanction in this period to take over enterprises and plantations and to plan the economy, but it appears to have been no more immune than other bodies from private interests.

At the end of April the social revolutionary movement was clearly at an end, with its most radical leaders imprisoned or in hiding. It had achieved the permanent destruction of a host of small states, and a bigger stake in the formal power structure for the pemuda organizations, the army, and some politicians. The cost however was not limited to the few hundred aristocratic victims of the social revolution, who included Indonesia's greatest pre-independence poet, Amir Hamzah. One consequence was the accelerated breakdown of power in East Sumatra among a number of competing badan perjuangan, better designed for fostering their respective economic and political interests than for protecting the region against Dutch attacks. Another was the embittering of inter-ethnic relations both within East Sumatra and beyond it. For the indigenous aristocracy and its numerous supporters among Malays and Simelunguns, the revolution had come to symbolize their bloody defeat at the hands of outside groups. The abortive export of the 'social revolution' to the northern districts of Tapanuli, moreover, led to fierce clashes in Sidikalang which by May 1946 had become exclusively ethnic, between Karo (with some Acehnese support) and Toba Bataks. About 300 were estimated killed in six weeks of fighting.

Except in Aceh, the results of the 'social revolutionary' movements were primarily negative. Anachronistic monarchies were eliminated, and pamong praja influence shaken, but no positive restructuring of the lower levels of society took place. In East Sumatra, and to a lesser extent Pekalongan, Marxists who rejected or ignored the moderate 'international' line played a substantial role. Their failure to turn the social revolution to greater account is largely a measure of the little control they had over events. They could provide a potent spark, but they had no disciplined cadres at their disposal to direct the flames. Thus on the one hand the developing anarchy and violence produced a strong reaction in the new as well as the old élite; on the other hand, the hardening of pemuda leaders led them to treat the 'revolutionary' PKI politicians with as little respect as they had earlier treated conservative Republicans. Increasingly they heeded their own interests as armed pemudas.

Undoubtedly the PKI would have been better-placed to take advantage of the November-March revolutionary situation if the most prestigious communists in Java had perceived the unique possibilities of that period. But their chances even then of bringing the revolution to a conclusion satisfactory to themselves do not seem high in view of the East Sumatran experience. Although condemned by their successors for not taking leadership of the revolution on a more radical platform, the top communists of 1945–7 may not have been altogether mistaken in their élitist mistrust of the constructive potentialities of the pemudas in arms.

The Parliamentary Revolution: (1) The Form

At the national level the principal beneficiary of the revolutionary ferment of late 1945 was Sutan Sjahrir. He had made himself the leading symbol of nationalist opposition to the Japanese, and of opposition equally to the Sukarno government and everything in it that smelled of Japan. Because he stood for change, because he was himself young (36), and because he talked the stirring language of revolution, he was supported by the Jakarta leaders of the pemuda upsurge. Elite politicians throughout Indonesia accepted that he was the right man, both personally and ideologically, to negotiate with the Allies, just as Sukarno had been the right man to negotiate with the Japanese. There was a lot going for Sjahrir in the last three months of 1945.

This should not allow us to minimize the remarkable achievement of the young socialist in this period. He not only brought about a

fundamental change from presidental to parliamentary government
and obtained the sympathy and ultimately the recognition of the
world powers; he also played the major part, with Amir Sjarifuddin,
in fashioning the machinery which linked the government of
Indonesia with its people remarkably effectively throughout the
remainder of the independence struggle. Thereby he ensured that
the 'revolutionary situation' was resolved on his own strictly
limited terms rather than serving any more fundamental social
transformation.

Besides his unrivalled credentials for dealing with the new forces
on the Indonesian scene, Sjahrir had the inestimable advantage, in
this fast-changing situation, of a precise and realistic vision of the
way ahead. The Japanese surrender, which had brought confusion
to most Indonesian nationalists, had been for Sjahrir the fulfilment
of years of planning. His manifesto *Perjuangan Kita* (Our Struggle),
written during October and promulgated on the eve of his accession
to power, cut like a knife through the continuing fog of revolutionary pemuda slogans and cautious older-generation appeals for calm.

The most striking feature of this remarkable document was its
emphatic and repeated rejection of nationalism. Those who attempted to use nationalism to arouse xenophobia among the masses
(Hitler, Franco, and Chiang Kai-shek, but not Sukarno, were
instanced by name) might gain easy initial successes, but they 'are
always enemies of the people', and their methods 'are always reactionary and conflict with progress and the social struggle the world
over'.[12] Sjahrir's approach was uncompromisingly international.
Indonesia's strategic situation and wealth, combined with its
underdevelopment, made it unusually dependent on the international situation. 'So long as the world we live in is dominated by
capital we are forced to make sure that we do not earn the enmity
of capitalism'.[13] The achievement of socialism would only be possible
on an international level. The working class in particular should
therefore beware of being led into an ardent nationalism which
prevented their understanding the international nature of the
workers' struggle.

The Indonesian revolution must not be purely national, and could
not be purely socialist. Its fundamental nature and purpose must
therefore be democratic. The demand for *kedaulatan rakyat*, and the
wide popular participation in the struggle, were for Sjahrir evidence
that the fundamental desires of the masses were for freedom from
'bureaucratic feudalism' and the virtual slavery of the peasant class.
Democratization would not only give substance to the revolutionary
struggle; it would also bridge the antagonism which then existed
between the people and the government. The formation or revitalization of truly representative councils at every level, and the

democratization of government agencies, would 'automatically' restore the authority of the government right down to the village level, and check anarchy at its source. The old pamong-praja would be removed from power immediately but gracefully, by giving them advisory or technical functions. For although Sjahrir was among the most emphatic of the national leaders in demanding an end to feudalism, he was also the most outspoken in condemning the physical attacks being made on the traditional rulers, together with Ambonese, Chinese, and Europeans. Change was only accept-able when it was orderly and peaceful.

It was imperative that there be some change in the Republic's leadership after the Allied landings on 30 September. Sjahrir's confidence in this new situation helped to ensure his own rapid rise to power through a 'democratic' adjustment to the Republic's structure. When the KNIP began its second full session on 16 October, Vice-President Hatta read a proclamation, the basic terms of which had been previously agreed among members, giving the KNIP legislative power in the transitional period before the repre-sentative bodies envisaged in the constitution could be established. Because of the emergency situation, these new powers of the KNIP would be exercised by an elected working committee (BP-KNIP, i.e. Badan Pekerja KNIP) between full sessions. Such was the demoralization and defensiveness of the politicians who had co-operated with the Japanese that they gave a free hand to Sjahrir and Amir Sjarifuddin, the two leading anti-Japanese figures in the Republic, to select its members. They drew up a list of fifteen of their leading supporters among 'anti-fascist' intellectuals, and secured their election as the BP-KNIP.

With this shift political initiative was firmly in the hands of Sjahrir and his associates rather than the cabinet. The former moved steadily to demolish what they characterized as 'fascist' elements in the Republican polity. On 30 October they proposed that political parties should be freely established provided they served the independence cause. Four days later this proposal was sanctioned by the Vice-President, who was much more prominent in the capital than Sukarno during this transition period. Hatta added the optimistic note that the parties should prepare for a general election in January 1946.

A general election had already been promised in the 1 November 'political manifesto', the clearest official statement of the Republic's position towards the outside world. Though signed by Hatta alone, this appears to have been a joint effort of the Vice-President and the new BP-KNIP leadership. Except in its careful defence of those who had co-operated with the Japanese, the manifesto closely followed Sjahrir's thinking. By appealing to the Atlantic Charter and the Dutch debacle of 1942, it rejected any Dutch claim to legal sovereignty. Nevertheless it took a very liberal stand towards Dutch capital and Dutch personnel. The Republic would assume all the debts of the Netherlands Indies Government, and would return all foreign-owned property.[14]

The BP-KNIP also devoted immediate attention to the 'democratization' of regional government in accordance with Sjahrir's blueprint. Its proposal, drafted on 30 October and promulgated on 23 November, was for regional national committees at the level of the residency, the kabupaten, and the autonomous town. These bodies would each elect a five-man working committee to join the appointed head of the region in daily government. In the residencies of Java and Sumatra a high priority was given to this law, and revitalized national committees were formed in most areas in December. This provided an opportunity to replace the older regional KNIs which were virtual extensions of wartime *Hokokais*, and to bring into government the new forces which had sprung up in late 1945. In a few urban national committees members were even elected, by an indirect process based on the neighbourhood associations (*tonarigumi*, renamed *rumah tetangga*) established by the Japanese. Although the reforms were accompanied by further stress on the sovereignty of the people, their merit lay not in any absolute standards of democracy to which they aspired, but in the opportunity for an orderly change of leadership within a framework set by a government which appeared to know where it was going.

The final steps in the transition to parliamentary government were taken on 11 November. The BP-KNIP announced that the President had accepted its proposal that cabinet ministers be made responsible to the KNIP, acting as a parliament. With that the first Republican cabinet was dismissed by Sukarno, to be replaced on 14 November with a new cabinet headed by Sjahrir and Amir Sjarifuddin.

This rapid series of events constituted a watershed of the first magnitude. It inaugurated what became known as the 'liberal' or parliamentary form of government which was to prevail against the Sukarnoist model envisaged in the 1945 constitution for the next twelve years. It gave leadership of the Republic to the type of 'modernizing' Western-minded intellectuals who were then thought to be the coming men of Asia, easy for Western observers to appreciate. Judged in terms of previous forms of government in Indonesia, it was the most revolutionary political change at the national level in the whole period 1945–50.

The Parliamentary Revolution: (2) The Power Struggle
Although Sjahrir's name has become inextricably associated with

the parliamentary and multiparty system, especially in the eyes of the many Indonesian opponents of such a format, it is striking how little the new form of government owed to democratic ideology, and how much to the jockeying for power among a handful of Jakarta leaders. The three major parties involved in this manoeuvering were Sukarno–Hatta; Sjahrir and his 'anti-fascist' young intellectuals; and the Kaigun group of older nationalists with whom Tan Malaka became associated. The eventual outcome was an alliance between the first two, with initiative for the time being firmly in the hands of Sjahrir. Since there was no place for Tan Malaka in this alliance, he quickly came to embody opposition to it.

Tan Malaka's earliest and most enduring connections, when he surfaced in Jakarta in August, were with the pemuda leaders Sukarni and Adam Malik, who had already been associated with his underground PARI before the war. In late August he also met Mr Subardjo, whom he had known in Holland twenty-seven years earlier. He assisted Subardjo as Foreign Minister, and through him was introduced to the other leading Kaigun figures, and to Sukarno.

Because, like Sjahrir, Tan Malaka had influential pemuda support and a revolutionary reputation untainted by co-operation with the Japanese, he was another potential beneficiary of the strong pemuda demand for change in October. The most influential politicians in the first cabinet, Subardjo and Iwa Kusuma Sumantri of the Kaigun group, were anxious to increase the revolutionary status of the cabinet by including Tan Malaka. Like Sjahrir, however, he decided against propping up this dying horse. He appears to have seen himself as an ideologue and symbol of the revolution rather than a cabinet-level politician. His supporters were to launch him publicly in December as *bapak* (father) of the Indonesian Republic.

In two meetings with Sukarno in September Tan Malaka greatly impressed the President with his command of revolutionary strategy, especially his emphasis on mass mobilization and national unity. Sukarno expressed his desire that Tan Malaka's strategy should guide the struggle if he and Hatta were arrested by the Allies. On 1 October Subardjo and Tan Malaka persuaded Sukarno to sign a 'testament' identifying Tan Malaka as his political heir. However, Hatta intervened to have the names of Sjahrir, Iwa Kusuma Sumantri, and Wongsonegoro added to the list of those by whom 'the leadership of the independence struggle will be carried on'.[15] This dilution of the testament, the rapidly apparent reluctance of the British to arrest Sukarno, and the growing assertiveness of the KNIP as a representative body, deprived these palace manoeuvres of political relevance. The main significance of the 'testament' was its use, much later, to discredit Tan Malaka as a devious anti-Sukarno plotter.[16]

Nevertheless there were more serious moves in October to make Tan Malaka president, as a way of raising the Government's standing with the 'revolutionary' pemudas and the Allies. Sukarni, Adam Malik, and perhaps Subardjo supported such a move. Sjahrir met Tan Malaka twice and offered to support him if he could demonstrate even one tenth of Sukarno's mass support. Sjahrir's emissaries in Central and East Java, however, reported that Sukarno was indispensable.

The fact that Tan Malaka was the only candidate being seriously suggested as an alternative president appears eventually to have brought Sukarno around to fearing him more than he feared Sjahrir, despite the similarity of outlook of the two older men. Sukarno became reconciled to the transition to relative inactivity as a 'parliamentary president', since it allowed him at least to continue in office. Sjahrir found the same compromise acceptable for different reasons. Power was effectively transferred to his hands, in terms the Dutch and British understood. Yet the enormous popular appeal of Sukarno as President, and the retention of the August constitution despite its inapplicability to the new structure, provided essential legitimacy within Indonesia.

The shift to a multiparty system was similarly pragmatic. In October Sjahrir was still thinking, like Sukarno and Tan Malaka, in terms of a one-party rather than a multiparty state. Sjahrir's party however was to be of a cadre rather than a mass type:

> Its membership need not be large, provided that it forms a tightly disciplined army efficient and modern in organization . . .[17]

Sjahrir's followers appear to have hoped as late as November that Tan Malaka might lead such a party. However it appears to have become clear to Sjahrir before 31 October that other parties with potential mass support were already in process of formation, and that there was no hope of absorbing them into his own type of élitist party. On the other hand he quickly abandoned any intention he might have had to organize a national election in January 1946. Without an extensive programme of political education, his own type of modernizing Marxist leadership could not hope to rival Sukarno's nationalism or the religious parties in a count of heads. One of the merits of the revolutionary situation was that it gave the initiative to an unrepresentative modern-minded élite.

Curbing the Social Revolution

Sjahrir's *Perjuangan Kita* had already attacked with astonishing fierceness the anarchic forces which had so successfully destroyed the Japanese régime and brought about his own rise. The pemudas were in danger of sinking 'to the level of wild beasts',[18] he wrote, and could in no way lead the revolution. The narrow composition of the cabinet he announced on 14 November offered further evidence of how little he trusted the forces which had brought him to power. Sjahrir and Amir between them monopolized all the five key political posts (Sjahrir taking internal and foreign affairs as well as the premiership). The remaining nine posts appear to have been filled with an eye to technical competence or acceptability to the Dutch rather than to any political support within the country. Having no substantial reputation or following, these ministers were entirely dependent on Sjahrir and Amir. Four of the eleven ministers were (Protestant) Christians, and the non-representation of Muslim interests brought immediate complaints.

Although he had come to power through perjuangan, Sjahrir quickly became identified with diplomasi. Diplomasi, however, towards the Allies, not the Japanese. The new government continued to favour the replacement by younger Marxists of officials and politicians who had co-operated with the Japanese. A BP-KNIP member and friend of Amir, Mr Hindromartono, was appointed Resident of Bojonegoro; a follower of Sjahrir, Mr Hamdani, Resident of Cirebon. They talked of forming soviets, and making these regions laboratories of democratic government. Many of the wartime supporters of Sjahrir and Amir Sjarifuddin took a prominent role in the social revolutionary wave in Java—particularly in the *Tiga Daerah*. The determination to avoid bloodshed and anarchy, however, meant that in practice the government invariably threw its weight against the social revolution. Sjahrir and Amir had insufficient trusted cadres of their own to restructure the government; they distrusted the forces engaged in pulling down the old order. Their insistence on presenting an appearance of ordered democracy to the outside world drove them in specific cases to side with the old pamong praja against social revolution.

Sjahrir's government was unable to control or direct the Pekalongan disturbances, which were suppressed independently by local army units. The government's dilemma was well represented, however, in its subsequent insistence on bringing the leading social revolutionaries in this region to trial, and making the hairline distinction between righteous revolution and criminality.

In the case of the 'social revolution' of East Sumatra, the government's opposition was unqualified. The disturbances there caught Sjahrir and Amir completely by surprise, and gave powerful ammunition to Van Mook in his attempt to demonstrate the Republic's lack of control over Sumatra. A high-level government delegation led by Amir Sjarifuddin flew to Medan in a British plane on 9 April 1946, in an attempt to bring Sumatra back to a safer path. Two prominent 'international' Marxists, Amir and Mr Abdul-madjid Djojoadinigrat, strove to convince the impatient revolution-aries of East Sumatra that the national revolution was no time for socialism:

as a Marxist . . . I want an egalitarian society with fair distribu-tion. But every theoretician of revolution must accept that that aspiration must be attained in stages . . . Mao Tse Tung once said, "Our struggle now must be directed to the first phase, with the second phase delayed for the time being".[19]

The social revolutionaries were guilty of Lenin's 'infantile disorder of radicalism'. Unity, discipline, and the power of the state were all important. Mr Hermani, secretary to the Interior Ministry, in-structed one pemuda audience,

although in our state the highest authority rests with the people, this does not mean that the people, ordinary men, sit in judgement or exercise the highest government, but people's sovereignty is exercised through people's representatives.[20]

Although such comments were frequently disputed, the delegation was remarkably successful in bringing the Sumatran *Persatuan Perjuangan* to adopt a pro-Government position, and in organizing an all-Sumatran KNI in Bukittinggi to reinforce the authority of the provincial governor, Mr Hasan.

The priorities of the national revolution, the caution of the Marxists who led it, and the organizational unpreparedness of the real social revolutionaries, prevented permanent restructuring of Indonesian society. Nevertheless the upheaval of 1945–6 had pro-duced a revolution in the manner in which authority was wielded. It had overturned the relationship between youth and maturity; between heroic spirit and legal expertise; between charisma and authority. Smail quotes a not untypical *camat perjuangan* ('struggle'-style district official) who

dressed with deliberate casualness and never wore the pamong praja uniform, let his hair grow long in the pemuda fashion of the revolution and always carried a pistol. If he had not done so, and not made a practice of speaking bluntly (rather than with priyayi politeness) no one would have paid attention to him.[21]

This was the outward sign of a fundamental shaking of the found-ations of Indonesian society, and above all of Javanese society. The intensely hierarchic structure of the latter was by no means per-manently or completely overthrown, but for the first time in centuries it appeared vulnerable. Having needed, in 1945–6, to invoke a different form of legitimation in order to survive at all, the Indonesian ruling classes consequently lost much of their traditional strength.

References

1 *Our Struggle*, trans. B. R. O'G. Anderson, Ithaca, 1968, p. 28.
2 *A Road With No End*, trans. A. H. Johns, London, 1968, p. 97.
3 E.g. Osman Raliby, *Documenta Historica*, Jakarta, 1953, pp. 176–8.
4 *Ibid.* p. 497.
5 *Our Struggle*, p. 27.
6 Ruth McVey, introduction, in Sukarno, *Nationalism, Islam, and Marxism*, Ithaca, 1970, pp. 5–10 and 16n.
7 Robert Jay, *Religion and Politics in Rural Central Java*, New Haven, 1963, p. 69. An Indonesian scholar has recently demonstrated the extent of this phenomenon in the Sragen Kabupaten of Surakarta, where 80 of the 180 lurahs were replaced in 1945–46. Soejatno, 'Revolusi dan Ketegangan2 sosial di Surakarta 1945–1950', paper presented to A.N.U. colloquium on the Indonesian revolution, Canberra, August 1973, p. 19n.
8 1 hectare $= 2 \cdot 47$ acres. The village studied by Jay (*ibid.* p. 44) had also reduced the lurah's bengkok to 5 hectares. Only 153 of its 735 families held more than one hectare in 1953. Larger bengkok's are still common in other areas.
9 Jay, *op. cit.*, p. 46.
10 One of the few ruling uleebalangs in Pidië to survive this affair was the ruler of Pineuëng, father of the Republican Governor of Sumatra, Mr Hasan.
11 Marxism was not completely absent. Husein al-Mudjahid, the pre-war PUSA youth leader who undertook the purge of uleebalangs throughout Aceh following the Cumbok affair, was a close friend of the veteran Islamic communist Nathar Zainuddin. At least some of the superficial language of Husein's 'long march' against the uleebalangs was derived through Nathar from Marxism. Husein's own understanding of Marxism was, however, negligible.
12 *Our Struggle*, p. 28.
13 *Ibid.* p. 31.
14 An abbreviated form of this manifesto is translated in Feith & Castles, *Indonesian Political Thinking 1945–1965*, Ithaca, 1970, pp. 50–55.
15 The Testament is reproduced in Muhammad Yamin, *Sapta Darma*, Jakarta, 1957, pp. 32–3.
16 Kahin, pp. 148–51 and 167–70, gives a version of this episode advanced by Hatta in his 1948 indictment of Tan Malaka and the July 3 Group. Tan Malaka was alleged to have 'forged' a document naming himself alone as heir to the presidency, and to have claimed in Central Java that it should now come into effect because Sukarno and Hatta were prisoners of the British. This allegation is gravely weakened by its absence from Government or other statements in early 1946, when the cabinet was desperate to pin something on Tan Malaka (see e.g. Raliby, pp. 287–9 and 341–5). Anderson, *Java*, pp. 278–80; Tan Malaka, *Pandangan Hidup*, Jakarta, 1952, pp. 99–103; and Sajuti Melik, in *Kompas* 28 June 1972, provide a more convincing picture.
17 *Our Struggle*, trans. B. R. O'G. Anderson, p. 30.
18 *Ibid.* p. 36.
19 Amir Sjarifuddin, as cited in *Soeloeh Merdeka* (Medan), 10 April 1946.
20 *Ibid.* 6 May 1946.
21 J. R. W. Smail, *Bandung in the Early Revolution*, Ithaca, 1964, p. 127.

Chapter Five

NATIONAL POLITICS IN THE
REPUBLIC, 1946–1947

> *Tan Malaka told Sjahrir at Banten that the
> consequences must be weighed in advance,
> for if one party was formed, various parties
> would arise like mushrooms after rain. But
> the above advice was not followed. Parties
> were formed, first of all by cabinet members
> themselves. . . but the government and the Sjahrir
> cabinet themselves feared the results of
> democracy.*
>
> Muhammad Yamin, 1948[1]

Sjahrir's rise and the transition to parliamentary government had
been accomplished within the small world of Jakarta élite politics,
affected only indirectly by the fighting going on in Surabaya and
elsewhere. Only after this transition did the new leaders begin in
earnest to form representative councils, political parties, and youth
organizations, to mediate between the government and the people.
The opponents of Sjahrir, ousted or ignored in his rapid rise to
power, sought in turn to demonstrate the unrepresentativeness of
the new government. Some political parties had already been in
process of formation before Hatta's 3 November announcement gave
them the green light, but no party began to link its national leadership with a mass base before December 1945. A more urgent
imperative than political support was to establish some degree of
control over and communication with the physical power of the
revolution—the armed pemudas.

Pemuda Organizations

THE ARMY
The potentially strongest, best-disciplined segment of armed
pemudas constituted the Republican army. Army units in each

kabupaten shared many features with irregular *pasukan:* their local autonomy (based on the PETA/Gyugun Company); their foraging for supplies, uniforms and weapons; the high value they placed on heroic spirit vis-a-vis orthodox military discipline and tactics; and their dependence on charismatic leadership.

It was a time when the idea of 'bapakism' and the individual unit's 'sovereignty' were widely accepted. *Bapak* (fathers) who were clever at leading their men, quick to satisfy their needs and their ideological orientations, judicious in fulfilling their material requirements, assumed very strong positions, and were obeyed as fathers. Usually they acted less as commanders giving orders than as fathers defending the interests of their 'children'. In such circumstances the bapak held a powerful position vis-a-vis his superiors. He could not be transferred . . . Thus the Army leadership could not control him. . .[2]

The government commenced the Herculean task of moulding such units into the military arm of the government only on 5 October (now celebrated as Armed Forces Day), when Sukarno decreed the formation of the TKR (*Tentara Keamanan Rakjat*, People's Peace-keeping Army) out of the quasi-military *Badan Keamanan Rakjat* which had existed only at the local level. Three months later it became the TRI.[3] These changes of name were accepted enthusiastically, new recruits were enrolled, and command structures began to form at residency level by a process of natural selection among the various ex-PETA/Gyugun officers.

Japanese training had been limited to field operations, mainly at platoon level, as a basis for guerrilla warfare. In looking for staff officers the government therefore turned to those with pre-war Dutch officer training, who were in any case spiritually closer to the nationalist élite than were the Japanese-trained men. In mid October a former KNIL Major, Urip Sumohardjo, was appointed to form an army general staff in Jogjakarta. He quickly drew up a paper command structure of 10 Divisions in Java, surmounted by three 'Commands' corresponding with Provinces. The effective TKR units continued to be the battalion and the company, however, and authority above that level was always tenuous.

The army commander, on the other hand, was designated from below. An all-Java meeting of TKR commanders on 12 November elected Colonel Sudirman as their leader. Sudirman, then 33 years old, had been a PETA *Daidancho* (battalion commander), and a pre-war Muhammadiah schoolteacher. He owed his election in part to his success in negotiating the acquisition in his Banyumas area of the largest supply of Japanese arms outside Surabaya; in part to his personal moral authority as an ascetic, strong-minded exemplar of traditional Javanese values, with a fatherly concern for his men's spiritual and material welfare. The incipient conflict between Japanese-trained and Dutch-trained officers was partly resolved by the surprisingly smooth relationship which developed between Commander Sudirman, the charismatic leader, and his technically more competent chief of staff.

In Sumatra the autonomous pattern was even more marked because of the absence of Dutch-trained staff officers. In each residency, TKR divisions were formed entirely on their own initiative. Only in January 1946 did Dr A. K. Gani, Resident of Palembang and representative of the Defence Minister in Sumatra, appoint an all-Sumatra commander. This was Suhardjo Hardjowardjojo, a Dutch-trained Captain in the pre-war royal guard of the Mangkunegaran (Surakarta). Suhardjo had no basis of support outside Lampung, where he had migrated in the 1930s, and even less leverage than Sudirman in Java over the essentially autonomous TKR/TRI divisions.

Amir Sjarifuddin's assumption of the Defence portfolio in the first Sjahrir cabinet immediately produced friction with the TKR and its new commander. Initially neither was prepared to recognize the other. The 12 November TKR Conference had, on the Japanese pattern, advanced its own nominee as Minister of Defence—the Sultan of Jogjakarta, Hamengkubuwono IX. Fortunately the Sultan was not eager to contest the position. The government for its part did not ratify the choice of Sudirman until 18 December, when it had exhausted all alternatives.

The army was a prime target of the government's 'anti-fascist' programme. Ex-PETA officers had already been antagonized by Sjahrir's biting attack on the 'traitors', 'fascists', and 'running-dogs' who had co-operated with Japan.[4] Amir's model was the Red Army, which he saw as a citizens' army loyal to the government and indoctrinated with socialist ideals. But although Amir attempted to educate the army in socialism, he had no effective way to enforce his will on unit commanders. Sudirman and the majority of PETA-trained officers in Java bitterly resented the 'fascist' slur cast on them, and rejected the attempt to introduce partisan ideology to the army. In their vision the military was above politics and shunned divisive alignments, in order to play a unifying role in the national struggle.

Because of this fundamental antagonism, Amir was obliged to build an armed base of government support in other ways. One way was to ally with sympathetic Dutch-educated officers in certain divisions, notably the West Java 'Siliwangi' division of which the pre-war KNIL Lieutenant A. H. Nasution assumed command in May 1946. This division was developed into one of the best equipped and disciplined in the Republic, absorbing most of the arms and the best trained men from the badan perjuangan in the Bandung area.

PESINDO AND ITS RIVALS

The new cabinet's other option was to consolidate its influence among the more educated armed pemudas sympathetic to its socialist, 'anti-fascist' approach. Here again it was Amir Sjarifuddin who played the major role. One of the most engaging personalities and persuasive orators in the Republican leadership, Amir also had more time and aptitude than Sjahrir for the organizational work of party-forming. At the time Sjahrir was preparing the cabinet list which was to begin the drift of pemuda support away from him, Amir was using his considerable powers to build a more permanent pemuda following for the incoming government and for himself.

The first all-Indonesian Pemuda Congress assembled in Jogjakarta on 10 November. As a demonstration of pemuda spirit and solidarity the congress was an enormous success, drawing hundreds of delegates from all over Java and renewing the *perjuangan* commitment at the very height of the Surabaya crisis. The goals of the principal organizers of the congress, to form a disciplined pemuda organization with a socialist and 'anti-fascist' programme, were less fully met. In the event only seven of the twenty-three pemuda groups represented accepted this programme and merged into PESINDO (Pemuda Sosialis Indonesia). These seven, however, included the most important early pemuda catalysts in Jakarta, Semarang, and Surabaya—API, AMRI, and PRI respectively. The emphatic rejection by PESINDO of all things Japanese, its sense of revolutionary purpose, and its close connections with the government, made it easily the strongest youth organization in Java. Its Jakarta leader, Wikana, represented pemudas in all the socialist led cabinets except the first.

The decisions of the Jogjakarta Conference were also received with enthusiasm in Sumatra. Most of the early youth groups there immediately declared themselves branches of PESINDO, primarily as a gesture of solidarity with the exciting pemuda developments at the centre. Powerful PESINDO branches developed, but without sharing any of the pro-government and especially pro-Amir partisanship of the parent in Java. In Sumatra PESINDO simply represented the revolutionary, 'modern', and relatively secular left-wing in each different residency situation.

The formation of PESINDO extended into pemuda ranks a similar polarization to that which *Perjuangan Kita* and the accession of Sjahrir created amongst élite politicians. Among pemuda organizations in Java which generally opposed PESINDO in national politics were the *Barisan Banteng* and Hizbullah. Both of these had roots in the Japanese period. Barisan Banteng (Buffalo Corps) arose directly from *Barisan Pelopor* (Vanguard Corps), the youth arm of Jawa Hokokai. It naturally assumed a close relationship with the PNI, although it was unable to retain an organization of much effectiveness beyond the Surakarta region. Hizbullah, the Japanese-trained Islamic youth corps of MASJUMI, was even less effective in national politics. Under the Japanese it had been organized on a purely local level. However it bore a heavy share of fighting at the front and wielded considerable influence at the local level.

Political Parties

In the ideological or programmatic sense in which political parties have been understood in the Anglo-Saxon world, the only true Indonesian political parties have been Marxist. Since the 1920s it was common for Indonesians to divide their political organizations into three groups, according to whether their basis was Marxist nationalist, or religious. For the religious groups, and to some extent also the nationalists, the party was primarily a way of ensuring representation of a cultural group. If Muslim parties spoke for the santri community, abangan Javanese and some non-Muslim outer islanders tended to seek a counterweight in nationalist parties. Insofar as it had a programme, Indonesian nationalism emphasized unity above precision.

THE PKI

If Marxist parties have often defined the practical issues in Indonesia, this was never more true than in the early years of the revolution. The Marxists' anti-Japanese background, their revolutionary credentials and expertise, the stirring language with which they spoke to the pemudas, gave them a dominant position. Therefore the most important divisions were those between Marxists.

At the end of 1945 it was abundantly clear that the most important cleavage was not between communists and social democrats. It was between those Marxists in both the above camps whose principal orientation was international, and those whose experience and sentiments were primarily or entirely Indonesian. For the former the primary issue was still the international struggle against fascism, and after that against international capitalism; the strategy was the united front with anti-fascist and bourgeois-democratic forces; and one of the assumptions was relative confidence in the Dutch and British Left, both now in power. For the more westernized Indonesian Marxists who had suffered in the resistance together with Europeans, the emotional bond of anti-fascism was initially stronger than anything binding them to their fellow countrymen in such groups as the Barisan Pelopor.

The great majority of Indonesians attracted to communism in 1945, on the other hand, saw it as the party of revolution *par excellence*, carrying on the defiant tradition of the 1926–7 revolt, prepared to match its rhetoric with action and to carry the revolution into domestic Indonesian social structures. The eventual success of the international Marxists in taming most of this group was one of the most important factors in curbing the whole social revolutionary movement.

It was representatives of the second, more impatient group who first re-formed the PKI on 21 October. Led by Mr Muhammad Jusuf, a young Marxist lawyer with no important position in the pre-war 'illegal PKI', the party issued a revolutionary programme to nationalize land and all key enterprises, confiscate large land-holdings, and introduce pure socialism. 'The Social Revolution is the only way to eliminate and destroy the exploitation of the common people', it declared.[5] Despite its lack of well-known national leaders, the party was already acquiring strong support in late December, especially in East Java, and established the *Lasykar Merah* (red militia) as its fighting arm. However in February 1946 during the first PKI Conference at Cirebon, Jusuf's supporters clashed with the local TRI (formerly TKR), chased them out, and took over the town for a week. When the army retook the town Jusuf and some of his followers were arrested. Demoralized by this event, the leaderless PKI in Java was gradually taken over by a group of older 'international' communists. In May 1946 the leadership was assumed by Sardjono. Party chairman in 1926, Sardjono had been taken from Dutch internment in Boven Digul to Australia in 1942 and had worked for Allied propaganda during the war. The PKI in Java was thus gradually transformed into a pillar of support for the government.

In Sumatra, on the other hand, the 'international' Marxist element gained an early following only in the south. A spontaneously-formed militant PKI in South Sumatra was crushed in the same way as the PKI-Jusuf, but more completely. In North and Central Sumatra, the PKI was able to flourish as the first party to win enthusiastic pemuda support. A PKI Sumatra executive was established in Medan on 18 November 1945, headed by Abdul Xarim M. S. In sharp contrast to the 'international' Marxists, Xarim had been prominent during the Japanese occupation as leading spokesman for the East Sumatran political propaganda organization. His principal colleagues, Nathar Zainuddin in Medan and Haji Dato Batuah in West Sumatra, were 'Islamic Communists' who had like him been active in the pre-1926 PKI. Both personally and ideologically these men were closer to Tan Malaka than to the eventual 'international' leaders of the PKI. In the two largest residencies, East and West Sumatra, the PKI was able to set the tone of the pemuda revolution, at least until the PNI and Muslim parties began to expand early in 1946. Although it remained strong, the Sumatra PKI suffered after March 1946 from its growing contacts with the PKI in Java, which curbed its early opportunistic radicalism.

PARTAI SOSIALIS (PS)

The most widely known and respected politician to consider himself communist in 1945 was Mr Amir Sjarifuddin.[6] He had been in contact with the 'illegal PKI' established by Musso in 1935, though Dutch and Japanese surveillance ensured that this was never a disciplined or coherent organization. On the other hand Amir had nothing but disdain for the unsophisticated and unknown Marxists who re-established the PKI in 1945. In terms of the anti-fascist struggle he had much more in common with Sjahrir. Amir's closest colleagues from the 'illegal PKI' underground or the pre-war GERINDO formed the *Partai Sosialis Indonesia* (PARSI) on 1 November. Three weeks later it was announced that Amir's PARSI would merge with Sjahrir's political grouping, PARAS, most of which was similarly derived from Sjahrir's pre-war party and wartime underground. At a fusion conference on 16–17 December a united Partai Sosialis (PS) was formed. Its leadership included, besides the associates of Sjahrir and of Amir, a third group of leftist intellectuals who had spent the war in Europe associated with the Dutch underground. The leader of this group was Mr Abdulmadjid Djojoadinigrat—lawyer, scion of one of Java's leading aristocratic families and member of the executive of the Dutch Communist Party. Abdulmadjid and his colleagues brought the added authority of European Marxism to the 'anti-fascist' international line which Sjahrir and Amir were already pursuing. They also brought a doctrinaire distrust of Tan Malaka, who had been condemned by the Comintern as a Trotskyist. The Socialists began to drift radically apart from Tan Malaka in December, until he was regarded with even more hostility than the Japanese 'collaborators'.

Until its communist and social democrat constituents again fell apart in 1948, the Partai Sosialis was the strongest of the parties supporting the government, especially in Jogjakarta and East Java. The PS accepted the argument of its leaders that the time was not ripe to implement socialism, that international support was necessary, and that unruly levelling movements from below had to be opposed. As its opponents repeatedly complained, its westernized leaders showed more faith in left-wing forces in the Netherlands than they did in the revolutionary fervour of the Indonesian people.

LABOUR PARTY

The third Marxist party, the Labour Party (PBI), underwent a transition similar to the PKI. Formed at a Congress of Workers on 9 November, it initially adopted a radical policy of worker control of industry, and on other issues also followed a line sympathetic to social revolution. No doubt this was in part because the November change of government threw the party into opposition through its association with the minister for social affairs in the first Cabinet, Iwa Kusuma Sumantri. In East Sumatra too the Labour Party was among the most revolutionary. During 1946, however, the 'international' communists returning from Australia and Holland gradually established control of the labour movement including the PBI, which followed a firmly pro-government line from mid-1946. It was however the least significant of the Marxist parties.

MASJUMI

The santri community was the most clearly identified and organized cultural group in Indonesia at the end of the Japanese occupation. MASJUMI had already established a working relationship throughout Java between the two great Muslim associations, Muhammadiah and Nahdatul Ulama. Its organized mass base far exceeded that of any of the parties discussed above. However the Islamic establishment needed to be prodded by younger activists before it took the plunge into revolutionary politics.

After a month's preparation, a Muslim conference met in Jogjakarta on 7 November 1945 to form a new political party making use of the name and local structure of the Japanese organization. It elected a new MASJUMI leadership comprising pre-war Islamic politicians rather than the heads of the religious associations as in Japanese times. The predominant element in the executive was that of the Muhammadiah-oriented, Dutch-educated intellectuals of the pre-war Jong Islamieten Bond and Dr Sukiman's Partai Islam Indonesia. Dr Sukiman himself became chairman. In its defence of private property MASJUMI's programme was the most conservative of the major parties. Muslim emphasis on doing things in a legal and moral (rather than 'revolutionary') style, generally had similar consequences at a local level. The most notable feature of the party's early stance, however, was its strong condemnation of Sjahrir's cabinet on the grounds of the absence of Muslim representation.

From its inception MASJUMI probably had the largest membership of any party in Java, although this by no means implied similar effectiveness in national politics. In Sumatra, Islam was even more of a social force, but there the party had a poor start. The Japanese at the surrender had only just begun to expand the West Sumatran

MIT (*Majlis Islam Tinggi*, High Islamic Council) to neighbouring areas. The MIT continued this initiative in December 1945 by convening an all-Sumatra meeting at Bukittinggi, which declared MIT a political party representing Muslim interests in Sumatra. Only in February and March 1946 did MIT branches in most residencies declare for MASJUMI.

THE NATIONALIST PARTY—PNI

Paradoxically the nationalist current, which ought to have enjoyed the greatest degree of continuity from the late Japanese period, was the slowest to become organized. The initial plan of the PPKI was that a PNI state party would accomplish a smooth transition from the Japanese period by absorbing the Japanese Hokokais and other propaganda bodies. The suspension of the PNI state party by Sukarno on 31 August as a result of leadership difficulties halted its development in the more accessible parts of Java. In Sumatra, where the forceful Dr A. K. Gani had been appointed leader, the PNI carried on as a state party claiming Sukarno as its head. Its failure even there to generate mass support or enthusiasm was indicative of the weakness of the whole state party idea. The Japanese political/propaganda bodies had essentially been élite organizations of leaders from all streams of society, mediating between the Japanese and the people. They had neither the capacity nor the will to arouse mass support for a specific cause. The pemudas, although anxious for unity in principle, were not inspired by the sort of rhetoric a state party could provide, especially when most of its leaders had been prominent figures under the Japanese. Even in Sumatra the PNI state party was quickly surpassed by Marxist and Muslim parties except in Dr Gani's own Palembang.

In the wake of Sjahrir's attack on the 'collaborators', the closest followers of Sukarno in Java seemed initially demoralized. Only in December 1945 did some former members of Sukarno's pre-war parties (PNI and PARTINDO) form a new party, SERINDO. In January 1946 SERINDO sponsored a Conference at which a new PNI (Partai Nasional Indonesia) was formed by its fusion with the state party groups in Sumatra, South Sulawesi, and parts of Java. As with MASJUMI, the new PNI leadership elected at this conference reflected the prevailing anti-Japanese and radical mood. The chairman elected was Sarmidi Mangunsarkoro, who had not been politically prominent under either the Japanese or the Dutch. His assets were a strong position in the Taman Siswa school system, the potential basis for a PNI youth wing; an anti-Japanese stance; and a major role in the BP-KNIP which brought Sjahrir to power. The official programme of the party was a vague 'socio-national democracy'. Its real heart was a nationalism which rejected the

Western models to which Sjahrir and the Marxists (and in a different way the Muslims) were alleged to adhere, in favour of a syncretic political style respecting traditional Javanese attitudes and structures. On this basis the potential constituency of the PNI was very large indeed, especially when indirectly linked to the magical charisma of Sukarno. But in the first year of the revolution this essentially conservative philosophy had little appeal for revolutionary youth. It was some time before the PNI made its expected impact in national politics.

Despite its Javanese orientation the PNI's strongest local bases were initially in the outer islands. In South Sulawesi and South Sumatra this was the legacy of the PNI state party. Dr Gani also took the initiative in forming a PNI youth wing, NAPINDO, which became one of the strongest fighting groups both in South Sumatra and East Sumatra. In the latter residency its strength rested on two of Dr Gani's pre-war GERINDO colleagues with a big following among Japanese-trained guerrillas.

Diplomasi and Perjuangan

Some relationships between these national parties and the *pasukans* and *badan perjuangan* which exercised physical power at the grass roots could be expected to grow from common cultural identity or loyalties built up under the Japanese. Since pasukans themselves were slow to form effective links above the city or regency level, however, it was not until well into 1946 that parties had any reliable control over branch and pemuda supporters. Nevertheless the parties immediately demanded a voice in government on behalf of the religious or cultural group they felt they represented. MASJUMI and PNI opposed Sjahrir's cabinet in the first place because it denied representation to themselves and their respective cultural orientations, not because they disapproved of its policies.

The consuming issue in Republican politics, the conflict between diplomasi and perjuangan, was only incidentally an issue between parties. It was between the government, whatever its party complexion, and the opposition. Every government of the Republic was committed to negotiating a settlement with the Dutch, and relying on international sympathy as its major card at the negotiating table. Internally this policy implied moderation. Foreign financial interests could not be alienated by premature expropriation; spontaneous 'social revolutions' or disorders could not be permitted to undermine the government's credibility as an instrument of order. Once the potentiality of Sjahrir's 'anti-fascist' revolution in Allied eyes had been exhausted, the diplomasi strategy necessarily involved a defence of the status quo.

The pemuda movement, on the other hand, insisted that independence had already been proclaimed and was not subject to negotiation. It had only to be defended by heroic action. Bargaining with the enemy and protecting his property was highly suspect, particularly if conducted by older leaders who spoke a different language. Although Sjahrir initially was immune from this charge, the government's shift to Jogjakarta on 4 January 1946 left him isolated. The Allied and Dutch presence in Jakarta had become pervasive and even dangerous. KNIL soldiers attempted to assassinate both Sjahrir and Amir Sjarifuddin at the end of December. The centre of national politics therefore moved to the free air of central Java, where the revolution was an intoxicating reality. As foreign minister with primary responsibility for negotiations Sjahrir however remained in Jakarta. Diplomasi became personally identified with him to an ever greater degree.

It would be wrong to characterize the perjuangan opposition as essentially a pemuda matter. Amir Sjarifuddin's success with PESINDO had assured the Socialist government of a very strong pemuda base. The attraction of PESINDO for the better-educated youth was that it went beyond 'cheap nationalism . . . the attitude of a frog under a coconut shell. We are building a world state'.[7] 'International' Marxism enabled such youths to feel that the revolution was part of something much wider and nobler than attacking Dutchmen, Eurasians, and Chinese, part of whose culture they had already come to share.

Only one politician of important national status adhered to the perjuangan path to independence with conviction and consistency—Tan Malaka. He matched Sjahrir in his ability to bring a Marxist training to bear on the revolutionary potentialities of a particular point in history; but he came to opposite conclusions. Having lived an underground existence for twenty years he was an inveterate political loner, enjoying the freedom as well as the inconvenience of the prophet. He remained always in the background, never even beginning to form the mass party he advocated. It was he who articulated the inchoate desire for perjuangan, and thereby provided direction and ammunition for the diverse, demoralized elements thrown into opposition by Sjahrir's rise—the dismissed first cabinet, and especially its Kaigun members; the unrepresented MASJUMI and PNI; the army leadership antagonized by *Perjuangan Kita* and Amir's defence ministry. The combination of these powerful elements with the emotive perjuangan groundswell almost overwhelmed the government in 1946. Against it the government had only two weapons: exploitation of the internal diversity of the opposition; and appeals to national unity in the face of external danger. In a society where traditional holistic notions of the state have never been fundamentally shaken, the latter appeal has seldom failed to rescue governments from their opponents. It is ironic that the socialists and communists, who suffered most from this tactic in the long run, were the first to make use of it in 1946.

Tan Malaka and the Persatuan Perjuangan

At the time of the independence proclamation Tan Malaka was badly out of touch with Indonesian realities. His 24 August meeting with Mr Subardjo was his first direct contact with Indonesian élite politics for decades. His first pamphlet, *PARI*, apparently written in early September,[8] was still preoccupied with his fantastic pre-war dream of linking Indonesia with Australia and other Southeast Asian countries in the proletarian republic he called ASLIA—a step towards world federation. Already however he saw the paths to freedom and socialism as one. He had long rejected the orthodox insistence on prior bourgeois revolution. The first priority was the mobilization of a single party (PARI), the only guarantee of the necessary unity for the coming struggle. Once this party was established in the main centres, the workers, the peasants, defence, youth, and women (in that order) should be organized through a system of co-operatives and syndicates. Only then could the fight begin against traitors within the camp and imperialism outside.

As we have seen, Tan Malaka's early plan to effect this type of strategy from above broke down when Sjahrir and Sukarno established what amounted to a working relationship in early November. The difference in attitude between both the latter leaders and Tan Malaka became very clear in December, when the old revolutionary's second pamphlet, *Muslihat*, appeared.[9] By this time Tan Malaka had witnessed personally some of the Surabaya fighting, Sjahrir had begun negotiating with Van Mook, and the multi-party system was in being. In *Muslihat* Tan Malaka attacked the government's assumption that international recognition was the major goal. With Surabaya in mind, the immediate task was to organize and unify the perjuangan to drive the Dutch into the sea. Since the chance for a single party had already been lost, unity would be achieved through a *Volksfront* (popular front) organized for total war. To ensure maximum commitment to the struggle, workers would immediately obtain the control of production, and poor peasants would get land, though only at the expense of foreigners and traitors. Now, as in the 1920s, Tan Malaka was ready to sacrifice whatever Marxist principles seemed to stand in the way of maximum revolutionary unity.

In the two months following the appearance of this (still anonymous) pamphlet, Tan Malaka rose from shadowy obscurity to become one of the best known leaders in Indonesia. He was firmly supported on the one hand by his pre-war pemuda disciples, Sukarni, Chaerul Saleh, and Adam Malik, who withdrew from PESINDO in December disenchanted with Sjahrir and Amir; and on the other by the ousted politicians of the first cabinet or the Kaigun—Subardjo, Iwa Kusuma Sumantri, Yamin, and Sajuti Melik. At three January meetings in Purwokerto and Surakarta this group organized a *Persatuan Perjuangan* (Struggle Union) which rapidly attracted the support of all major popular organizations. In Yamin's words[10] it 'drew the People and the attention of the perjuangan as a magnet draws the surrounding metal'. The Minimum Programme proposed by Tan Malaka and adopted by the PP on 27 January ran as follows:[11]

1   Negotiation on the recognition of 100 per cent Merdeka (Independence)
2   A People's Government
3   A People's Army
4   Taking care of European internees
5   Disarming the Japanese
6   Confiscation of enemy rights and properties
7   Confiscation of enemy industry (factories, workshops, etc.), and agriculture (plantations, mines, etc.).

In expanding on the first of these points PP spokesmen emphasized that 100 per cent independence must be the *pre-condition* for negotiation.

We are not willing to negotiate as long as the enemy is still in our country. If we are willing to hold negotiations, we are doing it against the will of the general public. Therefore, as long as one single enemy remains in the country, as long as there is an enemy ship on our shore, we must continue to fight.[12]

Impractical as this might seem in the vast Dutch-occupied areas outside Java and Sumatra, it was the fighting talk the militant pemudas longed to hear from their leaders. The double attraction of the '100 per cent Merdeka' slogan and the appeal for total unity made the Persatuan Perjuangan irresistible. On both points the PP stood in direct contrast to the highly unrepresentative Sjahrir cabinet, and it was therefore regarded as an open challenge by that cabinet. However its leaders did not attack Sjahrir openly, and the pro-Sjahrir PESINDO and Partai Sosialis participated in it. Indeed it was impossible for any popular group to stand outside the PP, in view of the popularity of its slogans and the necessity at the residency level for a forum in which the powerful badan perjuangan could work together. In West Sumatra the Partai Sosialis actually promoted the local PP, while in Priangan (West Java) PESINDO rapidly took control of it. In some remoter areas, particularly in Sumatra, the PP assumed a semi-governmental role, as the most up-to-date representative body for the various organizations holding physical power. Although the cabinet undoubtedly opposed the Persatuan Perjuangan everywhere, it was only at the national level that its oppositionist character was obvious or necessary.

The last two points of the PP minimum programme, though much less publicized than the first, were an equal contradiction of the government's promises to foreign capital. Yet it is noteworthy that they contained no threat to propertied Indonesian interests, and their justification was entirely in nationalist terms without a hint of Marxism:

> Why should the factories and the agricultural estates be con-
> fiscated before freedom is obtained 100 percent? Why should they
> be distributed among the masses? Because if they have become the
> properties of the masses, they will be able to fight as lions if the
> enemy ever comes back.[13]

Lacking time and inclination to organize a base among the Indonesian underprivileged masses, Tan Malaka played the same game of élite politics as the cabinet he opposed. Although he expressed post facto support for the 'social revolutions', he was even less able than Sjahrir to turn the levelling sentiments within them to account. In this respect the most that could be said for the PP was that, like the KNIs reorganized by Sjahrir, it provided a means to make local government more representative of the forces in society at a particular moment—January/February 1946.

The government's conviction that it would have to respond positively to the realistic Dutch proposals of 10 February made a showdown with the PP inevitable. Four days before these proposals became public Sjahrir had already travelled to Jogjakarta for unsuccessful talks with PP and other leaders on concessions from the Republican side. Instead the PP slogan, 100 per cent Merdeka, was taken up and echoed at rallies throughout Republican territory, especially at celebrations to mark six months of freedom on 17 February 1946. The TRI commander General Sudirman spoke strongly about the sacred duty of resistance at one PP rally. Sjahrir was deluged with telegrams to the same effect. A majority of the BP-KNIP became convinced that the Sjahrir government could not continue with its existing programme and membership. Sjahrir's resignation was formally accepted by Sukarno on 28 February, at the commencement of a critical session of the full KNIP in Surakarta.

In the eyes of Sukarno, Hatta, and other key leaders, Sjahrir's diplomasi was the only practicable policy. The crisis had therefore to be resolved solely by broadening the cabinet. On the other hand Sukarni and Chaerul Saleh insisted on behalf of Tan Malaka that policies were more important than people, and that the manifestly popular PP Minimum Programme must become the basis of the new cabinet. The PP leadership announced that it would boycott a cabinet formed on any other basis. Given the conviction of most leaders even within PP ranks that diplomasi was a painful necessity, this pure perjuangan stance opened the way for the PP's isolation and defeat. Sjahrir was able to entice four MASJUMI politicians and one minor PNI figure into disregarding the PP line taken by their respective parties. With their addition the new cabinet he formed on 12 March looked somewhat broader than its predecessor, without diminishing the power of the Partai Sosialis over key posts and policies. The new government did not explicitly denounce the popular PP programme. It simply adopted Sukarno's five point programme, which had a similar sound to that of the PP but sufficient vagueness to ensure complete freedom of manoeuvre.

This government crisis enabled Sukarno to return for the first time since independence to his remarkable role as manipulator and arbiter of opposing factions. In the crisis of the previous October Sukarno had been a principal butt of pemuda criticism, and 'opposition' had been able to win a victory which proved to be unique. The President's removal from direct political responsibility had proved a blessing for him. No longer was he held by the Allies as primarily responsible for pemuda violence, nor by the pemudas as primarily responsible for diplomasi. That role now fell to Sjahrir and Amir. Sukarno was free to build his image in the heartland of the Republic as the central symbol of unity and freedom. During December and January he was constantly moving about the whole Javanese-speaking area from Banten in the west to Malang in the east, addressing vast crowds in every centre. The other major Republican leaders—Hatta, Sjahrir, Amir, Tan Malaka—were not Javanese in fact, in language, or in style. None of them could approach Sukarno's ability to appeal directly to the masses in terms of Javanese imagery and symbol. Sukarno's capacity to make the Republican struggle real to simple people, to hold crowds spellbound with his oratory, was unique and indispensable.

By February the President had regained the comfortable middle ground of Republican politics. At every moment of crisis he supported the government and diplomasi, yet he spoke the language of perjuangan and encouraged the opposition to trust him. 'If it should ever turn out that Sjahrir is not maintaining the demand for 100 per cent Merdeka that all of you, my brothers, want, then I have the right to dismiss him', he told a cheering crowd on 17 February.[14] Moreover, the pemudas most bitterly opposed to Sjahrir (the Barisan

Banteng and Bung Tomo's BPRI, as well as many central Java TRI leaders) had a warm and long-standing respect for Sukarno. Though Sjahrir had helped rescue Sukarno in October, from now on it would be Sukarno who would rescue Sjahrir.

The Second Sjahrir Government, and Opposition

Having weathered this crisis, the government sought to drive the PP into oppositionist isolation so that it could be destroyed. The KNIP discussions had revealed the strength of resistance among some Tan Malaka followers to the sort of concessions Sjahrir was preparing to make to the Dutch. Action would have to be taken before these concessions became public, to prevent their becoming popular martyrs of 100 per cent Merdeka. The first step was the withdrawal of all pro-government forces from PP ranks, accomplished in time for the next major PP congress at Malang on 15 March. As the conference drew to an end two days later on a defiantly perjuangan note, government forces moved in. PESINDO units and the military police (which Amir Sjarifuddin had built into an organization loyal to his ministry rather than army headquarters) arrested all the key PP leaders who lacked any protective armed following—Tan Malaka, Sukarni, Chaerul Saleh, and Abikusno.

Realpolitik as harsh as this was a considerable blow to romantic early notions of the revolution as liberation. When the government finally attempted to justify the arrests on 1 April, it naturally argued in terms of the dangers of opposition at a moment when unity was essential. The arrests were nevertheless generally regarded for what they were, 'a policy of the central government . . . in order to be able to continue its negotiations with the outside world'.[15] At their trial two years later some of the victims claimed that the action had been instigated by the Dutch and announced in advance by Dutch radio.[16]

Bitterness was intensified by the government's heavy-handed attempt to curb the turbulent 'social revolution' of Surakarta. As a traditional rival in every field, it was not surprising that Surakarta should attract opponents of the central government which had made its home in Jogjakarta. Surakarta was moreover the headquarters of one of the strongest PP elements, Dr Muwardi's Barisan Banteng, which claimed 10,000 members in the city alone. It was the Barisan Banteng which led the attack on the frivolous young Susuhunan of Surakarta, kidnapping him for three days in January to indicate displeasure at his insufficient dedication to the struggle. Pressures for the abolition of the monarchy reached a peak in April 1946, as virtually every district refused to take further orders from the Susuhunan. In this predicament the young prince, together with his somewhat less abject royal colleague the Mangkunegoro, naturally appealed to the judgement of the central Republican government.

The crisis was handled by Dr Sudarsono, who had emerged as the third Socialist Party strong man with his appointment to the Interior Ministry in Sjahrir's second cabinet. He decreed that the status of the *swapraja* (monarchy) must be resolved in a democratic and orderly manner by elected representative councils. His PS colleague Soebadio was appointed chairman of a committee to organize the elections. The swelling revolutionary tide was not to be stayed by such manoeuvres, however. Both sides understood the dynamic of the situation: the Barisan Banteng demonstrated it by continuing to organize massive anti-swapraja rallies; Sudarsono by arresting Dr Muwardi and the other leading figures in the movement. Here Sudarsono went too far, bringing upon the government the accusation that it was fostering factionalism and division instead of unity. General Sudirman personally intervened to have the prisoners released, and even the government's representative in Surakarta forbade further arrests without his permission. The government was forced to accept the abolition of royal powers as of 1 June in favour of a ruling committee in which the local TRI strongman, Colonel Sutarto, had the largest role.

Hitherto Sjahrir's government had resisted using the military to suppress social revolution. Both in terms of its own anti-fascist and democratic assumptions and the likely effect on the Allies, the cure would have been as bad as the disease. Amir Sjarifuddin had been seriously disturbed at the declaration of martial law by the TRI in East Sumatra in the wake of the 'social revolution', and had insisted that civil government be immediately restored there. In Surakarta, however, the government's authority had been repudiated, and it had no choice but to put the best face on a situation of effective military control. A state of emergency was proclaimed for Surakarta on 6 June and extended to the whole of Java the following day. Although rationalized in terms of Dutch-Indonesian fighting and a massacre of Chinese at Tanggerang (West Java), the declaration appears to have been intended to divert attention from the government's humiliation in Surakarta and to facilitate tougher action in the future.

If a subsidiary aim of the decree was to placate the TRI with a formal role in government, it was unsuccessful. The mutual suspicion between Amir Sjarifuddin and General Sudirman was kept alive by Amir's attempts to mould the TRI into a progressive 'people's army'. On 19 February he inaugurated an 'education staff' for the army dominated by Socialist and MASJUMI politicians. This body in turn appointed fifty-five 'political officers' at the end of May without consulting the army command. The new officers were to educate each TRI unit in the goals of the revolution. The Marxist coloration of the new military academies Amir established also conflicted with the popular army view of being above politics. Finally the choice of divisional commanders throughout Java created a series of crises between the followers of Sudirman and of Amir from March until late May 1946. The government *razzias* of 3 March and 23 May had only embittered an already clear-cut confrontation.

The 3 July Affair

Military opposition to Sjahrir, Amir, and Dr Sudarsono was strongest precisely in the TRI Divisions at the political centre of the Republic—the Third (Jogjakarta) Division under Major General Sudarsono and the Fourth (Surakarta) under Colonel Sutarto. Both these officers had come to power despite the Defence Ministry. They shared the blend of traditional and revolutionary Javanese values symbolized supremely in Sudirman. After the government's setback in Surakarta there is little doubt that this central military group, supported by the Barisan Banteng and some opposition politicians, were seeking an opportunity to separate the Socialists from Sukarno and force them out of power.

The occasion was provided by a speech by Hatta on 27 June, making public for the first time what had been the Republic's negotiating position since March—the *de facto* recognition of the Republic in Java and Sumatra only. Leading politicians had long been aware of these terms, but the public announcement of such a betrayal of 100 per cent Merdeka was a favourable moment to strike against Sjahrir. On the evening of the speech Sjahrir, Dr Sudarsono, and others travelling in their party were imprisoned in Surakarta by Major A. K. Jusuf, a former Jakarta pemuda leader. Jusuf had been authorized both by his own commander, Maj. Gen. Sudarsono, and by Sutarto in Surakarta. Both men evidently felt their authority to be as least as legitimate, in populist terms, as that of the Prime Minister.[17]

It was more of a pemuda-style 'daulat' operation than a military coup. Having passed the judgement of the people on Sjahrir, the plotters evidently expected Sukarno to form a new government of national unity. They had been misled by the President's public rhetoric. In practice Sukarno was convinced that diplomasi was the only possible policy and Sjahrir the most acceptable man to conduct it. He immediately proclaimed martial law and took government powers into his own hands. He demanded angrily, but in vain, that Sudirman act to release the Prime Minister. On 30 June he made a masterful broadcast pointing out the harm such lawlessness did the Republican cause. This left the opposition in confusion and disarray. Sjahrir was released the same evening. This allowed the government to send police to arrest all the leading opposition politicians (except Tan Malaka and Sukarni, who had remained in detention throughout the proceedings).

The situation was now slipping away from the military conspirators. In a belated countermove which followed talks with Sudirman, and presumably had his blessing, Maj. Gen. Sudarsono now ordered the release of the newly-arrested opposition politicians. A show of force was organized for 3 July, but once again it relied fatally on trying to persuade Sukarno to form a new government. Since the military themselves appeared not to have made plans beyond the original kidnapping, they were forced to fall back on Muhammad Yamin. He at least had a plan for an alternative government, even if it was little more than a return to the first cabinet with the addition of Tan Malaka. However the last-minute attempt to mobilize a massive demonstration failed completely. The pathetic group which accompanied Gen. Sudarsono and Yamin to present their petitions to Sukarno was arrested without difficulty. Major Jusuf was foiled in a new attempt to seize Hatta and Amir Sjarifuddin.

The wave of arrests which ensued, totalling about a hundred, removed from the political scene most of the leading opposition politicians. General Sudirman also lost some influence, although he retained his post and a seat in the State Defence Council which held supreme executive power during the emergency period. He was able to ensure that few military men except Sudarsono himself were sacrificed. Sjahrir emerged from the crisis more than ever identified with diplomasi and divisive internal policies. The real beneficiary of the crisis was Sukarno, who had again demonstrated his power and effectiveness as a symbol of unity. The spectre of open conflict between rival armed forces in the Republican heartland placed a new importance on this ability to accommodate conflicting pressures. Whatever life remained in the 'anti-fascist' democratic revolution of the Socialists as well as the 'social revolution' of some Tan Malaka supporters was more than ever sacrificed to the need for unity.

Bulldozing Parliament
When the BP-KNIP called for a return to parliamentary-style government in mid August 1946 it was once again Sjahrir whom Sukarno designated as cabinet formateur. Sjahrir was still regarded as indispensable to fruitful relations with the Dutch and British, but he was no longer in a strong internal position. In the interests of diplomasi itself it was now imperative that the broadest range of politicians be drawn into cabinet and thereby made to share responsibility for the approaching compromise with the Dutch. After lengthy negotiations the third Sjahrir cabinet was announced on 2

October. Amir Sjarifuddin, retaining the Defence portfolio, became the only major source of PS strength in internal affairs. Two other key ministries, Interior and Finance, were surrendered to a pro-Sjahrir faction of MASJUMI (Mr Muhammad Roem and Mr Sjafruddin Prawiranegara), and Prosperity to the leader of the Sumatran PNI, Dr A. K. Gani. The leadership of MASJUMI and PNI continued to oppose the cabinet and its diplomasi policy, largely because they could not regard the eleven members they nominally had in it as truly representative of their parties. Nevertheless this was for the first time a true coalition of diverse social forces. To that extent it was less capable of decisive reforming action.

This cabinet successfully negotiated the Linggajati agreement in November 1946 (see pp. 109–11), whereby the Republic, recognized as speaking for Java and Sumatra, would co-operate with the Dutch to build a sovereign, federal United States of Indonesia. Linggajati immediately became the major issue of Republican politics. The 'international' Marxist parties which supported it—PS, PKI, Labour Party, and PESINDO—formed a coalition called the *Sayap Kiri* (Left Wing) on 14 December. On the other hand the major elements of the old PP opposition, who still considered themselves the political 'outs', opposed ratification of the agreement. The PNI, MASJUMI, the remaining Tan Malaka supporters at liberty, BPRI, and Barisan Banteng formed the *Benteng Republik* (Republican Fortress) coalition against Linggajati. The only major absence from the former opposition was General Sudirman, who advised his soldiers to struggle on regardless, leaving the politicians to argue about treaties. As one organization after another declared its attitude to Linggajati at the end of the year, it began to look as if the Sayap Kiri would not be able to muster enough support in the KNIP to have the agreement ratified.

Once again Sukarno had to intervene to save diplomasi. On 30 December he announced a plan to increase membership of the KNIP from 200 to 514 in such a way as to give a clear majority to the Sayap Kiri. The PKI and Labour Party would each be advanced to major party status, while eighty extra seats would go to workers and peasants (in practice mainly SOBSI and BTI).

This presidential act raised a furore in the BP-KNIP, not only because of its implications for Linggajati, but also because it marked the first clear departure since the parliamentary revolution of October 1945 from the principle that legislative power was shared by the KNIP. In a curious reversal of the 1945 position, the Socialist Party now fought for wider presidential prerogatives and their opponents for the rights of the KNIP as defined in Hatta's October 1945 decree. Outnumbered, the Socialists left the BP-KNIP on 17 January 1947 while a vote was passed to annul the decree.

Table 1   KNIP and BP-KNIP membership, 1947

	Old (1946) KNIP	New (1947) KNIP	New BP-KNIP
Socialist & PESINDO	35	35	7
PKI	2	35	3
Labour Party	6	35	3
Workers	—	40	3
Peasants	—	40	4
PARKINDO (Protestant)	4	8	1
Partai Katolik	2	4	—
Sayap Kiri & allies	**49**	**197**	**21**
MASJUMI	35	60	6
PNI	45	45	5
Partai Rakyat (Tan Malaka)	—	(in other categories)	2
Benteng Republik	**80**	**105**	**13**
Sumatra	1	50	5
Kalimantan	4	8	1
Sulawesi	5	10	1
Moluccas	2	5	1
Lesser Sundas	2	5	1
Chinese	5	7	1
Arabs	2	3	1
Eurasian	1	3	1
Other categories	49	121	1
Allegiance scattered	**71**	**212**	**13**
TOTAL	200	514	46

This stalemate between president and 'legislature' increased the urgency for a session of the full KNIP, which had not met for over a year. The existing KNIP membership was convened at Malang on 25 February 1947, while the additional appointees of Sukarno's decree were kept in attendance until their status was settled. The latter group included fifty representatives of regions, parties, and organizations in Sumatra, many of whom had been grateful for the opportunity to leave their turbulent home situations.

In opening the crucial KNIP session Sukarno insisted that he was not a president of the French or American type but a 'President a la Indonesian revolution . . . guiding and leading the people'.[18] One of his supporters proclaimed, 'Our President is the President of the Revolution; whoever opposes the Presidential Regulation No. 6 opposes the revolution'.[19] Nevertheless the majority of the KNIP was clearly not impressed. The debate was tense. Hatta only decided the issue on the third day by making it a straight question of confidence in the leadership. 'If you are not satisfied with the leadership of the President and Vice-President let us look for another President and Vice-President'.[20] Once again the opposition could not bring itself to overthrow Sukarno. The BP-KNIP withdrew its defiant motion and the 314 new KNIP members were able to take their seats to debate Linggajati.

Ratification of the agreement with the Dutch was now a foregone conclusion. The Benteng Republik opposition withdrew before the motion of assent was carried on 5 March by 284 votes to two. This victory for diplomasi was qualified however, by a second motion, proposed by the South Sulawesi spokesman Manai Sophian, that the government should support the Republican struggle in Borneo and East Indonesia. The appointment of twenty-eight representatives of these areas to the new KNIP in itself defied the Dutch view that Linggajati had ended Republican claims outside Java and Sumatra.

This was the last plenary session of the KNIP until late 1949. It elected a new, enlarged BP-KNIP roughly reflecting the strength of the parties at Malang. The government naturally held a secure majority within it, and the Sayap Kiri alone had almost half the seats (see Table 1).

The Socialists Divide and Fall

One of the unexpected consequences of this expansion of the Sayap Kiri's representation was a further decline of Sjahrir's authority within it. The PKI and Labour Party had been given representation equal to Sjahrir's Partai Sosialis. In May 1947 the Sayap Kiri itself gave equal voting power to its three major constituents. The Labour Party was now led by Setiadjit, a communist from the wartime Dutch underground. Both it and the PKI were therefore more Moscow-inclined than was Sjahrir.

Even within the PS the cleavage between Sjahrir's and Amir Sjarifuddin's followers rapidly deepened during 1947. Sjahrir, with Hatta, had been expelled from the Perhimpunan Indonesia in Holland when it came under communist control in 1931. There was always, therefore, some mutual suspicion between Sjahrir and the communists who returned from Holland in 1946, which became more obvious as the 'anti-fascist' cause faded. Led by Abdulmadjid, this group placed its support behind the alternative PS leader, Amir, who had never had to make a choice between the communism he often professed and the contradictory elements in his character.

The preoccupation of Sjahrir with diplomatic manoeuvres, his physical isolation in Jakarta, and his distaste for mass meetings, allowed the more Moscow-inclined Marxists gradually to assume control of the rank-and-file of both the PS and the Sayap Kiri as a whole. 'Marx House', a political training centre established jointly by the whole Sayap Kiri in a former sugar estate near Jogjakarta, had produced 400 cadres by May 1947, most of them in practice oriented towards Moscow. SOBSI (the all-Indonesian Labour Federation) was reorganized in November 1946 to give communists, many of them recent returnees from Australia, a decisive voice. The BTI (Indonesian Peasant Front) was at first led mainly by Sjahrir followers, causing the MASJUMI element within it to withdraw early in 1947 to form the rival STII (Sarekat Tani Islam Indonesia). Moscow communists increased their influence within the BTI during 1947, partly as a result of one of its founders, Ir Sakirman, entering the PKI. Communists did not take control, however, until 1948.

The factionalism which was increasingly evident within the small group of Sayap Kiri leaders during 1947 was more a matter of personality and attitude than of specific policy. The growing isolation of Sjahrir from the coalition as a whole, together with the unpopularity he had earned as the exemplar of diplomasi, appears to have convinced the opposing faction that it was time to depose him. On 26 June 1947 three Moscow-inclined members of cabinet—Amir Sjarifuddin (PS), Abdulmadjid (PS), and Wikana (PESINDO)—backed by a majority of the Sayap Kiri, withdrew their support from Sjahrir. They argued that he had gone too far in compromising the Republic through diplomasi—the same charge which brought down every revolutionary government.

The major parties bargained for several tense days over the formation of a new cabinet, under the threat of imminent attack by the Dutch. All parties now accepted that in view of Dutch belligerence there was no practical alternative to Sjahrir's policy of conciliation. If Sjahrir was now too little in touch with Republican realities to be useful, Amir was almost equally known and trusted by the Dutch and the great powers. A broad coalition under his leadership appeared to be called for. MASJUMI hostility toward the Defence Minister, however, kept both the party leader, Dr Sukiman, and the pro-Sjahrir 'religious socialists' of the previous cabinets from joining this one. Amir was able to woo another faction of MASJUMI (some politicians of the pre-war PSII) with a generous share of portfolios and the release of its leader, Wondoamiseno, from prison. Amir Sjarifuddin's communist allies controlled only about ten of the thirty-four places in this PS-PNI-Labour-PSII cabinet, and only Amir's Defence Ministry was a key one. Nevertheless this cabinet marked the highest point in the movement of the revolution towards orthodox communism.

Amir's cabinet had to cope both with the Dutch military offensive of July 1947 and with the subsequent diplomatic pressure to legitimize Dutch conquests, culminating in the humiliating *Renville*

agreement of January 1948. This agreement provided the opportunity for Amir's enemies to act against him. Leading the field was
MASJUMI,[21] for whom Amir represented all that was unacceptable
in a prime minister—a left Marxist, a Christian, and the man
responsible for splitting MASJUMI itself. Some MASJUMI ministers
had joined the cabinet in November 1947, as a tactical move, and
they resigned again on 16 January in protest against Renville. The
PNI followed two days later, bringing about the government's fall.

International calculations were not absent from these moves.
Sjahrir had been representing the Republic at the United Nations
following his fall. His firmest supporter in MASJUMI ranks, Mr
Sjafruddin Prawiranegara, led the Republican mission which was
refused admission to an ECAFE conference in the Philippines in
November. Both were struck by the effect on the Republic's position
of the 'two-camp' doctrine in the Soviet bloc and cold war thinking
in the West. It was becoming clear that in terms of acceptability
to America and its clients the advantage of Amir's 'anti-fascist'
record was now outweighed by the danger of being identified as a
communist fellow-traveller. Hatta's return in January from Sumatra,
where he had been for the whole of Amir's ministry, helped shift
Presidential support from Amir, whom Sukarno had backed in the
July crisis, back to the forces around Sjahrir.

Amir resigned as premier on 23 January 1948, after half his
cabinet had defected. He was later criticized by the harder-line
Stalinist, Musso, for the 'very important error . . . that the cabinet
resigned voluntarily, without offering any resistance whatever. . .
The communists isolated themselves in the opposition'.[22] One of the
reasons for this 'error' was Amir's confidence that the strength of the
Sayap Kiri in the BP-KNIP was now sufficient to ensure a new
cabinet not very different from his own. Sukarno surprised him by
naming Hatta formateur of a 'presidential' cabinet not responsible
to the BP-KNIP. In theory it was to be an emergency cabinet of
national unity, but Hatta made clear that the Sayap Kiri would
have to accept the loss of its key position including the defence
portfolio. The Marxists, with the exception of Sjahrir's immediate
followers, preferred the perilous path of opposition. Hatta took over
the controversial defence ministry himself, while the Sultan of
Jogjakarta became minister of state with special responsibility for
defence co-ordination. The other key portfolios were divided between
MASJUMI and PNI, with a minor post each for Protestant and
Catholic parties and for Sjahrir's followers in the PS. As if to
emphasize the purely tactical nature of opposition to Amir's
diplomacy, the new cabinet announced as its foremost point of
policy, 'To carry out the Renville agreement and continue negotiation upon the basis which has been reached'.

National politics—the making of governments, the conduct of diplomacy, the verbal definition of goals—involved a remarkably small number of men in Jogjakarta and Surakarta. Almost all of these accepted the necessity of diplomasi when faced with the alternative: a guerrilla war in which they themselves would be the first losers. Only those militarily and psychologically prepared for an endless, destructive, hit-and-run guerrilla resistance could be consistent about defying both Holland and the great powers. In practice only Tan Malaka and some military men were in this category among national leaders, although the communists also joined it after their fall. Only occasionally did the demand for total struggle whatever the cost, which had its basis among armed pemudas at local levels, interact to an important degree with national politics. Once, in late 1945, this revolutionary groundswell was sufficient partially to overturn the national leadership, though only because its demands temporarily coincided with those of diplomasi. Pemuda leaders of the TNI and badan perjuangan continued to be powerful at local levels, but rapidly became too pre-occupied with the 'front', or with defence of their own newly acquired vested interests, to exert a radicalizing influence on national politics. Perjuangan, moreover, which had obtained such startling victories against demoralized or apathetic Japanese soldiers, experienced nothing but defeat from the Dutch in the years 1946 to 1948. In its original spontaneous form, perjuangan rapidly lost momentum after March 1946.

The justification of the overthrow of every cabinet by its intolerable concessions to the Dutch, therefore, was a political tactic increasingly irrelevant to the real issues. The striking theme in the politics of late 1946 to 1948 was the growing importance of unity and its symbols in national politics. Having come to power on a divisively revolutionary and democratic programme, Sjahrir himself was forced by 1947 into almost total reliance on Sukarno, the embodiment of those forces of nationalism and unity which he had derided as conservative in 1945. Sjahrir and Hatta, the two chief architects of diplomasi, were entirely justified by their quest for rapid national independence in making use of Sukarno's prestige in one manoeuvre after another. The internal consequence, however, was their alliance with forces which were conservative in their essence and not simply as a revolutionary tactic. Although the various changes of government made little difference to the Republic's outward policy, the replacement of Amir Sjarifuddin and his friends by MASJUMI, PNI, and 'non-party' men was of profound importance for the direction of the revolution. It meant the separation of the revolution of Sukarno, Hatta, and Sjahrir from the only force with the capacity as well as the will to bring about more fundamental and permanent social changes than those already accomplished. The full significance of the shift was not apparent until much later.

References

1 Muhammad Yamin, *Sapta Darma*, p. 272.
2 A. H. Nasution, as translated in Anderson, *Java*, p. 236.
3 As the need to disguise the army receded, its title was changed to *Tentara Keselamatan Rakjat* (People's Security Army) on 7 January, and *Tentara Republik Indonesia* (TRI) on 25 January 1946.
4 *Our Struggle*, pp. 28–9.
5 Cited Anderson, *op. cit.*, p. 218.
6 Various authorities have either rejected Amir's 1948 statement that he had been a communist since 1935, or have argued that he and the other communists outside the PKI were involved in a deliberate deception. Both misunderstandings rest on the same gratuitous assumption that Indonesian communism in 1945 was already the disciplined monolith it was to become in the 1950s. Nothing could be further from the truth. For almost two decades prior to 1945 there had been no functioning party hierarchy within Indonesia, so that the enlarged group who considered themselves communists in 1945–6 could not be expected to share a common strategy as regards party formation.
   Amir's 'communism' appears to have been no secret in 1945 (e.g. *Semangat Merdeka* [Aceh] 22 November and 7 December 1945). It required no great sophistication subsequently to see the diplomatic advantages of keeping this quiet at least when talking to Westerners, given the anxiety of Dutch enemies to exaggerate communist influence in the Republic, and of American friends to play it down. Compare W. K. H. Feuilletau de Bruyn, *Naar de Sovjet Republiek Indonesia*, The Hague, 1947, with Wolf, pp. 84–7, and to a lesser extent Kahin, p. 220.
7 Pramoedya Ananta Toer, *Tjerita dari Blora*, p. 296.
8 Tan Malaka, *PARI*, Bukittinggi, 1946. The date 7 September 1945 is given within the text (p. 45).
9 Described in Anderson, *Java*, pp. 284–8.
10 *Sapta Darma*, p. 113.
11 *Ibid.*, p. 112. Tan Malaka's very similar original proposal is cited in Anderson, *Java*, p. 290.
12 Tan Malaka's address to Purwokerto meeting, 4 January, cited in Kahin, p. 173.
13 *Ibid.*, *loc. cit.*
14 Cited in Anderson, *Java*, p. 313.
15 *Soeloeh Merdeka*, (Medan), 10 April 1946. Also *Semangat Merdeka*, (Aceh), 28 March 1946.
16 Yamin, *Sapta Darma*, pp. 64 and 114–5. Also Anderson, *op. cit.*, p. 326n. The ritual quality of such allegations is however evident from Sjahrir's identical charge after he was 'kidnapped' on 27 June; Kahin, p. 189n.
17 A reflection of this is Iwa Kusuma Sumantri's indignant denial of the 'kidnapping' charge: 'It was an official arrest carried out by Major A. K. Jusuf on legitimate authority, i.e. the Jogja Division Commander R. P. Sudarsono', *Sedjarah Revolusi Indonesia*, Vol. II, p. 142n.
18 A purportedly full text of Sukarno's speech is in *Kedaulatan Rakjat* (Jogjakarta), 25 February 1947. Although this does not quote Sukarno as saying 'the President himself is regarded as the representative of the

whole people' (Kahin, p. 202), such a claim would be strikingly consistent with his July 1945 view (above, p. 20).

19 Ir Sakirman, cited in *Kedaulatan Rakjat* 26 February 1947.

20 Cited in *Republik Indonesia. Daerah Istimewa Jogjakarta*, Jakarta, n.d., p. 196

21 The bitterness of some MASJUMI politicians at what they regarded as the capture of the revolution by the Left was already suggested by a covert statement from the party's maverick vice-chairman, Abikusno, to a high Dutch official in May 1947. If the Dutch occupied Java militarily, he reportedly suggested, they 'could expect support from his side and his party'. *Het Dagboek van Schermerhorn*, Vol. II, p. 534.

22 Translated in Ruth McVey, *The Soviet View of the Indonesian Revolution*, Ithaca, 1957, p. 62.

Chapter Six

ENCIRCLING THE REPUBLIC

*The Dutch were convinced that Indonesia,
and especially the Republic, was not in a
fit state to carry the responsibility of
nationhood.*

H.J. van Mook, 1950[1]

Dutch Policies

Dutch strategists were forced to a recognition of the Republic in
Java and Sumatra by the fact of their own weakness. Government
calculations at the end of 1945 were that it would take over a year
to assemble anything like the 75,000 soldiers Van Mook and his
military advisers agreed were necessary for the reconquest of Java
and Sumatra. The few thousand Dutch troops available in late 1945
were not even allowed to land in the two major islands, because the
British believed they would antagonize Indonesians without
assisting the Allied Forces. The British insisted that negotiations
begin with the Republic, in order to forestall criticism from the
Indian Government and at the United Nations (where the issue was
first raised by Ukraine on 21 January 1946).

The strength of Van Mook's position was that he was able to make
a virtue of necessity, rather than continue fulminating against a
British betrayal like his military commanders, Helfrich and Van
Oyen. Van Mook has been described as a latter-day Daendels
(the Napoleonic ruler of Java): a pragmatic 'enlightened despot'
impatient of the outmoded constraints the Dutch constitutional
system imposed on Indonesia, yet distrustful of popular democracy
in such a diverse, politically-inexperienced land.[2] As soon as he
perceived, in November 1945, that little could be accomplished
militarily in Java and Sumatra for the time being, he began to urge
the diversion of troops to the other islands:

Dutch authority can be established firmly in the Great East [i.e. Sulawesi, Bali, and all islands to their east], Borneo, Riau, Bangka, and Billiton with limited means (5 to 8,000 men), while production can be speedily restored . . . In two months time we would be able to occupy this area wholly with our own forces . . . by this means there would be rapid consolidation of an economically important area with a population which in general is still well-disposed. In consequence our economic position as well as our international position would be strengthened, while our own men would moreover enjoy the moral encouragement of their first real success.[3]

The political counterpart of this military strategy was federalism. Even before the war Van Mook had been among those favouring a strongly decentralized basis for constitutional advance. He became a sincere and untiring champion for federalism as the only solution for post-war Indonesia. That he was able to gain his government's full backing for this policy, reversing a long tradition of centralism in Batavia, was a product of hard political reality. Only such a strategy would enable the Dutch to accept the inevitable negotiations with the Republic in Java while building their own power elsewhere. Van Mook was well aware of ethnic minority fears of Javanese hegemony, which could be exploited to maintain such a system.

Discussions in Europe between the British and Dutch Governments (December 1945 – January 1946) eventually produced a progressive-sounding Netherlands declaration based on Van Mook's federal strategy. For the first time The Hague publicly accepted the principle of ultimate self-determination for Indonesia, after a transitional period which Van Mook later defined as 'within the working life of the rising generation'.[4] In the meantime the Netherlands proposed to construct 'a Commonwealth of Indonesia . . . composed of territories possessing different degrees of autonomy'.[5] This position allowed Van Mook to recommence negotiations with Sjahrir on 10 February 1946 in the hope of accommodating the Republic as the representative of Java within such a Commonwealth.

In view of strong British pressure for agreement, and the need to retain great power sympathy, Sjahrir now dramatically compromised his initial negotiating position. He had first to arrest Tan Malaka and undermine the Persatuan Perjuangan with its insistance on one hundred percent Merdeka. Then on 27 March he secretly proposed that the Republic enjoy *de facto* recognition in Java and Sumatra only, and co-operate with Holland in setting up a federal Indonesian 'free state' which would be linked to the Netherlands in a political union (*staatsverband*).

The two parties' positions were now remarkably close. Van Mook himself thought they could meet. In April 1946 two of Sjahrir's ministers and his cabinet secretary accompanied Van Mook to Holland, confident that a realistic agreement would be finalized. But Van Mook had underestimated the difficulties of his fellow progressives in the Netherlands cabinet. With the first post-war election due on 17 May, Labour and moderate Catholic politicians were unwilling to make concessions which would have played into the hands of the Dutch Right. As an authoritative Dutch writer has pointed out, the failure of the discussions at the Hoge Veluwe (14–24 April) 'lay exclusively on the Dutch side'.[6] The Indonesians went home saddened by what they took to be a reactionary drift in Dutch politics. The neglect of this opportunity for an early agreement proved tragic for both sides. Sjahrir's government lost the opportunity to demonstrate positive dividends from its unpopular diplomasi, and was forced to pursue a harder line thereafter. The Netherlands lost not only the goodwill of moderate Indonesians, but also the opportunity to retain a political union with Indonesia, rather than the international treaty relationship on which the Republic subsequently insisted.

Dutch Strategy in Outer Indonesia
This setback directed Van Mook's efforts towards building his federal system in those parts of Indonesia where Dutch power permitted. Although in a position to know better, Van Mook had been one of the Dutch negotiators most reluctant to allow Republican claims over Sumatra. Sumatra, Borneo, and 'the Great East' were the three large 'governments' which the Dutch had established outside Java in 1938 in an ineffective move towards decentralization. Van Mook now conceived of these same regions as three elements in a prospective federation, to provide a credible balance to the fourth element, Republican Java. Sumatra was, it is true, more difficult for the Republic to govern centrally than Java, but there were no grounds for the Dutch to think they could prise it away from the Republic altogether. Dutch influence was limited to the offshore islands of Bangka, Billiton, and Riau, occupied with little opposition early in 1946. Positive Dutch moves had therefore to be limited to Borneo and 'the Great East'.

The gap which the Japanese Navy and the Australians had created, dividing Borneo and eastern Indonesia from Java and Sumatra, continued to grow. While British pressure and Indonesian arms were forcing the Dutch to a realistic acceptance of the Republic in the latter, they continued to treat its supporters as traitors in the former. Those nationalists in Borneo and Sulawesi who continued to act in the conviction that the Republic rather than NICA was the legitimate government were driven underground. This was to have the most serious consequences in South Sulawesi, where the pemuda movement for the Republic was strong and popular. The Dutch initially attempted to isolate the leading Republicans from the rajas, and finally arrested Dr Ratulangie and his six principal assistants on 5 April 1946. Those of the rajas who made it obvious that their sympathies continued to lie with the Republic were also eliminated—the Datu of Luwu and the Arumpone of Bone were exiled; the Datu of Suppa was killed.

By beheading the Republican movement in this way the Dutch lost any capacity to influence pemuda militants. After their initial failures against Dutch arms in early 1946, most pemudas had either gone underground in Sulawesi of fled to Java. In November, when the monsoon change provided a following wind, twelve Bugis *prahus* (schooners) set sail from East Java carrying arms and South Sulawesi pemudas who had received officer training in Java. Thus strengthened, the guerrilla movement made effective administration impossible for the Dutch in most areas of South Sulawesi. Having gone so far in denying any legitimacy to the Republic outside Java and Sumatra, local Dutch officials now appeared to feel they had no alternative but to unleash terror in the region.

A state of war was declared in South Sulawesi on 11 December 1946 and a detachment of 120 Indonesian 'special troops' was sent there under Captain 'Turk' Westerling, a Dutch commando specializing in counter-insurgency. For three months Westerling's men went through the region killing and terrorizing. His practice was to call together all the men of a suspected village, to demand that the 'extremists' be produced for execution, and failing this to begin shooting men identified by spies. If necessary the same effect was obtained by entirely arbitrary 'executions'. The worst authenticated atrocity occurred on 1 February 1946 in a village where three KNIL soldiers had reportedly been killed. The 'special troops' arbitrarily shot down three to four hundred men in this single village.

A Dutch Parliamentary enquiry of 1969 estimated that about three thousand Indonesians may have been killed in such operations, most of them by others imitating Westerling's methods.[7] Although a few voices were raised at the time, Dutch officials were remarkably unanimous in commending Westerling's work, without which they could see no way to achieve their aims in South Sulawesi. Westerling's ability to strike terror into his opponents owed much to the similarity of his style to that of the Indonesian *jago*. He relied on espionage and manoeuvrability rather than firepower, and he strove to develop a supernatural mystique around his person. In South Sulawesi he let it be known that he was a Turkish Muslim (he had been born in Istanbul); in Java he made clumsy use of the *Ratu*

Adil concept; in Sumatra he autographed some of his victims as 'The White Tiger'.

This terror ended pemuda activity in South Sulawesi. It also made a farce of Dutch claims to allow the voice of the people to speak. Only as the memory of Westerling's activity began to fade did the representatives of Muslim Sulawesi begin again to express themselves strongly within the Dutch-inspired federal structures.

Before these structures could be erected, the interim period of Allied military government had to end. At a meeting in Singapore on 25 May 1946 Van Mook persuaded the British to treat the outer islands separately from Java and Sumatra, and transfer full authority there to the Dutch on 15 July. Preparations were put in train immediately for a conference of delegates from all areas outside Java and Sumatra, to open the day after the transfer ceremonies, at Malino, near Makassar.

The Malino Conference (16–22 July 1946) brought together thirty-nine Indonesians selected by the Dutch. A considerable number were 'self-governing' rajas, while many representatives of Christian Ambon and North Sulawesi, and the less advanced Dayaks, Torajas, and Papuans were also predictably anxious to retain a strong Dutch connection. The conference naturally did what was expected of it. It endorsed federalism and commenced the task of building two new states in Borneo and the 'Great East'. Yet the calling of such a meeting amidst a blaze of publicity, and the need to appear to be listening to its counsels, set the Dutch on an irreversible path to democratization in the 'Malino area'. Even of this timid first conference Van Mook could claim 'it was a revelation for the Dutch—at least for me', to hear delegates insisting on rapid progress to independence.[8]

The strength of Republican sentiment among Muslims of South and East Borneo made the execution of Dutch plans there impossible. The eastern state alone was erected, at a larger conference in Den Pasar, Bali (18–24 December 1946). Its composition was important, as the same delegates acted as a 'parliament' for the new state for the following three years. Fifteen delegates were appointed by Van Mook. The remaining fifty-five were elected by councils in thirteen autonomous regions of the 'Great East'. These councils were either federations of ruling rajas, modelled on the *Paruman Agung* of Bali, or direct Dutch appointees. Nevertheless nationalist sentiment was stronger and better organized than at Malino. Delegates obtained important changes in the draft constitution of the state. They changed its name to Negara Indonesia Timur (State of East Indonesia) or NIT, and its anthem to 'Indonesia Raya'. They attacked strenuously the last-minute Dutch exclusion of Western New Guinea from the state. There was some muttering about Westerling's purges in South Sulawesi. The strength of pro-Republican sentiment was indicated by a narrow (36–32) defeat, for the NIT presidency, of Mr Tadjoeddin Noor, an avowed Republican who had been chairman of the Sulawesi PNI until that party was declared illegal on 8 September 1946. Tadjoeddin's supporters became a vocal opposition within the NIT Parliament, especially when relations with the Republic were discussed.

The choice for president fell on Tjokorde Gde Rakè Sukawati, long a conservative representative of Bali in the Volksraad (1924–42). He selected as prime minister Nadjamoeddin Daeng Malewa, an ambitious politician who had broken with the main nationalist current in 1939 through his championing of South Sulawesi regional interests. The first NIT cabinet was conservative, with pro-Dutch Christian, Chinese, and Eurasian minorities heavily over-represented and Republicans not represented at all. Real decision-making in any case remained in the hands of Dutch advisers and officials in most matters.

In comparison with the total self-reliance of the Republic, the NIT was a lame piece of window-dressing, justifying the parody Negara Ikut Tuan (follow-the-master-state). In terms of the previous experience of its inhabitants, on the other hand, or the pattern of contemporary decolonization in other parts of the world, it represented remarkable progress. The conservative character of its government had the incidental merit of lulling the deep suspicions felt by pro-Dutch Ambonese of anything 'Indonesian'. Yet there were many within the NIT who asked with reason how much political progress the Dutch would have allowed them but for the challenge posed by the Republic.

Linggajati—False Interlude
The negotiations which had broken down at Hoge Veluwe began again in Jakarta on 7 October. Britain had determined to withdraw its troops by December 1946 and insisted that at least the principles of agreement be reached by then. Another British diplomat, Lord Killearn, was offered to smooth the way. The main improvement over the situation in April, however, was that the Dutch negotiators were now in a position to make decisions. Elections had taken place, giving the Catholic Party the leading role in cabinet under Prime Minister Beel. The Labour Party continued to hold the colonial portfolio through Jonkman, who was more cautious than his predecessor but saw no alternative to the existing policy of compromise. On 14 September three commissioners-general left Holland for Jakarta: Schermerhorn, the outgoing Prime Minister (Labour), as chairman; Van Poll (Catholic Party); and De Boer (former chairman of the KPM shipping line). They were given extensive power to act

together with Van Mook in the name of the Netherlands Government.

Both sides desired agreement, and were willing to avoid the hardest questions in order to achieve it. On 14 October a ceasefire was arranged on all the 'fronts' around the Allied-occupied urban enclaves in Java and Sumatra. For three months this provided a real lull in the continuing hostilities. Negotiations with the Republic about the future of Indonesia were successfully concluded on 12 November at the hill resort of Linggajati (near Cirebon). The Netherlands recognized *de facto* Republican authority over Java, Madura, and Sumatra, including the Allied enclaves. The Republic and the Netherlands agreed to co-operate in establishing a federal United States of Indonesia by 1 January 1949. Its three components would be the Republic, Borneo, and Eastern Indonesia. The emotional issue of a tie with the crown was eventually resolved through a union symbolically headed by the Dutch Queen, comprising the Kingdom of the Netherlands and a sovereign United States of Indonesia as equal partners.[9]

Not resolved were the hard questions of the balance of power in the transition period. What would be the role of the Dutch and Republican armed forces? What guarantees existed for pro-Dutch elements within the Republic and pro-Republican elements outside it? How and when would the enclave cities in Java and Sumatra be surrendered to the Republic? Furthest from resolution was the question of the states to be formed in Borneo and East Indonesia. The Dutch had recognized no Republican claims over these areas, and acted on the presumption that they remained under full Netherlands sovereignty in the transitional period. The NIT was immediately formed without reference to the Republic.

On 12 May 1947 an autonomous constitution was also granted to West Borneo, where the dashing and very pro-Dutch young ruler of Pontianak, Sultan Hamid II, had sufficient influence to make this possible. The Republic protested strenuously against these moves. Politically Sjahrir's government could not be seen to be abandoning the Republican struggle in these areas. Diplomatically it believed the Linggajati Agreement's provision for Dutch-Republican co-operation in building the USI extended to the formation of these component states.

The six month delay in reaching this agreement had eroded the basis of mutual trust which might have overcome such difficulties. Neither side was prepared to place its faith in the goodwill of the other, and mutual attempts to prepare for a breakdown of negotiations did much to contribute to such a breakdown. The Republic sought to ensure it would not be without international advocates in the event of Dutch armed action. Haji Agus Salim, deputy

Republican Foreign Minister, was feted in India and the Middle East (March–June 1947), and signed treaties of friendship with Egypt and Syria. This was taken in Holland to mean that the Republic did not accept its status under Linggajati, as a mere part of a not yet constituted international entity. Pemuda military pressure on the Dutch also revived again in January 1947.

For their part, the Dutch made a poor secret of their preparations to eliminate the Republic militarily should Linggajati fail. Less than two weeks after agreement had been reached, Schermerhorn consulted the generals about the 'military alternative' should Linggajati be rejected in Holland. They replied confidently that all main cities could be occupied in a fortnight, though a complete conquest would take five or six months.[10] In the event the Dutch Cabinet and Parliament did reluctantly approve the agreement in December, but only with a number of unilateral qualifications and interpretations. The most serious was a demand advanced by Jonkman that New Guinea (West Irian) should be excluded from the United States of Indonesia to serve as a refuge for disaffected Eurasians.

Until Linggajati was approved by the Republican KNIP (see above pp. 96–8) and eventually signed on 25 March 1947, public speculation about the alternatives continued. Paradoxically, however, it was only after the signature that Dutch policy-makers began to accept military action as something virtually inevitable. The main reasons for this shift appear to have been economic. During the long delay over ratification of Linggajati, the optimistic mood which could have facilitated drastic change in Dutch-Indonesian relations was allowed to evaporate. Dutch capitalists began to point out that they would not return to their pre-war enterprises except under protection of Dutch arms. Meanwhile Java and Sumatra continued to be a heavy drain on Dutch finances particularly after the build-up of troops there was complete in early 1947. Smit estimates that the Dutch could not have afforded to retain their military strength in Java and Sumatra beyond the end of 1947 without access to the resources of these islands.[11] On 7 May the two key cabinet ministers, Beel and Jonkman, arrived in Jakarta with a pair of financial experts, determined to end what they considered an untenable deadlock. In a top level meeting (14–16 May) the economists argued that military occupation of Java would resolve the financial crisis by freeing 300 million guilders in exportable commodities. Although there were several voices pointing to the gloomy prospects of extensive guerrilla warfare, terror, and counter-terror, this conference nevertheless set Netherlands policy decisively on a 'war unless . . .' course.[12] The change of emphasis was at first barely perceptible beneath continuing earnest appeals for reason. Gradually, however, the psychological preparation for war appeared to develop a momentum of its own.

The commission-general's note to Sjahrir on 27 May was for the first time cast in threatening terms, in accordance with an agreement before the two ministers left Jakarta four days earlier. The commission 'had reached the last stage of its negotiations', and demanded a reply within a fortnight to a spelling-out of the Dutch interpretation of Linggajati. During the ensuing two months Sjahrir, and after his fall Sukarno and Amir Sjarifuddin, granted one after the other of the Dutch demands as they perceived the seriousness behind them. However it appeared that Van Mook, having once accepted the possibility of a military solution to the deadlocked discussions, became increasingly anxious to get on with it. 'No alternative is conceivable', he cabled on 17 July, 'which would not have results at least as harmful.'[13]

War

At midnight on 20 July 1947 the well-prepared Dutch attack began. From Jakarta and Bandung two strong divisions moved out to occupy most of West Java. From Surabaya two brigades moved towards the eastern point of Java, and Madura. Smaller forces simultaneously began the occupation of the rich plantation areas of East Sumatra (around Medan), the oil and coal installations near Palembang, and limited areas near Semarang and Padang.

The objectives of these attacks were far from clear, beyond the immediate one of securing key economic resources. The Hague assured Britain and America that it was a 'police action' designed to suppress disorders outside the Republican government's control and to enforce the terms of the Linggajati agreement. The areas to be occupied would be strictly limited. Van Mook, however, publicly asserted that his government was no longer bound by Linggajati. Schermerhorn, as chairman of the commission-general, had protested against the offensive because it was conceived in too limited terms. 'Since Jogja is the spiritual centre of the disease', he cabled, 'military action will only reach goal if this repeat this Republic is brought down by it'.[14] Once it became clear that Jogjakarta's reaction to the attack was not capitulation but resistance and scorched earth, Van Mook and the other members of the commission came round to the same view. Van Mook insisted that all Java be occupied and a new amenable Republican leadership installed.

International pressures on The Hague, however, made this course impossible. Britain and America made clear their disapproval of a military solution. When the question was brought before the UN Security Council on 31 July, the Netherlands deemed it wise to accept the call for a cessation of hostilities. The vital points in the areas originally envisaged for the operation had in any case been secured. Instructions were given to arrange a ceasefire, which was announced by General Spoor for the Dutch and Sukarno for the Republic on 4 August.

Despite the great Indonesian superiority of numbers, the Dutch advance met remarkably little opposition. The Republic had long since resolved that its best defence against much superior arms, training, and organization would be tactical retreat after withdrawing or destroying vital supplies, in order to prepare for lengthy guerrilla resistance. Relatively few units of the TNI (Tentara Nasional Indonesia—the new title for the TRI augmented by irregular units) were captured. On the other hand the rapid Dutch advance in the wake of aerial attacks caused confusion, demoralization and panic in Republican ranks:

> The retreat of most of these [TNI] units was in all directions. Often commanders did not know where their men were. . . One certainty was that units, or groups, or even individuals who were split up, all went towards their own place of origin, their base. Similarly with their commanders. Fathers sought their sons, and sons their fathers.[15]

By the time of the ceasefire announcement the Dutch commanded the major cities and roads in the areas of East and West Java they sought to control. Where possible TNI units retreated into safer Republican territory. In West Java, however, the Dutch began a major pincer-movement after the ceasefire, when their troops moved south from Cirebon and east from Bandung to take Tasikmalaya and Garut on 10–11 August. Later, in October, they occupied the south coast of West Java. As the West Java commander, Nasution, records, 'our position was grim, for there was no further possibility of retreat'.[16] Cut off from the Republican stronghold in central Java, the Siliwangi Division discovered it could move with remarkable freedom within and even across Dutch-held arteries. Within the area of West Java the Dutch now claimed, the Siliwangi built up several well-established pockets where Republican government continued to function. They gained valuable experience in the conduct of guerrilla operations from these virtual sanctuaries.

To a lesser extent similar operations were possible in other areas. The Dutch advance had been limited to the main roads. Yet on 29 August, four weeks after the ceasefire, Van Mook announced a unilateral demarcation line joining up the most advanced posts, regardless of the degree of Dutch control of the intervening territory. Many Republican units were within the so-called 'Van Mook line'. A few, in addition to the relatively powerful Siliwangi, managed to retain their positions despite subsequent Dutch operations.

The 'Indonesian question' had now become a major concern of the United Nations. Sjahrir made his way to New York where he dramatically put the Indonesian case before the Security Council. In itself this was a major advance for the Republic's claim to be the legitimate voice of Indonesia. After voting to hear Sjahrir, the Council refused the same privilege to the representatives of the NIT, West Borneo, and the areas newly under Dutch control. Continual complaints from both Dutch and Republican sides about ceasefire violations kept the issue before the UN. In effect a fitful war was continuing within the 'Van Mook' line, as the Dutch sought to establish their control, and Republican pemudas to intimidate potential co-operators.

United Nations involvement in the dispute was continued through a three-nation 'Good Offices Committee'. As this committee, comprising representatives of Belgium (appointed by the Netherlands), Australia (appointed by the Republic), and America (appointed by the first two), did not reach Indonesia until late October, a committee of career consuls stationed in Batavia was asked to report immediately on alleged violations of the ceasefire. Undoubtedly the effect of all this was to make it virtually impossible for Holland to take advantage of its military superiority to destroy the central Republican government. At a time when progressive men everywhere, including Holland, saw in the United Nations a harbinger of a more peaceful world, recognition by this body was the strongest card remaining to the Republic.

In its peace-making task, however, the UN Good Offices Committee was faced with an even wider gulf of mistrust than existed in 1946. The committee had to labour mightily before both parties agreed to sign, on 17 and 19 January 1948, a declaration known as the Renville Agreement, because it was negotiated on the neutral territory of the USS *Renville* anchored off Jakarta. The agreement was, however, entirely synthetic. The Dutch accepted it because it legitimated the 'Van Mook line' and demanded a cessation of Republican military activity within it. The Republican leaders signed it under considerable US pressure because American goodwill was essential to them, and because the US chairman of the Committee, Graham, was able to persuade Amir Sjarifuddin that the Dutch would be obliged by the agreement to hold fair and internationally supervised plebiscites in the conquered areas within a year. In the short run Renville appeared a humiliation and a cheat for the Republic, forcing them to relinquish territories they had not lost, in return for assurances which proved illusory. In the long run, however, it enabled the Republic to retain that international concern for its survival which was its ultimate salvation.

The Extension of Federalism

Van Mook's primary political purpose in advocating the offensive had failed. The Republic was not forced into a position where it would accept the role designated for it by the Dutch within the United States of Indonesia. Van Mook could not afford to sit still. In the newly-conquered areas he now encouraged regionalist movements to break with the Republic, in the hope of demonstrating that Jogjakarta did not represent the true voice of Indonesian national aspiration. While 'non-violent' Republicanism was allowed to exist in the conquered territories, the encouragement given to Federalism there would also ensure that the Republic had a relatively smaller voice in whatever USI might eventually arise.

The task of encouraging such anti-Republican sentiments was much facilitated by the chaos and division left behind by retreating Republican *pasukans* (units) in many areas. The mutual suspicions which had caused the death of countless Indonesians in the *bersiap* time were again heightened to murderous levels by the panic and humiliation wrought by the Dutch offensive. The scorched-earth policy emphasized by the Republic as a major defensive measure had unexpected results in practice. Many of the most strategic installations were unharmed, sometimes because they were too solidly-built for unskilled saboteurs. Violence was directed instead against people whose loyalty to the Republic was questionable, who had fallen foul of particular pasukans, or who simply had property which could be used by the retreating units. Chinese were vulnerable on all counts and suffered very badly, especially in the Sukabumi and Tasikmalaya areas of West Java.[17] Prominent Indonesians who lacked any protecting link with pasukan or party were also affected by this wave of frustration and anger. The effect was to convince many moderate Republicans who strongly supported the goal of total independence that the Republic was incapable of ensuring the security which would make that goal feasible.

Bitterly divided East Sumatra provided some of the saddest examples of brutality. Passions aroused during the 'social revolution' of March 1946 were now unrestrained by government or TNI authority. Many of the aristocrats arrested in 1946 were killed as they left their places of detention, whether or not they were seeking to contact the Dutch. Thousands of refugees fleeing the Dutch army were killed as they entered Tapanuli or the Karo plateau.[18] Part of the reason was the regalia, jewellery, and gold of the ill-fated rajas of East Sumatra, which had intensified mutual suspicions among pasukans as soon as it had fallen into their hands. When refugees were found carrying property of this sort they were immediately accused of enriching themselves instead of staying to fight the

Dutch. The property changed hands, but its bitter legacy continued. The killings of 1947 had the double effect of driving many Republicans to seek reluctant refuge in Dutch-occupied East Sumatra, and of further bedevilling the politics of Tapanuli, where the strongest East Sumatra pasukans had retreated. By far the most troubled area of Republican Sumatra, Tapanuli in 1948 provided a sad contrast with the reconstruction the Dutch were able to show in the comparatively opulent plantation area of East Sumatra.

Although its main base of support was the Malay, Simelungun, and Karo aristocracy which had suffered in the 'social revolution', the federalist movement in East Sumatra was therefore able to win some support from Republican ranks. An anti-Republican movement had already been organized before the offensive, with Dutch encouragement, from among the conservative Persatuan Sumatera Timur (East Sumatran Association) which Dr Mansur had led in the late Dutch period. Its aim in both periods was to promote the interests of the indigenous peoples of East Sumatra as against more dynamic and numerous 'immigrant' Indonesians. Although its leading members were all aristocrats, the movement showed little enthusiasm for restoring the rajas whom the 'social revolution' had overthrown. Still less did the Dutch. An opposition Malay group was formed to defend the historic position of the rajas, and the unbending Sultan of Deli flew to Holland to protest to Queen Wilhelmina that the Dutch had broken their treaty obligations towards him. But the revolution had run too deep to allow the clock to be turned back. Federalism in East Sumatra had to be a protest against the way the 'social revolution' had been executed, not against its aim.

A demonstration was organized in Medan only ten days after the Dutch offensive began, to request the establishment of an East Sumatran 'special district' outside the Republic. Van Mook moved swiftly to give his support. By October Dr Mansur's lobby for the special district had been recognized as a provisional constituent assembly, with a few Dutch-appointed additions. On Christmas day 1947 the Negara Sumatera Timur (State of East Sumatra), or NST, was formed. Dr Mansur took his oath a month later as Wali Negara (Guardian of the State). As with the NIT before it, Dutch advisers and secretaries played the key roles in government. Yet the NST was by no means the artificial creation which its short life might suggest. It had real support from one section of a deeply divided region.

Because this 'indigenous' section was a minority of East Sumatra's population, even had it been united, there was no elective element in the early stages of the NST. In the conquered areas of Java which contained a dominant non-Javanese population, on the other hand, the Dutch made some novel democratic gestures. A hasty plebiscite was organized in Madura on 23 January, in which the adult male population was asked to decide whether to sever relations with the Republic and choose Raden A.M. Tjakraningrat as head of an autonomous Madura. Madura was a rice-deficient island which had suffered partial famine since the Dutch blockade had hit its imports. Moreover Tjakraningrat had been the principal Republican official on the island, and the majority of village and district officials remained with him after the Dutch conquest. Thus whatever the educated minority thought of it, the plebiscite was bound to be received in the villages as a vote for the established order. Not surprisingly, it was affirmed overwhelmingly. Madurese ethnic or regional resentment of Javanese, however, was never very signifi- cant, and therefore the federal idea had in principle few supporters.

West Java was the most portentous of Dutch experiments. The Dutch conquest had been designed in part to embrace the whole Sundanese-speaking area, leaving in Republican hands the less digestible Bantenese at the western corner of Java. Within the Dutch-controlled portion of West Java, the twelve million Sundanese formed a clear majority. In the 1930s the Sundanese 'Pasundan' movement led by Oto Iskandar di-Nata had been both the strongest regionalist party in Indonesia and the one most clearly integrated into the mainstream of the nationalist movement. The experience of late 1945, when Oto had been killed and much of the ruling Sundanese establishment pushed aside by younger, often non- Sundanese politicians more acceptable to the pemudas, had sharpened aristocratic suspicions of the Republic. Yet the mood of the Sundanese élite appeared still to be that of the pre-war Pasundan movement—favouring participation in the Republican movement, but on terms fixed by Sundanese. Having failed in an early (May 1947) crude attempt to evoke Sundanese separatism, and with the attention of the United Nations now upon them, the Dutch had little alternative but to seek a broader political base through partial accommodation to this mood.

After two preparatory conferences in October and December 1947, indirect elections were organized at the end of January for fifty-three members of a third West Java conference. Another forty-seven members were appointed by the Dutch. When the conference met a month later to discuss the formation of a West Java state, a majority of delegates were broadly nationalist, and a minority of thirty-five were sufficiently Republican to oppose the formation of a separate state unless by the sort of plebiscite pre- scribed in the Renville agreement. A close election for Wali Negara went in favour of an eminent Republican, Raden A.A.M. Wiranata Kusuma. Interior minister in Sukarno's first cabinet, Wiranata

Kusuma was still living in Jogjakarta at the time of his election, as chairman of the Republic's largely decorative 'High Advisory Council' of elder statesmen. His ceremonial departure from Jogjakarta on 19 March, to assume the highest office in the new state of Pasundan, marked a new stage in the hitherto icy relationship between the Republic and the Dutch-created states. It was no surprise that the first prime minister of Pasundan was Adil Poeradiredja, leader of the pro-Republican faction in the third-conference, which became the parliament of Pasundan.

A similar transformation was coming over the Negara Indonesia Timur, the oldest of the federal states. Its first prime minister, Nadjamoeddin, had been indicted for corruption in September 1947 and arrested in Jakarta on his return from New York, where he had failed to gain a hearing from the United Nations. Nadjamoeddin was a shrewd businessman as well as an ambitious politician, and had a reputation long before accepting the prime ministership for not always keeping the two roles separate. Only the patronage of his pre-war superior Van Mook had enabled him to withstand earlier Dutch official attacks. The timing of his fall appears to have been chosen by resentful cabinet colleagues, and particularly by the able but arch-conservative Ambonese leader, Dr Soumokil, who began proceedings against Nadjamoeddin in his capacity as Minister of Justice. Republican sources however argue that the Dutch dropped Nadjamoeddin because he grew too critical.[19]

The stop-gap ministry of Dr Warouw proved to be too narrowly-based on rightist pro-Dutch elements. It fell when the NIT Parliament met on 9 December 1947, not least because its endorsement of the Dutch military offensive was deemed too fulsome. The premiership passed to an able and pragmatic young Balinese prince, Anak Agung Gde Agung. Some moderate Republicans were for the first time included in his cabinet, which showed its colours in a 23 December statement qualifying the earlier NIT support of the Dutch military action. Attitudes were changing within the NIT parliament, even though its composition did not change between 1946 and 1950. A major cause was the increasing activity of Republican pemudas within 'legal' channels. During the Westerling purges, East Indonesians had appeared to face a choice between the Dutch and the guerrillas. Once guerrilla resistance was crushed, however, Republican pemudas began to gather behind the legal but non co-operating Partai Kedaulatan Rakjat (People's Sovereignty Party) founded by Andi Burhanuddin and Henk Rondonuwu in November 1946. At the end of 1947 this group joined co-operating Republicans in a broad NIT-wide federation (GAPKI) headed by the leading Republican spokesman in the NIT Parliament, Arnold Mononutu.

In the freer political atmosphere of 1947–8, NIT politicians had to take account of the pressure exerted by this active Republican movement. The NIT Government itself grew steadily closer to the Republic. In February 1948 it despatched a delegation to Jogjakarta which was answered by a Republican mission to Makassar under Mr Sartono. To the dismay of militant non co-operators, Jogjakarta itself had now recognized the legitimacy of the NIT. In the aftermath of the Renville agreement the Republic had already decreed that its supporters were free to take part in elections and act as officials in the Dutch-supported federal states.[20] The bitter dividing line between Republicans and federalists was crumbling, enhancing Jogjakarta's diplomatic position but damaging and confusing the perjuangan.

The transformation of violent resistance into non-violent opposition was of course part of the Dutch objective in allowing Republican activities within the federal states. The intervention of the United Nations also increased the importance of presenting a democratic and popular image. But a more important reason was Van Mook's belief that once freed from terror and intimidation the Indonesian people would choose order and reconstruction in co-operation with the Dutch in preference to the desperate freedom of the Republic. In this he was fundamentally mistaken.

References

1 H. J. van Mook, *The Stakes of Democracy in South-East Asia*, London, 1950, pp. 224–5.

2 C. Smit, *De Indonesische Quaestie. De wordingsgeschiedenis der souvereiniteitsoverdracht*, Leiden, 1952, pp. 104–5.

3 Van Mook telegram of 6–7 November 1945, in *Enquêtecommissie Regeringsbeleid 1940–1945*, Vol. 8 A & B, *Militair Beleid 1940–1945, Terugkeer naar Nederlandsch-Indië*, The Hague, 1956, p. 665.

4 Alastair M. Taylor, *Indonesian Independence and the United Nations*, London, 1960, p. 19n.

5 The full 10 February statement is reproduced in David Wehl, *The Birth of Indonesia*, London, 1948, pp. 110–1.

6 C. Smit, *De Liquidatie van een Imperium. Nederland en Indonesië 1945–1962*, Amsterdam, 1962, p. 35.

7 Tweede Kamer der Staten-Generaal, Zitting 1968–9, *Nota Betreffende het Archiefonderzoek naar gegevens omtrent Excessen in Indonesië begaan door Nederlandse Militairen in de periode 1945–1950*, The Hague, 1969, Appendix 2, pp. 2 and 11. Raymond ('Turk') Westerling, *Challenge to Terror*, London, 1952, pp. 116–7, also estimated three to four thousand deaths from all 'anti-terrorist' operations in South Sulawesi, although he claimed only 600 were caused by his own group. By late 1947, however, the Republic brought before the UN a complaint of 20,000–40,000 killings, and subsequent Indonesian commentators felt obliged to repeat the higher of these two figures. Local Indonesian officials have recently admitted the relative accuracy of the Dutch figures, however.

8 Van Mook, *op. cit.*, p. 220.

9 An English translation of the agreement is in Charles Wolf Jr., *The Indonesian Story*, New York, 1948, pp. 175–8.

10 *Het Dagboek van Schermerhorn*, ed. C. Smit, Groningen, 1970, p. 143.

11 Smit, *De Liquidatie*, p. 60.

12 *Ibid*. pp. 61–4. *Dagboek van Schermerhorn*, pp. 530–2.

13 *Dagboek van Schermerhorn*, p. 770.

14 *Ibid.*, p. 771, cable Schermerhorn to Jonkman 17 July, 1947.

15 A. H. Nasution, *Tentara Nasional Indonesia* Vol. II, Jakarta, 1968, p. 92.

16 *Ibid.*, p. 93.

17 The UN-appointed Consular Commission reported what it considered a reliable estimate: that 1,000 Chinese were murdered, 10,000 missing and 100,000 homeless as a result of Republican 'scorched-earth' activities. *Security Council Records, 1947, Supplement 4*, p. 18.

18 Although these killings are no secret in Sumatra, they do not yet appear to have found their way into the literature. My sources here are a number of interviews, and letters of September–October 1947 in private possession.

19 Compare the Republican interpretation of these events in *Republik Indonesia. Propinsi Sulawesi*, Jakarta, n.d., p. 135, with Alers, *Om een rode of groene merdeka*, Eindhoven, 1956, pp. 148–50, who considered the action of Soumokil was 'certainly not instigated by Netherlanders'.

20 Two decrees to this effect, dated 3 February 1948, are cited in Nasution, *TNI* Vol. II, Jakarta, 1968, pp. 117–9. Nasution regrets their tendency to 'destroy the line of demarcation between patriot and traitor'.

Chapter Seven

GOVERNMENT REFORMS, COMMUNIST REVOLUTION

> *... private initiative and 'auto-activity' in
> the people may be said to have ceased completely,
> while state enterprises and those 'supervised'
> by the state are incapable of meeting the people's
> needs.*
>
> Sjafruddin Prawiranegara, 1948[1]

Strikingly few concrete social, economic, and administrative reforms became law during the revolutionary period. Profound changes took place, but for the most part they came about by spontaneous pressures from below and gained no legislative sanction. The nationalist politicians who controlled the central government were obliged to direct all their efforts towards political survival. The plans for economic and social transformation which had been for so long nurtured in the nationalist movement had to be either postponed, or piously invoked as aspirations having little relation to political reality. As we have seen, the Marxist-dominated governments of Sjahrir argued against rapid social change, in theory because national revolution preceded social revolution, and in practice because moderation was a prerequisite for international recognition. Paradoxically the centrist Hatta government had more to show in terms of progressive legislation, in part as a defence against the increasingly programmatic Marxist opposition.

Despite the changing shape of cabinets, however, there was a high degree of continuity in positive Republican planning for economic and administrative matters. Vice-President Hatta consistently played the leading role, assisted by a relatively small group of cabinet ministers and BP-KNIP members. The two years of relative stability which began with the serious Dutch-Indonesian negotiations of late 1946 and ended with the Madiun rebellion of

September 1948 gave these men their best opportunity to build the sort of society they wanted. Insofar as we can judge the direction of the Indonesian revolution from the actions of its official leadership, it is to these years we must look.

Administrative Reforms

The Dutch colonial administration had been dualistic. The Dutch-staffed *Binnenlands Bestuur* had provided a strict and centralized hierarchy of governor, resident, assistant-resident and controleur, all appointed by and responsible to their superiors. Parallel to the lower two ranks was an Indonesian aristocracy in the process of conversion to a bureaucracy. The process was most complete in Java, with its hierarchy of bupati (regent), wedana, camat, and lurah (village head). The Japanese had completed the bureaucratization of this Javanese aristocracy, removing the hereditary element, while they abolished the two lowest levels of what had been the Binnenlands Bestuur. A unified and centralized bureaucracy resulted, with only the ranks equivalent to Resident and above filled by Japanese. By replacing these top positions with Indonesians, the Republic arrived at what in theory was a monolithic administrative hierarchy, responsible only to the centre.

Sumatra under the Dutch and Japanese had a much more variegated pattern of 'self-governing' rajas, hereditary chiefs and adat heads. Except in East Sumatra, where 'self-governing' rajas were retained, the Japanese subordinated all of these to an administrative hierarchy staffed by Japanese down to the assistant-resident (*bunshucho*) level and Indonesians below that. The 'social revolution' of March 1946 removed the element of dualism which had persisted in East Sumatra into the Republican period. Thereafter Sumatra, like Java, was governed in theory by a centralized bureaucracy. Its uniformity was accentuated during the first central government mission to Sumatra in April 1946, when the designation and function of officials in Sumatra were altered to the Javanese bupati-camat system, as 'an indication that in every respect Sumatra does not want to be divided from Java'.[2]

The administration of Islam, previously in the hands of 'self-governing' rulers, bupatis, or local Islamic councils, was theoretically centralized with the establishment of a Republican Ministry of Religion in January 1946. In practice Islamic authority at least in Sumatra tended to lie with the local branch of MASJUMI in the initial period following the overthrow of the traditional rulers. Only gradually was a separate religious bureaucracy built up under the Ministry.

Replacing the various regional councils which had possessed limited powers under the Dutch but purely 'advisory' functions under the Japanese, were the KNIs of the Republic. These had been formed at each level out of existing Japanese bodies, and then reformed in December 1945. The legal relationship between the theoretically appointed official in charge of each region and the theoretically elected KNI was imprecise, beyond the fact that the working committee of each KNI was to 'assist' the relevant official. In practice the KNIs played a mediating and legitimating role between the pasukans which held physical power and the government official who held legal authority.

In reality, revolutionary conditions ensured that all legal authorities in cities and towns held office at the sufferance of popular organizations. In Sumatra the central and even provincial governments had virtually no control over the choice of officials, especially during 1945-6. What might in theory have been (and later became) a somewhat rigid administrative structure was in practice extremely responsive to pressure from below, and central governments were naturally more concerned at increasing their control over it than building checks to its power. Apart from West Java, which tended to go its own way once Jakarta and Bandung were firmly in Dutch hands, the remainder of Java formed a coherent geographic and cultural unit, inevitably influenced by developments in Jogjakarta. In Sumatra, on the other hand, neither the political parties nor the administration in the separate residencies had much contact with each other, let alone with Java. The tour of Sumatra led by Amir Sjarifuddin and Mr Hermani, secretary of the Interior Ministry, in April-May 1946, was the first attempt by the central government to build institutions in that island responsive to Jogjakarta control. They organized a meeting of an all-Sumatra KNI in Bukittinggi at which policies and personalities acceptable to Jogjakarta were promoted. The meeting resolved that three deputy governors should be appointed for North, Central, and South Sumatra, since the authority of Governor Hasan in Pematang Siantar (where he had retreated from the strong Allied presence in Medan) could not hope to influence the south. The significance of the all-Sumatra government rapidly declined, even after it moved to more centrally-located Bukittinggi in 1947, and it was abolished in favour of three separate provinces in April 1948.

After a second Amir Sjarifuddin visit to Sumatra in December 1946 it was decided to begin sending experienced officials from Java to reinforce the Sumatra administration. In January 1947 the Interior Ministry announced that five officials with the rank of bupati, 300 lesser officials, and thirty doctors and other specialists had been selected. Later in the year the key Jogjakarta departments of Finance and the Interior sent commissioners to Bukittinggi with junior minister rank, to attempt to channel a percentage of Sumatra's relative affluence towards the central government's purposes. Hatta's presence in Sumatra throughout the second half of 1947, together with a brief visit by Sukarno in June 1948, did much to bring central government influence to bear directly on Sumatran problems. Finally the considerable logistic effort of bringing fifty delegates from all residencies and parties in Sumatra to attend the Malang KNIP meeting in February 1947 did more than anything else to acquaint Sumatrans with politics at the 'national' level.

The Republic, from a starting point of almost total regional autonomy and spontaneity, was directing its efforts to strengthening central control. The Dutch, meanwhile, were proceeding in the opposite direction from a starting-point of thinly-disguised central control by a military-backed Dutch bureaucracy. Not only the federal system itself, but the sophisticated, highly varied pattern of local autonomy which the Dutch developed within the Negara Indonesia Timur, provided a challenge which the Republic could not ignore. Already in February 1947 the Sayap Kiri proposed as part of its post-Linggajati 'National Programme' a combination of strong central government with the fullest autonomy for regions, in order to meet the challenge of federalism.

The Republic's endeavour to show its earnestness about regional autonomy culminated in law number 22 of 8 August 1948. This provided for very complete autonomy at three distinct levels: Provinces (of which there were now three in Java, plus the Jogjakarta special region, and three in Sumatra); kabupatens (the regions governed by bupatis) and large municipalities; desas (villages) and small towns. The appointed administrative hierarchy would largely disappear, and residents, wedanas, and camats cease to exist. Each of the three levels would have its elected executive head and legislature. The government did not even begin to put this idealistic legislation into practice until after the transfer of sovereignty. It remained an aspiration to be bargained over in the 1950s and 60s. In its idealization of local autonomy, however, it was in basic conflict with the thrust of the revolution. Decentralization appealed to some of the older generation who appreciated the local variations of customary law or who feared to lose their local influence or opportunities in a centrally-controlled state. To the educated youth who made the revolution, on the other hand, the important, emotive symbols were all national.

Economic Trends

Whatever its professions about long-term policy, the Republican government was also forced by circumstances into a steady expansion of its economic role. When Japanese-controlled factories, plantations, or utilities were taken over by their workers in the early stage of the revolution, there was a tendency for workers to feel that the installations had become theirs. Sometimes production continued with brilliant improvization; sometimes there was simple pillage of the moveable property. The mood of nationalist enthusiasm, however, made it relatively easy for officials armed with letters from Sukarno or Hatta to persuade workers to accept at least nominal government authority. Given the weakness of Indonesia's middle class it was never even a remote possibility that private enterprise would fill the gap left by the Japanese. The choice was between government authority or some degree of worker control. If Sjahrir's government had contemplated the latter at all, it must have been dissuaded when workers' control was taken up as the policy of the pro-Tan Malaka Barisan Buruh Indonesia (Indonesian Labour Front). Borrowing the jargon of European Marxism which Abdulmadjid and his colleagues had brought from Holland, the government began to condemn notions of worker control as 'anarcho-syndicalism'. Government leaders quoted Lenin to show that the State was 'the instrument for destroying every effort of the capitalist'.[3] On 20 March 1946 the government announced that all enterprises formerly controlled by the Japanese government would now be managed by the regional governments of the Republic.

This did not mean that government enjoyed the exclusive revenue from such installations. In Java the only really profitable ones were the government monopolies of pawn-shops, salt, and opium, which did bring in revenue to Jogjakarta. Saleable produce or stockpiles on estates remote from Jogjakarta were much less likely to profit the government directly. Sometimes they helped finance a local TNI unit or a pasukan of another sort.

Sumatra was where the real wealth lay, in the form of stockpiles of rubber, tea, pepper, and coffee which had accumulated since access to world markets had been closed by the war. Export of these stocks to Singapore and Malaya through Chinese intermediaries was able to flourish under the British Military Administration, and continued even during the Dutch blockade. Initially the export took place under the auspices, or at least with the approval, of the local governments concerned, and helped to keep them in reasonable financial condition. However the 'social revolution' in East Sumatra and a decline in the authority of the resident in Lampung undermined this system during 1946. The TRI/TNI and other badan perjuangan increasingly took over rubber and other stocks themselves for export to Singapore, to buy weapons or uniforms. Not suprisingly there was widespread corruption, and derisory prices were obtained by pemuda leaders who took it on themselves to negotiate a deal in Singapore. In Palembang and Aceh, stronger local governments continued to benefit directly from this trade, and indirectly it certainly kept the standard of living of the whole political élite relatively high in comparison with Java. However the vital foreign exchange which these exports should have been earning the young Republic was squandered. Virtually none of it was ever used for the purposes of the central government,[4] except insofar as the Indonesian agency in Singapore was able to solicit contributions from Sumatran dealers. The increasing foreign diplomatic commitments of the Republic from 1947 had to be financed by the export of limited government stocks of opium and gold by chartered plane to Thailand, and by borrowing. The most important foreign loan was acquired in January 1948 from an American film magnate, Mathew Fox, in return for the 'sole agency' of Republican exports to the United States.

In both Java and Sumatra the first year of the revolution was the period of greatest affluence. In comparison with the terrible shortages of the late Japanese period, most Indonesians probably experienced distinctly better conditions. Stocks of rice, cloth, and other essentials which the Japanese had stored in each district against a final Allied onslaught generally fell into local government or army hands, in addition to large quantities of occupation money. This provided an initial capital for government, as well as relief for the population.

The exhaustion of stockpiles, the tightening Dutch economic blockade during 1947, and the run-down of services all brought steadily worsening conditions. The heaviest blow was the loss of the wealthiest areas in the Dutch military action, and the further disruption of communications that this entailed. Jogjakarta region, a normally rice-deficient area with its population abnormally swollen with officials and now refugees, was afflicted by acute shortages of everything, reaching crisis proportions when the Madiun rebellion isolated it from the wealthier areas to its northeast. Even in Sumatra the comfortable days ended decisively with the Dutch action. The peasant population, which had suffered most under the Japanese, was less affected by the mounting poverty than salaried officials and soldiers. The revolutionary anger of 1945, when a suffering people had seen their leaders in comfort, was therefore progressively removed.

The central government continued to collect some traditional revenues: from the government monopolies, from a special war profits tax introduced by the Japanese, and above all from taxes on the peasant rice crop. Nevertheless the gap in revenue could in the long run be filled only by printing money, with all its inflationary consequences. Jogjakarta issued the first Republican currency on 29 November 1946, to replace the old Japanese rupiahs and rival the hated new 'NICA money'. It held its value for about a month before a steady inflation began. Unable to obtain sufficient of these Jogjakarta notes for its purposes, the Sumatran government quickly issued its own currency. Following the Dutch offensive of July 1947 all the isolated residency, and even kabupaten, governments in Sumatra, as well as the Banten enclave in Java, began to put out crude notes with nothing behind them but whatever faith or fear local officials could inspire. As one example of the consequent inflation, the presses of the Tapanuli residency boosted their monthly output from Rp. 100,000 in August 1947 to 109 million in December 1948.[5]

The situation of the Republic made economic decentralization and improvization inevitable. Yet this decentralization was widely seen as at best a weakness and at worst a criminal diversion of vital national resources to private purposes. The effect of the revolution was to portray government, in an abstract sense divorced from personalities, as the only legitimate repository of economic power. The potential role of the central government in the economy was greatly increased by the experience.

Economic Policies
The most remarkable feature of Republican legislation and policy projection in the economic field was its caution and conservatism despite the background of revolution. With the exception of two junior ministers in Amir Sjarifuddin's huge cabinet, none of the economic portfolios was ever given to a Marxist or a member of the Sayap Kiri. The Marxists believed they should concentrate on power rather than policy in the national stage of the revolution, and therefore clung to defence, foreign affairs and internal affairs. Relatively conservative members of the PNI and MASJUMI virtually monopolized the economics and finance ministries. The Sayap Kiri's own programme was reformist, demanding nationalization only of the largest banks and the most vital branches of production. The Trade Union federation SOBSI spelt out gas, electricity, mining, transport, and the banks for nationalization.[6]

Official government statements on the economy were yet more imprecise, avoiding specific references to nationalization altogether. Beyond assuming the functions of the pre-war government, it promised to extend its activities in industry and commerce in competition with private enterprise. Emphasis was placed on economic planning, though this bore little relation to the realities of the revolutionary situation. A ten year plan was proposed in April 1947 by an economic planning board headed by Hatta and the PNI's Dr A. K. Gani. Amir Sjarifuddin's ministry published a more urgent three year plan. Omitting nationalization, these plans stressed three other cherished goals of the nationalist movement: industrialization; transmigration, from over-populated Java to the other islands;

and co-operatives. In the meantime at least, nothing could be done about the first two. Rural co-operatives, very close to the heart of Hatta, were strongly encouraged through the formation of government-supported boards in every kabupaten within the immediate orbit of Jogjakarta. They did not initially flourish, however. Excessive Japanese use of the *gotong-royong* (mutual help) principle for wartime exactions had made the peasants wary of such schemes. The general reaction was a reluctant acceptance of co-operatives as yet another burden imposed from above.[7]

As in every other sphere during the revolution, the most important changes in economic policy were brought about by pressure from below. The most persistent end organized pressure was directed against agricultural estates in land-hungry Java. The major cash-crops of the central Java region—sugar, tobacco, and, as a wartime expedient, cotton—were grown on peasant land in alternation with the peasants' own rice crops. For peasants in areas affected by these plantation crops, the right to do as they pleased with their land, free of the conditions imposed by Dutch estates under colonial government, was the real essence of independence. Only in such areas where they had a common, clear-cut objective, did peasants give active support to the Barisan Tani Indonesia (Indonesian Peasant Front), or BTI. The BTI was initially dominated by followers of Sjahrir and remained loyal to the government until the split in the Socialist Party, when communist influence began to predominate. In general the politicians who led it were free to formulate whatever pro-government policies they wished, but on the issue of the estate lands there was consistent pressure for change from below.

The first victory of the BTI was in the Madiun Residency in March 1946. With the resident's approval all existing leases between the estates and the peasants for the planting of estate crops were cancelled. New leases were drawn up for the 1946–7 planting year on terms drafted by the BTI itself. The main concentration of sugar, tobacco, and cotton estates, though, was in the former princely lands of Surakarta and Jogjakarta. Special legislation for these areas in 1918 had recognized individual peasant rights to land, where previously all land had been regarded as the property of the ruler. Peasant rights were limited, however, in lands suitable for sugar, by the ruler's continued *conversie-recht* (right of conversion), whereby he could arrange the lease of peasant land in his domain to estates on an alternating basis with peasant crops. The boards set up to administer sugar and other estates in the name of the Republic continued to operate on the basis of this law of 1918.

Peasants in the Jogjakarta area brought the issue forcibly to the government's attention in April 1946 by destroying cane and blocking irrigation channels on land planted in sugar. The Jogjakarta regional government made some minor concessions and promised a new law regulating estates within three years. In early 1948 demands gathered momentum again, this time centred in the Klaten kabupaten of Surakarta, the biggest concentration of sugar land. The BTI, now represented in the BP-KNIP, pressed for the abolition of the *conversie-recht*. When discussion of the issue was cut short by a presidential decree of 3 March regulating *conversie* for the coming year, the BTI organized a very effective series of peasant demonstrations throughout Surakarta and Jogjakarta, culminating on 1 April. The BP-KNIP hurriedly passed Law No. 13 of 26 April 1948, annulling those sections of the 1918 law relating to *conversie*. In theory this made farm owners fully masters of their land, though doing nothing for the landless peasants who had provided most of the demonstrators. The effect was also counterbalanced by a decree imposing on lurahs the obligation of ensuring that sufficient cash crops were produced to meet the government's needs. Nevertheless this did amount to a meaningful and popular land reform, a unique example of government response to peasant pressure. Land reform was not part of any of the government programmes, and the BTI itself had no specific proposals beyond this one.[8]

Political Polarization

> But the extremely valuable lesson for me and for our Party, even though a very bitter one, is that there was no support from the people because we diverged from our own strategy.
> If we had been able to carry out our plans peacefully. . . I am certain that our policy would have been accepted and have become state policy, without bloodshed taking place.
>
> Suripno, in prison, 1948[1]

In 1948 it was the turn of the powerful Marxist mainstream to play the dangerous role of opposition. Like Tan Malaka, the Persatuan Perjuangan, and the Benteng Republik, the pro-Moscow Marxists had now to try to make up in popularity what they had lost in power by reverting to a 100 per cent Merdeka line rejecting compromise with the Dutch, and by supporting economic and social demands from below. In terms of organization, commitment, and even arms, they were much stronger than any previous opposition. But as their cadre formation had proceeded in factories, plantations, and military units, the objective potential of Indonesian society for fundamental renewal had waned. Inflation and government instability had increased the relative value of rice, reducing or even reversing the gap between rice-growing peasant and urban élite. Grass-roots resentment of the authority figures of the Japanese regime had given way to polarization along more primordial lines. Above all, the strength of the Sukarno-Hatta leadership as a symbol of Republican unity and identity had grown with each succeeding crisis. Whoever was now identified as opposing this leadership risked coming into conflict with the force of nationalism itself.

If Tan Malaka's weakness in facing the government had been the lack of adequate organizational support, the communists of 1948 made the opposite mistake of trusting too much in the relative depth of their cadre structure in relation to other parties. The essential ingredient which drove them on to the bloodiest confrontation in the Republic's experience, however, was the application of international cold war politics to a delicate domestic situation.

The Sayap Kiri (left wing) progressed steadily into a full oppositionist stance following Amir's fall from power. Amir himself was angered at the way his MASJUMI opponents had used the Renville issue to bring him down, and at the 'traitorous' role of Sjahrir's faction. The decision of the latter to support Hatta's government in defiance of Socialist Party policy brought the festering sore within that party to a head. On 13 February Sjahrir's followers left to form a separate Partai Sosialis Indonesia (PSI). The new party had a strong head, including most of the PS representatives within the BP-KNIP, but a weak body. Its departure did little to weaken the Partai Sosialis as a mass organization, but much to emphasize its oppositionist character. Gone was the special relationship which Sjahrir had with Hatta (and through him Sukarno), and with the Western powers. Gone, too, were many highly-placed officials and intellectuals who had supported the PS because it was the party of government, of order, and of pragmatic moderation, rather than out of any socialist commitment.

For a few weeks the PS, now unquestionably led by Amir, continued to behave as if its fall from power was a temporary aberration. It demanded the return of a cabinet responsible to the BP-KNIP and broader than what it contemptuously called the 'MASJUMI Cabinet'. However until early March it continued to support the Renville agreement, implying a greater concern with realistic diplomacy than with internal popularity. The Sayap Kiri's transformation on 26 February into the Front Demokrasi Rakyat (People's Democratic Front), or FDR, implied a shift of priorities from parliatary to mass struggle, but the new federation's programme remained moderate.

Was the FDR's abrupt repudiation of Renville and of compromise with imperialism in March 1948 a response to the pressures of opposition, or to new instructions from Moscow? Advocates of the latter explanation point out that two Indonesian communist delegates to the communist-dominated Calcutta Youth Conference (12–21

February 1948) experienced there the full force of the 'two-camp' doctrine, rejecting neutrality or compromise with imperialism, which had dominated Soviet thinking since September 1947. The Indonesian delegates joined in the conference's denunciation of the Renville agreement, and their report must have exerted considerable influence on some FDR members. Moreover the outbreak of militant communist action following the Calcutta Conference, in Malaya, the Philippines, and Burma, as well as Indonesia, suggests at least a common awareness of the new tough line. On the other hand the domestic unpopularity of diplomasi was if anything increasing with the repeated humiliations of 1948, and it would have been very difficult for any party remaining long in opposition to ignore these pressures from below.[10]

Despite the 'two-camp' doctrine, Soviet polemic did not during 1948 consign the Republican government to the 'imperialist' camp. For its part the FDR carefully refrained from the sort of opposition which could be construed as stabbing the Republic in the back. Like Tan Malaka in 1946, the FDR strove to demonstrate the Cabinet's unrepresentativeness by concentrating on unity fronts and unity programmes. On 20 May the FDR, MASJUMI, and PNI celebrated together 'National Awakening Day' (the founding of Budi Utomo in 1908), with mutual assent for a set of objectives intended as the basis for a full 'national programme'. Without the intervention of Moscow, such tactics looked to have a good chance of bringing the FDR back into the cabinet.

On 26 May however, the Soviet Union announced that it had ratified an agreement with the Republic for an exchange of consuls. The agreement had been negotiated in Prague on Sukarno's instructions in January 1948, but Amir Sjarifuddin's government had delayed ratification lest it upset the final stages of the Renville negotiations. One of the provisions of Renville, at least as interpreted by the Dutch, forbade independent foreign relations by the Republic. When Hatta's government took office the treaty had been shelved altogether, since Hatta, like Sjahrir, was acutely sensitive to the danger of pushing America even further on to the side of the Dutch. The unilateral Soviet announcement now appeared to force Hatta publicly to accept or repudiate Soviet friendship. After some hesitation Hatta did neither, simply recalling Suripno, the young communist who had been asked to act for the Republic after attending a Prague youth forum.

This apparent truckling to American foibles at the expense of consummating the first great-power recognition of the Republic was too good a target for the FDR to resist. The FDR's onslaught, however, identified it for the first time with Russia on a major internal controversy. The gulf between the Front and the government widened to the point that a cabinet change no longer seemed feasible. 'From this point on', as Ruth McVey puts it, 'the problem created by the polarization of Indonesian political life began to assume a hopeless aspect'.[11]

This identification of the FDR with a foreign power appeared to give new purpose to the 'national communists' and other assorted leftists of the 1946 opposition. With Tan Malaka and his most prominent supporters still in jail, ideological leadership was provided by a former member of the Dutch Parliament, Rustam Effendi, who had defected from the Communist Party on his return to Indonesia in January 1947. On 6 June his party joined the larger Partai Rakyat, Dr Muwardi's Barisan Banteng, and a couple of minor parties all acknowledging some loyalty to the ideas of Tan Malaka. The new federation, Gerakan Revolusi Rakyat (Movement of People's Revolution), or GRR, continued to oppose negotiations with the Dutch and to demand nationalization of Dutch properties—policies now shared by the FDR. The primary concern of the GRR, however, was to vilify the FDR leaders as Dutch agents who had sold the Republic at Linggajati and Renville, and to demand the rehabilitation of the patriots whom these traitors had consigned to prison. Although in numbers the GRR could not rank with the three major political forces (FDR, PNI, MASJUMI), the bitterness of the polemic in its newspaper *Murba* did much to exacerbate the political climate. As early as 7 April *Murba* had published what it claimed was a secret FDR plan to sabotage the Republic. Once again the Republican Left prepared to tear itself to pieces.

Despite the growing polarization, the 20 May initiative for a national programme was carried forward principally under FDR pressure. By 24 June the major parties had agreed on a lengthy if imprecise programme covering every aspect of state policy. Vital industries should be nationalized without compensation. A new agrarian law was demanded, stressing private ownership without 'feudal' relics. More land should be made available for the peasants.[12] As an instrument of unity, however, the national programme was stillborn. Its main significance was its subsequent use by the communists as legitimation for action on the land question.

The fading of FDR hopes to re-enter a unity cabinet coincided with increasing emphasis on building a following among workers and peasants. At a series of meetings throughout Republican Central Java in June the FDR leaders explained a programme of agrarian and labour reforms, and attacked details of Republican administration. Communists began to talk as if they had just discovered the peasant mass of Indonesia: 'It could be said that up until today we have never given attention to the peasants and workers as basic revolutionary forces. What we have fed them with has been nothing but high-sounding words'. [13] The fluidity and spontaneity which had given educated pemudas such a key revolutionary role in 1945–6 had indeed passed. 'Perjuangan' and '100 per cent Merdeka' were no longer sufficient slogans for the more institutionalized political life of the Republic in 1947–8. Yet even the FDR was still far from having the sort of organization which could mobilize a significant section of the peasantry. The BTI's campaign against the *conversie-recht* had been the first exercise of this sort, limited in its effects to estate lands in Surakarta and Jogjakarta. Attention then shifted to a rural strike at Delanggu, in the heart of the same area, which for the first time brought national political forces dramatically into conflict in the villages.

The strike appears to have begun without any outside instigation, in a sack-making factory and a cotton plantation at Delanggu. Responsibility for both enterprises was in the hands of the government-appointed Badan Tekstil Negara (State Textile Agency) in Surakarta, against which an initial demonstration had been organized on 19 May. Over 500 Delanggu workers, organized by the local BTI amd SARBUPRI (Plantation Workers Union) branches, descended on Surakarta to press their demands. They argued that inflation had reduced their wages to a fifth of the appropriate level, yet they received no rice and cloth allowances like other civil servants. In addition they demanded union representation in the BTN. When the demands were not fully met, the sack factory workers and 17,000 SARBUPRI members on Delanggu plantations began their strike on 26 May. Interrupted for abortive negotiations on June 1, the strike began again on June 23. By this time the national SOBSI leadership had come out in strong support of the strikers,[14] while the (MASJUMI) Minister of Prosperity had entered the negotiations on the side of management. MASJUMI sent its peasant union affiliate, STII, into Delanggu to work the idle fields, an action which by 10 July had led to some nasty clashes with strikers and at least one death. Before the strike was settled in favour of the workers on 16 July, units of the West Java Siliwangi Division and the Tentara Pelajar had come to the defence of the STII, occupying several villages of Delanggu.[15]

The Delanggu affair inaugurated a series of FDR-backed strikes on a smaller scale among organized workers. Its greater significance, however, was the new stage it marked in the polarization of political forces down to the village level. At the grassroots this conflict was no longer a question of national politics or international ideologies, but the clash of the two Javanese cultures, santri and abangan. Delanggu cast the first dark shadow of the primordial antagonisms which political conflict could arouse within the Javanese village.

Military Rationalization

The Renville Agreement, sanctioning the shrunken boundaries of the Republic, made some sort of rationalization of the army imperative. The Republic was responsible for supporting 350,000 regular TNI members, and in theory also an uncertain number (reckoned by Nasution[16] as 470,000 in Java alone) of irregular units which nominally had been included within the TNI since June 1947. Because it could not hope to pay or equip more than a fraction of these units, the Republican government had little control over them. The universal call to arms of 1945–6 was not appropriate to the more stable military situation of 1948. The unwieldy units gave rise to frequent clashes over territory and supplies, but had proved ineffective against serious Dutch military action. Moreover if the army of the United States of Indonesia was to be formed by a federation of the TNI and KNIL, the leading TNI officers must be of sufficient technical competence to ensure that they at least held their own.

A special problem was created by the evacuation of TNI units from Dutch-held areas. One area of acute conflict was the Batak homeland of Tapanuli, to which both regular and irregular Republican units had moved when the vastly richer plantation area of East Sumatra was taken by the Dutch. A state of virtual civil war between rival war-lords existed in Tapanuli for much of 1948, reaching a peak between September and November. In Java the most radical upheaval was the '*hijrah*' (retreat)[17] of about 22,000 men of the relatively well disciplined and equipped Siliwangi Division from 'Dutch' to Republican territory in February 1948, in obedience to the humiliating Renville terms. The predominantly Sundanese Siliwangi clashed frequently with local Javanese units over territory and supplies, and also over the forceful way in which it sometimes acted to defend what it took to be the Hatta government's interest against rebellious local units. There were clashes, however, with the equally pro-government Tentara Pelajar. The Siliwangi commander later complained, 'Gradually every person who spoke Sundanese came to experience actions and attitudes of enmity from the society around him'.[18]

The movement towards rationalization of the TNI began with a BP-KNIP resolution of 20 December 1947, before the fall of the Amir Government. For the following six months the military was in turmoil over rival schemes for implementing the motion, all involving personalities more than principals. The earliest schemes under Amir were considerably influenced by a young group of Dutch-trained officers led by Colonel T. B. Simatupang. By apparently demoting Sudirman to commander of Mobile Forces, erecting an elaborate structure under the Defence ministry to replace the Supreme Command, and by dropping Urip Sumohardjo altogether for his opposition to Renville, these moves renewed the old suspicions of 1945. The change to the Hatta government intensified the search for a professional army as opposed to a political one, and altered the political coloration of some Defence ministry favourites. In mid-February 1948 Colonel A. H. Nasution arrived in Jogja ahead of the Siliwangi *hijrah* he commanded. His experience with guerrilla operations behind the Renville line lent weight to the new recommendations he formulated for the army. These called for the reduction of territorial forces to three divisions in the Republican heartland, plus an additional mobile reserve unit, comprising the Siliwangi. While the former should aspire to a ratio of one gun to three men, the latter should be fully equipped and capable of offensive operations. The bulk of Amir Sjarifuddin's TNI-Masyarakat ('Social TNI'—the successor of the badan perjuangan) would be demobilized, along with the regular units least responsive to military discipline.

Whatever the military merits of such drastic pruning, it was a complete political impossibility short of civil war. Moreover the reshuffling of posts in the reorganized central command structure exacerbated the mutual suspicions between factions of the army. Since Nasution's own Siliwangi was given effective élite status, there was grumbling that the Javanese units were being made a second-class army, and even that the new schemes were part of joint planning with the Dutch for a new Federal Army. The completion of legislation for the new scheme in a presidential decree of 4 May aroused a storm of military protest. Thirty battalion commanders waited on the President on 1 June to demand its recall. One of the points of the FDR-PNI-MASJUMI 'national programme' outlined on 20 May was an implicit rejection of rationalization. A number of the existing Divisional Commanders, notably Colonel Sungkono in Kediri and Colonel Sutarto in Surakarta, simply refused to relinquish their commands. Reorganization moves appeared to break down altogether when General Sudirman unilaterally circulated all the existing commanders to instruct the suspension of rationalization in view of the growing threat from the Dutch.

Increasing political polarization at the national level threw further doubts on the rationalization programme, especially in view of the loyalty of many commanders to the former defence minister, Amir Sjarifuddin. Initially the FDR was less critical of the programme than was the GRR, whose unruly armed supporters were among the first to be scheduled for demobilization. The FDR had the most to gain from a general military refusal to accept rationalization, yet too close an identification with the military opposition could make the Front vulnerable to charges of treason. The FDR appears to have realized this dilemma, seeking to retain its armed strength without drawing attention to its tactics by attacking rationalization frontally. Purely military pressures, however, were building up to a crisis.

The centre of military rivalry was perennially turbulent Surakarta, where no central government had ever established a reliable basis of control. A two-day battle had already taken place there at the end of March 1948, when the Senopati Division and Tentara Pelajar had decided to punish notoriously lawless units of the BPRI (Badan Pemberontakan) and Barisan Banteng. Both commanders were captured after a fight, and the BPRI's Lieutenant Colonel Mardjuki was executed on the spot on the charge of corruption. Perhaps in revenge, the Senopati commander Colonel Sutarto was murdered on 2 July. Despite his earlier association with the Tan Malaka-inclined coup attempt of 3 July 1946, Sutarto's friendship with the veteran communist Alimin had subsequently aligned him with the FDR in national politics. The real issues in Surakarta, however, were local military rivalries.

Surakarta had also become the main centre for the Siliwangi newcomers. Tension between them and the Senopati mounted steadily, especially when the latter discovered in May that they were to be almost completely demobilized under the new order. A series of kidnappings and murders between members of the two units reached the point of open warfare in early September, when this local conflict was overtaken by the crisis in national politics.

Musso's Eighty Days

Suripno, the communist who had negotiated the consular convention with Russia, flew back to Bukittinggi on 3 August 1948. On 11 August he arrived in the Republican capital. With him was an Indonesian 'secretary', who soon revealed himself as Musso, one of the leading promoters of the abortive 1926 communist rebellion. Apart from a secret visit to Indonesia in 1935 to establish an underground PKI network, Musso had spent virtually all the intervening period in Russia as a loyal follower of Stalin. His despatch to Indonesia at this critical juncture can only have been intended to convey to uncertain Indonesian communists the full force of the new Soviet two-camp doctrine, with its rejection of bourgeois leadership of the Asian Revolution.

The rapidity with which the experienced, well-known politicians of the FDR fell into the hands of this newcomer was a remarkable example of Moscow's growing power in international communist affairs at that time. Musso lacked the political sophistication of Abdulmadjid, Tan Ling Djie, or Amir Sjarifuddin; he had no longer revolutionary record than Alimin, and his understanding of Indonesian politics was limited. His main assets were his forceful, fiery oratory, his reputation among members of the 1935 underground PKI including Amir Sjarifuddin, and his authority as an interpreter of current Soviet thinking. Nevertheless it is difficult to believe he would have been allowed to guide the FDR on what proved a disastrous course but for the demoralization of existing leaders, particularly Amir. The perils of opposition were many. The various attempts of the FDR to regain a place in cabinet had proved fruitless, and the government threatened gradually to eliminate the armed strength of the FDR, leaving it at the mercy of an antagonistic professional army. Amir and his colleagues had already acknowledged the error of their former moderate policies. Even the 'bourgeois' revolution was now in peril. The Renville agreement, now denounced by Russia, had been a bitter disappointment, because America had failed to force the Dutch to abide by its terms. Musso arrived as if from the clouds, untainted by discredited policies of the past, bearing a confident blueprint for a new and certain path to victory.

Two weeks after his arrival in Jogjakarta, the PKI accepted Musso's leadership and his *Jalan Baru* (new road) policy. There must be a single party of the working class, taking the leading role in a national front which must in turn control the government. Although the revolution was still in its national stage, leadership could not be entrusted to the 'national bourgeoisie' because of its susceptibility to imperialist blandishments. In domestic affairs the *Jalan Baru* did not change so much as reinforce, with more explicit and aggressive language, the existing trends in FDR policy. Capitalism must continue to exist in Indonesia, under state control, to promote the economic development necessary for the later socialist revolution. Feudal and foreign privileges on the land should be abolished, however, and the land of 'rich peasants' confiscated. In foreign policy Musso insisted on a firmer reliance on the Soviet Union, whose power in Asia had been gravely underestimated by Indonesian Marxists in the past. Musso's optimism about support from Russia, taken together with the apparent failure of America to fulfill its earlier promise, was one of the factors which induced Marxists to accept the new path.

Swiftly the other constituents of the FDR accepted Musso's call for a single working class party. The Labour Party on 27 August, the Socialist Party on 30 August, and PESINDO on 2 September announced their fusion with the PKI. SOBSI and the BTI accepted the *Jalan Baru*. Amir Sjarifuddin, Tan Ling Djie, and Abdulmadjid of the Socialist Party, and the Labour Party leader Setiadjit, all announced that they had been secret members of the Communist Party since before the war. Amir's claim came as a shock to all but a few Republicans, particularly as he was widely known to be a practising Christian. Amir's communism had, in fact, only been possible because effective control of Indonesian communists by Moscow had previously been so slight. He had been able to follow his own political lights rather than those of party functionaries he considered his intellectual inferiors. Musso's arrival forced him to make a clear choice for the first time. He appears to have shrunk from the prospect of relative isolation and denunciation by harder-line Stalinists, which would have followed his repudiation of Musso's leadership.

Paradoxically it was the existing PKI leadership of Alimin and Sardjono who showed least enthusiam for the new Musso line. Alimin, the grand old man of the party, was a close friend of Sukarno and had constantly stressed the need for unity and the inapplicability of the Soviet model in Indonesia. In the new, enlarged PKI polit-bureau announced on 1 September, he and Sardjono were given relatively unimportant positions in the propaganda secretariat, whereas young communists like Aidit, Lukman, and Njoto, all in their twenties, were advanced to key positions by Musso.

Before Musso's arrival, during the Delanggu disturbances, the FDR had cautiously adopted a position of supporting strike actions which were manifestly popular and well-grounded in worker demands. In August, however, Musso's new line showed immediately in the readiness of the PKI and its allies to foment action by workers and peasants as part of the party's role of revolutionary leadership. Strikes became endemic in the oil-refining centre of Cepu, a PKI stronghold, by early September, principally on political rather than directly economic grounds. In Madiun a strike of municipal clerical workers began on 13 September on the grounds of repeated rudeness towards workers by members of the military. The most significant change of emphasis, however, was the increased attention given to the peasant majority of the Javanese population. Addressing a BTI Congress on 4 September, Musso insisted:

> The agrarian revolution, the division of land to the peasants, must be carried out in this time of revolution. For this, the *desa* (village) administration must first be democratized . . . Feudal elements must be eliminated. *Bengkok* lands must be returned to the peasants to be worked by themselves.[19]

This was the most fundamental of revolutionary demands, striking at the very backbone of bureaucratic control in Java. It is significant that it was made only in this brief period when Musso brought outside communist influence on the PKI to its highest level.

Already in late August the communist press began reporting favourably on a wave of actions by left-wing peasants to distribute *tanah bengkok* to landless farmers. Such actions were reported first from the turbulent Surakarta residency, but by September they had spread to Kedu (Magelang-Purworejo area), and Jogjakarta. In what was regarded as a model action, one village in Kapanewon Manis-renggo (Jogjakarta) agreed to take over 19 hectares of bengkok as village property, to be worked by the poorest peasants. The latter would enjoy two-thirds of the product of the land, surrendering the remaining third to village funds, from which the pamong desa would be paid a normal salary.[20] In the arid hill country of Pacitan and Gunung Kidul, where the colonial government had maintained teak forest reserves, the demand was added for distribution of this reserve to poor peasants.

Such actions were justified in terms of the agreed 'National Programme', with its demand for ending feudal remnants in the village. No more than in the 'unilateral action' on land reform in 1964–5, however, did national-level unity slogans of this sort soften the profound tensions which were building up in the countryside. In many villages the upheavals of 1945–6 had been used either by the abangan element (of which PESINDO became a militant expression) or the santris to oust their rivals from power. The rising tensions of 1948 presented an opportunity to turn the tables once more. Although some correlation undoubtedly existed between economic status and *aliran* (santri villagers tending to be among the least poor), the latter was vastly more important in popular consciousness. The land reform campaign thus tended to become transformed at the village level into a traumatic struggle between opposed cultural identities.[21]

At all levels it was Islam which provided sternest opposition. On 7 September a BTI leader complained in the BP-KNIP that the MASJUMI leader Sukiman had given secret instructions as Interior Minister that the land reform actions should be put down by force. According to PESINDO sources, MASJUMI speakers at a rally in Lodoyo (Blitar area) on 12 September attacked the communist programme for abolishing tanah bengkok, and suggested MASJUMI members buy arms to protect themselves. The following day the government arrested the leading leftists of Lodoyo.[22]

Allegations of MASJUMI-backed government repression such as the above form the substance of subsequent communist reconstructions of the Madiun affair, which insist that it was a simple defence against the provocation of the Hatta government. Certainly Hatta had not taken the threat posed by Musso's return in a passive spirit. On 17 August an amnesty was announced for all those being tried for complicity in the 3 July affair, thus strengthening the GRR in its crusade against the Stalinists. Only Tan Malaka, Sukarni, and Abikusno, against whom there had been insufficient evidence for any trial, remained in prison. When addressing the BP-KNIP on 2 September Hatta for the first time explicitly denounced communism and a Soviet-oriented foreign policy as dangerous for

Indonesia. Two weeks later he attacked the 'suicidal policy' of the
PKI, and announced the release of Tan Malaka and the remaining
GRR prisoners. Directly or indirectly the government probably had
some connection with the mysterious disappearance of five PKI-
inclined military officers in Surakarta on 7 September, and operations
against leftist units in Blitar and Nganjuk on 12 and 13 September.
That the government was preparing for a possible showdown with
the communists is certain; that it was sufficiently far-sighted,
cynical, and well co-ordinated to try to provoke such a showdown is
highly improbable.

The exact nature of communist plans is still more problematic.
In accordance with the *Jalan Baru*, the new PKI invited the PNI
and MASJUMI to join it in a broad national front which might
then form the government. What Musso openly called his 'Gottwald
plan' (referring to the destruction of non-communist Czech parties
in February 1948) could hardly have been expected to appeal to the
other major parties, however. Having failed to build an effective
national front in May, the more experienced PKI politicians at
least must have seen that they were now unlikely to woo the PNI
and MASJUMI. The whole emphasis of Musso's new line was in fact
that the PKI did not have to wheedle its way back into government.
On the contrary the right-wing parties should be the supplicants,
for without the workers' leadership 'bourgeois' revolution would
inevitably fail. A regular columnist pointed out in the party newspaper that the national bourgeoisie of Indonesia were even weaker
than their counterparts in India, China, and the Philippines, and
could not aspire to a neutral position between the socialist and
capitalist camps.

> The national bourgeoisie must unite with the Workers and
> Peasants in one Front with Workers and Peasants. . . . If not? If
> not the national bourgeoisie as a factor in the revolution will
> disappear completely. The Workers and Peasants will confront
> the imperialists directly.[23]

The implications of all Musso's speeches was that bourgeois leadership of the revolution was intolerable and temporary. Amir
Sjarifuddin had been gravely in error in surrendering the reins of
government without a fight, and the communists must now regain
the leadership by one means or another.

This confident and aggressive tone must at least have prepared
communists psychologically for an overthrow of the government.
The new PKI leaders would also have been very foolish had they
not made preparations for the armed confrontation towards which
Musso's stance, the military rationalization measures, and the
relentless polarization of political views were leading. Various

FDR/PKI strategies for revolt were published by its enemies. One of these, said to have been drawn up as early as July 1948 but captured after the revolt, was accepted as authentic by Kahin[24], who was in Jogjakarta at the time. This contingency strategy for 'rebellion or separate government' allegedly centred on the evacuation of FDR troops from the Dutch 'front', the concentration of strength in centrally-located Madiun residency, and the stimulation of diversionary 'Wild West' activities in Surakarta. That some such plans existed at least after Musso's arrival is almost certain, but scepticism is necessary about an alleged text of this plan which so conveniently laid all the difficulties of the Republic at the door of a scheming PKI.

All indications are that whatever plans the PKI was preparing were for a longer term, sometime early in 1949. By that time, it might have been assumed, the 'bourgeois' leadership would already have been eliminated by the Dutch in a second military action, leaving the PKI to compete with or absorb the army during the final guerrilla struggle. It seems very unlikely that the experienced leaders of the FDR/PKI could have sought directly to challenge Sukarno as the unifying symbol of the Republic, unless he had first been discredited by some Dutch action. Musso himself, however, was a considerable liability to the execution of any realistic communist strategy because of his insensitivity to the particularity of the Indonesian situation.

Whatever the plans of both government and PKI for an eventual confrontation, neither side could predict or control the march of events in September, particularly in turbulant Surakarta. The spiralling military rivalries in that city reached a new crisis on 7 September with the kidnapping and presumed murder of the five 'opposition' TNI officers. Another officer investigating their disappearance was himself kidnapped two days later. The Senopati Division accused the Siliwangi of the kidnappings and demanded that the men be returned by the 13th. On that day the Senopati launched an abortive attack on Siliwangi headquarters in which at least thirty died.[25] Meanwhile PESINDO members captured the Barisan Banteng and GRR strongman, Dr Muwardi, who was never seen again. In retaliation Barisan Banteng attacked PESINDO headquarters on the 15th. Fighting then became general, until on 17 September the reinforced Siliwangi was able to drive the main Senopati Division and PESINDO forces out of the city.

General Sudirman, true to his constant preoccupation with military solidarity, appealed to both sides in Surakarta to resolve their differences. After a visit to Surakarta Sudirman urged that the Siliwangi be withdrawn from the city to prevent further friction. Pressure was brought to bear by Nasution and the tough, anti-communist military police commander Colonel Gatot Subroto, however, with the result that the government intervened sharply on the side of the Siliwangi. On 15 September Gatot Subroto was appointed military governor of the Surakarta region under martial law. When, with his encouragement, the 'opposition' forces in Surakarta were driven out, the government had won the first battle before war had been declared.

In areas of PKI strength, PESINDO reacted quickly to the set-backs of its allies in Surakarta. On 15 September the two leading propagandists of the MASJUMI peasant union STII were seized while attending a conference in Purwodadi.[26] Around Madiun a propaganda offensive by PESINDO was reported, to the effect that the Sukarno-Hatta government had abdicated leadership. News of the strong and successful Siliwangi action in Surakarta appears to have convinced the top PESINDO leaders that the final test of strength had arrived. The strongest PESINDO units in East Java had already begun to concentrate around Madiun, its national head-quarters. In the small hours of 18 September PESINDO took over vital installations in Madiun on the instructions of its national leader, Sumarsono. In concert with the pro-FDR Brigade 29 of the TNI (formerly the Biro Perjuangan), it captured or killed the leading pro-government officers in Madiun, including almost the whole staff of what was intended to become the new East Java Division in the rationalized TNI. At 10 a.m. Madiun radio announced the formation of a National Front government for the Madiun residency, headed by Sumarsono as military governor. The 'rebellion' was still at the level of a regional coup, though Sumarsono appears to have given it national implications by urging over the air that his revolutionary example be followed all over Indonesia.[27]

Musso, Amir Sjarifuddin, and Setiadjit had left Madiun on 9 September during their speaking tour of Republican centres in Java. In a typically tough speech to a large Madiun rally Musso had berated the communists for letting the revolution fall into bourgeois hands, and demanded that 'elements which oppose the course of the revolution must be purged'.[28] The leaders could not, however, have anticipated the rapid military developments in Surakarta. By 18 September their tour had taken them to Purwodadi, whence they hurriedly returned to Madiun on hearing about the coup. There is no doubt that all were suprised, and all with the possible exception of Musso dismayed, by Sumarsono's action. In a frank postscript to the affair Suripno wrote:

The prevailing circumstances finally brought us to consider the affair a *fait accompli*. We all felt pressured into solidarity with our comrades at Madiun – particularly as the reports we received about the actions of the Siliwangi, MASJUMI, etc. intensified the feeling of comradeship.[29]

In any case the government moved first to portray the coup as a revolt against the national leadership. Early on 19 September PKI leaders in Jogjakarta were arrested, most of whom, even including General Secretariat member Tan Ling Djie, had no knowledge of the events in Madiun. The same evening Sukarno declared war on the PKI in one of his most blistering speeches. Quoting from an alleged FDR directive of February 1948, he asserted that the chaos in Surakarta and the coup in Madiun were both part of a sinister plan by the PKI to replace the Republic by a Soviet government under Musso.

My beloved people, in the name of the struggle for Indonesian independence I appeal to you at this moment of such crisis . . . for you there are two choices: follow Musso and his PKI who will bring the hopes of Indonesia Merdeka to bankruptcy, or follow Sukarno-Hatta who with God's permission and help will lead the Republic of Indonesia to become an independent Indonesia. . . .

My brothers, my people, arise!

The insurgents, who lack the patience to await the people's decision at a general election, want to overthrow our government, to destroy our state! Let us join together to wipe out these insurgents![30]

In East Java the Government had no reliable military units. The rationalization measures had alienated all divisional commanders there, especially the commander in Kediri, Colonel Sungkono, on whose support the communists probably reckoned. The new men Jogjakarta had been promoting were all eliminated by the rebels. Sukarno however gambled on appointing Sungkono as Military Governor of East Java, with special responsibility to retake Madiun. At the same time Colonel Gatot Subroto's responsibilities as Military Governor were extended to cover most of Central Java. Under his overall command, the Siliwangi troops in Surakarta were already mobilizing to move eastward against the communists, grateful to be given a patriotic role to play after so long as the 'outsiders' in Central Java.[31]

This full-blooded government response to the Madiun coup, before the PKI leadership had even declared its hand, is not difficult to understand. Negotiation or delay as advocated by General Sudirman[32] might have saved countless lives, but at the expense of feeding Dutch propaganda that the Republic was powerless against communism, and ensuring US support for Dutch intervention. The

Dutch government indeed made an offer of 'assistance' to Hatta on 20 September. Moreover the greatest chance for success in the vital military rationalization policy was to isolate and defeat the opposition on the field of battle. If Jogjakarta moved with more unity and vigour against the communists than it did against the Dutch, this was no more than a correct estimate of its priorities for survival. The internal viability of the Republic was thrown sharply into question at Madiun.

If Sukarno had hoped to force Musso into a corner by his speech, he succeeded brilliantly. Hardly an hour after Sukarno had finished speaking Musso replied over radio Madiun, with a speech which has been described as 'probably the worst piece of political psychology that Indonesian history knows'.[33] He attacked Sukarno and Hatta as no Indonesian has publicly attacked his President before or since:

> the ruling group has used our revolution to enrich themselves. During the Japanese occupation they became Quislings, slaves of Japan, romusha dealers and heiho propagandists. More than two million Indonesian women became widows, because their husbands became romushas. *Now they are going to sell Indonesia and its people forever to the American imperialists!* . . .
> Can people like that say that they have the legitimate right to govern our Republic? . . .
> Sukarno asked the people of Indonesia to choose: Sukarno or Musso.
> The people must answer: Sukarno-Hatta, slaves of Japan and America! Indeed, 'evil men will remain evil to the end'.[34] The people will certainly answer, 'Musso has always served the people of Indonesia'.

This speech lends support to the view that Musso, if not his communist colleagues, was dogmatic enough to welcome Sumarsono's precipitate action. 'The people of Madiun', he argued, 'have carried out the obligation of our National Revolution, that it must be led by the people themselves and by no other class.'[35]

Musso's speech removed any chance for compromise, and the communists prepared for civil war. On 20 September they issued their revolutionary programme, calling for a complete overhaul and replacement of the bureaucracy, arming of workers and peasants, the takeover of banks and factories, and the distribution of land to the tillers. Progressive forces throughout Java and Sumatra were urged to join in resisting the Sukarno-Hatta government.

In reality though, the political polarization taking place in the Republic's Javanese heartland was unrelated to events elsewhere. The FDR leaders in Sumatra and Banten, who had not yet felt the impact of Musso nor accepted the idea of fusion into an enlarged PKI, immediately disavowed any intention to rebel. They thereby avoided arrest, or even dismissal from official posts. The PESINDO units in Sumatra which had followed Sarwono S. Sutardjo in a communist direction were in any case relatively weak. The strongest military support for the FDR in Sumatra was to be found among the former East Sumatran units which had retreated into eastern Aceh, but these were locked in a conflict with the Aceh government of Daud Beureu'eh in which they felt themselves the champions, not the opponents, of Jogjakarta.

Even in Central and East Java communist strength was rapidly eroded from within. Many soldiers who might have been ready to fight to prevent the disbandment of their unit could not understand a political crusade now identified as opposed to Sukarno and Hatta. Some units disobeyed or killed their pro-PKI commanders. In Madiun the TRIP (East Java equivalent of the Tentara Pelajar—student army) was able to mobilize opposition after one of its members was killed in a PESINDO raid on 22 September. They formed a group called 'Patriot Anti-Musso' to circulate anti-PKI broadsheets in and around Madiun. One consequence was to draw TRIP and TP units elsewhere into more active opposition to the communists.

The most devoted popular support for the communists was found amongst the oil refinery and railway workers of Cepu. Thousands of workers, armed only with knives and sharpened bamboo, defended the town in two weeks of bitter fighting. Peasant support was less gratifying. The PKI did forcibly distribute bengkok or other village land to poorer peasants in at least the Wonogiri-Sukoharjo area which they controlled for several weeks, and attempted to do so more widely.[36] But such action was too hasty and ill-prepared to arouse committed support among a traditional populace. Typically it degenerated into killing or capture of the richest members of a village and plunder of their houses. As PKI forces were obliged to retreat from one area after another they began to kill the officials, and MASJUMI and PNI politicians, whom they had earlier captured. Many turned against the communists with the discovery of grisly scenes of mass execution at Dungus, Magetan (both near Madiun), Tirtomogo (near Sukoharjo), Wonogiri, and elsewhere. MASJUMI ordered its forces into action. The tension between santri and abangan militants erupted into killings of whichever was locally the weaker side.

The number of troops rallying to support the rebellion has been estimated at between ten and twenty-five thousand, though 35,000 were ultimately arrested by the government. The force effectively mobilized by Jogjakarta was also small. Most Republican units had no transport, minimal offensive capability, and little will to losing the fluid revolutionary situation which had been its greatest fight a civil war. Colonel Sungkono's forces in Kediri regained some territory but did not look capable of taking Madiun. The issue was decided by eight well-equipped battalions of the Siliwangi Division, who eagerly accepted their commission to retake the rebel headquarters within two weeks. In the event the communist forces left Madiun without a fight on 30 September, after failing to stem the Siliwangi advance at Ngerong and Magetan. Initially they moved to the mountainous area south of Madiun in search of a secure guerrilla base. There Musso left the main body, presumably after a disagreement. He was killed in a skirmish on 31 October, with only a handful of guards protecting him. The main force of about 2,000 men led by Amir Sjarifuddin was also harried from several directions by the Siliwangi, and began to strike north across Mount Lawu. They may have been hoping to reach the relative safety of the Dutch-occupied zone. At the end of November the top leaders were seized near the Renville line in the Purwodadi area. On 20 December they were summarily shot.

The Madiun affair was a terrible tragedy not only in its heavy toll of human life,[37] but also in the heritage of bitterness it created between Left and Right, between santri and abangan. Nevertheless it was a great advance towards the Republican government's immediate goals, both internally and externally. In purely military terms the kidnappings, killings, and local coups in August and September 1948 can be considered part of a steady deterioration in Jogjakarta's ability to control the area left to it under the Renville Agreement. What made the Madiun coup different from other crises was that it claimed justification by a higher revolutionary imperative, throwing out a political challenge to the fundamental legitimacy of the central government. It was precisely this which made it both possible and necessary for Jogjakarta to act decisively against it, thereby breaking the core of both military and political opposition. That all this was accomplished without any Dutch intervention greatly strengthened the Republic's standing with the US State Department. At a time of irresistible communist advance in China, it seemed to suggest that the Sukarno-Hatta government could be an anti-communist bulwark in Southeast Asia.

The first serious communist attempt to revolutionize the Javanese peasantry was a critical stage both for the PKI and for the Indonesian revolution. The rapidly escalating confrontation with the national government which accompanied it, however, made this attempt hasty, violent, and counter-productive. The PKI's discovery of the peasantry was permanent, but the party subsequently retreated from some of Musso's radicalism, at least in relation to tanah bengkok. Anti-communist forces were immeasurably strengthened by the Madiun affair. The PKI became politically isolated, opportunity. For Sukarno and Hatta, moreover, Madiun provoked a sharp conceptual break between national and social revolution. In 1945 the two had been seen as indivisible. Now social revolution was postponed indefinitely.[38] Although the direction of the revolution was far from settled, it had been jolted sharply to the Right.

References

1 As translated in J. O. Sutter, *Indonesianisasi: Politics in a Changing Economy, 1940–1955*, Ithaca, 1959, Vol. II, p. 529.
2 Mr Hermani, secretary of the Interior Department, as quoted on his return from Sumatra, *Merdeka*, 1 June 1946.
3 Amir Sjarifuddin, in speech of 8 June 1946, as quoted in Sutter, Vol. II, p. 378.
4 The major exception was a donation of gold from Aceh in 1948, intended to buy an aeroplane for the central government.
5 From table in *Perdjuangan Rakjat Tapanuli—S. Timur*, Medan, 1950, p. 62.
6 *Kedaulatan Rakjat*, 16 April 1947.
7 *Republik Indonesia, Daerah Istimewa Jogjakarta*, Jakarta, n.d., p. 448.
8 Law No. 13 is given in full in Mochammad Tauchid, *Masalah Agraria* Vol. II, Jakarta, 1953, pp. 240–50. Its background is discussed in *Republik Indonesia, Daerah Istimewa Jogjakarta*, pp. 501–7; *Republik Indonesia, Propinsi Djawa Tengah*, Jakarta, n.d., pp. 100–3; Anwas in *Pacific*, (Surakarta), 12 April 1948; and Sutter Vol. II, pp. 536–47.
9 Cited in Djamal Marsudi, *Menjingkap Pembrontakan PKI dalam Peristiwa Madiun*, Jakarta, 1966, p. 94.
10 This question is well examined in Ruth T. McVey, *The Calcutta Conference and the Southeast Asian Uprisings*, Interim Reports Series, Modern Indonesia Project, Ithaca, 1958.
11 McVey, *The Soviet View of the Indonesian Revolution*. p. 50.
12 For the full text of the National Programme see *Buruh* (Jogjakarta), 22, 23, and 25 June 1948.
13 Editorial by Supeno in PESINDO weekly *Revolusioner*, 29 June 1948. The previous (22 June) issue of the same journal complained in an article 'Democracy in the Village': 'Up to now there has been a general assumption which has changed little, that the *desa* has a static character which can with difficulty be changed'.
14 On 21 June SOBSI explained its support of strike action by arguing that the appropriate internal policy in a national revolution was anti-imperialism and anti-feudalism. SOBSI therefore authorized 'strikes which take the form of corrective-constructive action towards elements which endanger the national revolution'. *Buruh*, 22 June 1948.
15 The Delanggu strike is most fully covered in J. Jahmin, 'Kekuatan Sosial Kiri dan Persetudjuan Renville', Unpublished M.A. Thesis, Gajah Mada University, 1971, pp. 46–61.
16 A. H. Nasution, *Tentara Nasional Indonesia* II, Jakarta, 1968, p. 130.
17 The term *hijrah*, recalling Muhammad's retreat from Mecca to Medina prior to his final victory, was coined by Sudirman to emphasize its *reculer pour mieux sauter* aspect. T. B. Simatupang, *Laporan dari Banaran*, Jakarta, 1960, p. 184.
18 Nasution, *TNI* Vol. II, p. 165.
19 *Buruh*, (Jogjakarta), 4 September 1948.
20 For accounts of these actions see *Buruh* 21 and 30 August and 16 September 1948. *Jalan Baru* had suggested peasants would be better served by retain-

ing village land in corporate possession rather than permanently distributing it to poor peasants, because of the absolute land shortage in Java. This may explain the special praise for Manisrenggo.

21 For this aspect see Robert Jay, *Religion and Politics in Rural Central Java*, New Haven, 1963, pp. 27–9 and 73–6; and Pramoedya Ananta Toer, 'Dia jang Menjerah', in *Tjerita dari Blora*, Jakarta, 1952, pp. 277–340.

22 *Buruh*, 18 September 1948.

23 *Ibid.*

24 Kahin, pp. 269–71. Suripno's notes from prison, however, insist that Musso never mentioned rebellion since first showing a desire to return to Indonesia in March 1948, and that the typical communist reaction to attack in Surakarta was cautious rather than militant; Marsudi, pp. 81–6.

25 *Nasional*, (Surakarta), 16 September 1948, published a report from the city hospital that 31 were killed, of whom 3 were from the Siliwangi and 24 from the 'attacking army'.

26 The two men, Ir Sofwan and Hendrosudarmo, and four other prominent anti-communist prisoners, were shot on October 5 as the Siliwangi were about to enter Purwodadi. Only Hendrosudarmo miraculously survived his bullet wound. Information from Hendrosudarmo, July 1972.

27 Only A. C. Brackman, *Indonesian Communism. A History*, New York, 1963, p. 93, claims a verbatim text of this broadcast, without source.

28 *Api Rakjat*, (Madiun), 9 September 1948.

29 Marsudi, p. 93. See also Brackman, p. 100, and a somewhat similar point by Amir Sjarifuddin in Kahin, p. 285n.

30 Slightly different versions of this speech are given in full in *Republik Indonesia. Daerah Istimewa Jogjakarta*, pp. 284–6, and in *Siliwangi dari masa ke masa*, Jakarta, 1968, pp. 243–7. I have used the former, which appears to be similar to the text translated in Kahin, pp. 292–3.

31 This mood of release from a long frustration is well portrayed in *Siliwangi*, pp. 248 and 260–1.

32 The military commander sent Lt Col Suharto (later President of Indonesia) to Madiun to see whether compromise could be reached with the rebellious military units; Marsudi, p. 88.

33 H. J. H. Alers, *Om een rode of groene Merdeka*, Eindhoven, 1956, p. 190.

34 This phrase is a well-known Javanese proverb, *Ciri wanci lali ginowo mati*—literally 'a bad characteristic continues until death'. It is badly mistranslated in Kahin, p. 250.

35 Musso's speech was published in the Madiun newspaper *Front Nasional* and reproduced in Pinardi, *Peristiwa Coup Berdarah PKI di Madiun*, Jakarta, 1967, p. 91; and *Siliwangi*, pp. 248–50. Kahin, pp. 248–50, translates the whole.

36 Muhammad Dimyati, *Sedjarah Perdjuangan Nasional*, Jakarta, 1951, p. 203n. Selosoemardjan, *Social Change in Jogjakarta*, Ithaca, 1962, p. 178.

37 The degree of carnage may only be suggested by random statistics of varying reliability. The Dutch alleged in the UN that 8,000 people were executed by the TNI in Madiun. The Cepu hospital reported 4,000 deaths in the fighting for that town; *Nasional*, 9 October 1948. Jay, p. 28, was informed in 1953 that half the male population of Ponorogo (pop. 50,000) were killed by one side or the other, though this appears improbable.

38 Hatta, in his 2 September speech against the communists, stated 'The aim of the national revolution will fail if it is mixed with social revolution.' *Republik Indonesia. Daereh Istimewa Jogjakarta*, p. 282; cf Kahin p. 282. Sukarno, in a pamphlet issued shortly after Madiun, argued that it was a 'provoked social revolution, a social revolution that was forced years, perhaps decades, before its time'; translated Feith and Castles, p. 362.

Chapter Eight

THE VICTORY OF *DIPLOMASI*

The independence which we proclaimed on August 17 1945, and which has saturated our souls, will never be crushed by force.

Sukarno, 19 December 1948[1]

The Military 'Solution'

One of Holland's major difficulties in dealing with the 'Indonesia Question' was the traditional importance of colonial issues in metropolitan political life. The Republic's problem was not in making diplomatic concessions but in persuading its people to accept them. The Netherlands, on the other hand, had difficulty even formulating goals, because of the political pressures each move evoked.

In July 1948 the Dutch electorate passed judgement again. The Labour Party lost two seats, presumably because its flexibility on Indonesian matters had not been appreciated. The Catholic Party, having retained its dominant voice in the coalition, now resolved to take direct responsibility for Indonesian affairs for the first time. Its nominee for the portfolio of 'Overseas Territories' was the conservative Sassen, who made clear his desire for tougher policies not excluding military ones. He was also impatient to be rid of Van Mook, who was replaced in October by the former Catholic Party Prime Minister, Beel, now bearing the title 'High Representative of the Crown'.

While negotiations with the Republic continued in deadlock, the Dutch built unilaterally towards Van Mook's concept of a federal Indonesia. New federal states were erected in the Dutch-occupied areas of South Sumatra on 30 August and East Java on 21 November 1948, although neither had a viable popular base. On 8 July a committee known as the BFO (*Bijeenkomst voor Federale Overleg*—Federal Consultative Assembly) was formed from leaders of the federal states to discuss the future shape of the United States of Indonesia. In August, and again in September, it sent delegations to The Hague to negotiate the formation of an interim government. The Dutch were planning to inaugurate such a government by the end of 1948, with the Republic omitted altogether unless it accepted the minor role already defined for it. In mid-October the Dutch advanced for the first time a project for the USI, including Java and Sumatra, in which the Republic was not mentioned.

The fundamental differences between The Hague and Jogjakarta related as before to the balance of force during the period of interim government. Sassen, even more strongly than his predecessors, demanded that the Netherlands High Representative retain responsibility for security in the interim period. Hatta refused this. The Republic also insisted that the TNI retain its separate identity at least until more peaceful conditions modified the hostility the soldiers themselves felt towards absorption into a federal army.

Mutual distrust was kept alive on the Republican side by fear of a second Dutch offensive; and on the Dutch by the continuing activity of Republican armed units on the Dutch side of the Renville line. Besides the irregular units which had declined to evacuate after Renville, regular TNI units periodically crossed the line in Java. The most serious infiltration arose from internal Republican problems. After the Siliwangi battalion of Major Rukman had been involved in nasty fighting with local units in Surakarta, Siliwangi commanders decided to ease tension by sending it back to West Java.

> They were not sent off as the official army, but using the hammer and sickle emblem by way of disguise, as if they were just a 'wild' army, to pull the wool over the eyes of the Dutch as well as foreign observers.
>
> The despatch of the Rukman battalion . . . had the character of a rush, to prevent more serious clashes with comrades in the common struggle.[2]

The battalion clashed with Dutch troops in September 1948 when crossing the Slamet mountain, and letters of instruction from the Siliwangi's Colonel Sadikin were captured. Although the Siliwangi appears in reality to have acted entirely on its own, the Dutch naturally believed Hatta's government was systematically sending troops across the Renville line.

Much more alarming than the apparent duplicity of such incursions was the possibility that they might succeed. Intimidation of Pasundan officials was undermining the limited initial stability of that state. Dutch officials began to feel the initiative slipping from their hands. On 12 November Beel obtained from his top officials in each region a unanimous picture of deteriorating Dutch control. The meeting declared for immediate military action against Jogjakarta, lest the Dutch position deteriorate so much during December that action should become impossible.

Despite the element of deliberate alarmism in such views, the Republic's military position was in fact beginning to look brighter towards the end of the year. The TNI in Java was much more unified and battle-hardened after the crushing of the Madiun rebellion, though no less short of equipment. In Sumatra a brief visit by Hatta had brought the civil war in Tapanuli to an end on 28 November. Colonel Alex Kawilarang took over as commander of the feuding units in Tapanuli. Another competent young Dutch-trained officer from Java, Colonel Hidajat, had earlier taken overall command of Sumatra from the ageing and ineffective General Suhardjo. Nasution now occupied the same position in Java, and was directing most of his attention to the guerrilla operations which would follow another Dutch offensive. A major element in this strategy was the immediate return of the hijrah units as soon as the Dutch indicated their repudiation of Renville. It may have been preparations for such a return which alarmed Beel, when he cabled on 12 December that heavy Republican troop concentrations, including 14,000 south of Malang, 'were in a position to throw the Dutch-controlled territory into an untenable situation, at any moment of their choosing'.[3] He estimated that 12,000 Republican soldiers were already inside Dutch-occupied West Java.

Once again the Dutch were drifting towards war more out of frustration with other methods than a clear conception of the objectives to be achieved. Although the pragmatic foreign minister, Stikker, had postponed the grim decision during a visit to Indonesia (October-November), Sassen resumed the initiative when he in turn visited Jakarta at the end of November. To Hatta he made clear his unwillingness to make any concessions for the sake of bringing the Republic into his proposed USI. On 13 December Sassen persuaded the Dutch Cabinet to authorize military destruction of the Republic, although a bitter cabinet crisis arose from his tactics in doing so.[4] By launching a full-scale assault on the Republic at midnight on 18 December, without any serious attempt at compromise, and with the UN Good Offices Committee lodged a few miles from Jogjakarta for discussions with the Republic, Holland flew defiantly and suicidally in the face of world opinion.

Transition to Guerrilla War

This time Jogjakarta was the first Dutch objective. Its airfield was softened by bombing at first light on 19 December, and paratroops were dropped immediately thereafter. By mid-afternoon the Dutch had taken the Republican capital without serious resistance. They also captured Sukarno, Hatta, Sjahrir, and all the members of the cabinet then in Jogjakarta.

The TNI had prepared itself carefully for what it believed to be the inevitable Dutch attack. As Dutch paratroops were landing near Jogjakarta, General Sudirman rose from his sickbed to broadcast:

> We have been attacked. . . . The Dutch government have cancelled the cease-fire agreement. All the Armed Forces will carry out the plans which have been decided on to confront the Dutch attack.[5]

These plans called for strategic retreat from the main centres, scorched earth, and a prolonged guerrilla struggle on both sides of the former Renville line. Although as in 1947 there was grave disorganization and failure of communication, most units do appear to have headed for the positions assigned beforehand. There was little alternative as a refuge.

The political leadership, on the other hand, seemed strangely paralysed. Hatta had intended to lead a guerrilla government in Sumatra when the attack came, but had flown back to Jogjakarta to conduct the crucial negotiations with Sassen. Sukarno had always pledged that he would lead the guerrilla struggle to the last. 19 December confronted them with the most acute choice between diplomasi and perjuangan; between faith in international opinion or Indonesian strength. Predictably, and in terms of the surest path to independence correctly, they chose diplomasi. The Cabinet decided to remain to be captured in Jogjakarta. The presence of the Good Offices Committee at Kaliurang, the hill station above Jogjakarta, provided a powerful guarantee for the safety and the ultimate triumphant release of the Republican leadership. This appears to have tipped the balance in favour of caution. The failure of Sukarno and Hatta even to broadcast any exhortation to resistance,[6] however, was a remarkable testimony to their diplomatic preoccupations. Witnessing their painful hesitation before the Dutch attack, some of the key military officers in Jogjakarta could no longer accept the two men as the unquestioned symbols of the national struggle.

The Dutch offensive proceeded as swiftly and successfully as in 1947. All the large towns of Java were in their hands within a week, and all but a few in Sumatra by the end of December. Only Aceh, in northernmost Sumatra, remained a substantial stronghold for the Republic. Lacking any conceivable base of support in that most militantly Islamic region, Dutch strategists had to rely on the hope that it would drift away from the Republic by itself.

Yet none of Holland's objectives were achieved. Sassen and Beel had hoped that the Republic would disappear, and that pro-

minent former Republicans would come forward to represent the
newly-occupied areas in a federal structure on Dutch terms, as had
happened in East Sumatra and West Java in 1947. Nothing of the
kind took place. The immediate outraged intervention of the UN
Security Council ensured that the Republic continued to live as an
international entity. In the relatively homogeneous Javanese
heartland of the Republic, meanwhile, there were very few prominent
figures willing to break openly with the Republic. The Dutch had
high hopes of the four princely rulers, particularly the Sultan of
Jogjakarta. While his cabinet colleagues were arrested and exiled,
the Sultan was enticed with talk of a revived Mataram empire under
his sway. He continued to exercise his royal functions during the
Dutch occupation, and became indispensable as a channel of
communication between the guerrillas, the exiled leaders, and the
Dutch. In a 21 January statement, however, he carefully condemned
Dutch actions against 'our Republic', and announced his resignation
as head of the region. The inability of the Dutch to govern Jogjakarta without him was a remarkable demonstration of the inter-
dependence of ancient tradition and the revolution.

Only in Tapanuli was there sufficient disenchantment over the
terrorism of rival warlords to create a credible federal movement,
under Mr A. Abas. In general the political gains from the December
offensive were negligible.

Militarily it soon became clear that Holland's acceptance of a
Security Council ceasefire demand, effective from 31 December in
Java and 5 January in Sumatra, was the beginning rather than the
end of the war. The Dutch continued to attack Republican troop
concentrations wherever they could find them, and Republican
guerrillas to harass Dutch troops and Indonesian collaborators. For
both regular TNI units and the irregular units bordering on banditry,
the only alternatives were now guerrilla war or surrender. During
February the Dutch were placed increasingly on the defensive, As a
rule the TNI avoided frontal attacks. On 1 March, however, Lt
Col (later President) Suharto led a major attack on Jogjakarta, and
held most of the city for six hours before Dutch reinforcements
arrived.

The Dutch not only failed to establish effective control over the
newly-conquered areas; their hold over the Renville areas also
deteriorated. The Siliwangi Division completed its celebrated 'long
march' back to designated areas within Pasundan, while the Sungkono Division similarly infiltrated the former Renville line in East
Java. Even in Borneo, guerrillas under Hassan Basry who had
retained their arms in the Hulu Sungei area above Banjermasin
became more active. On 17 May Basry proclaimed himself Republican military governor of South Kalimantan (Borneo).

Alternative Leadership

The detention of its leading members left the Republic's civilian leadership weakly placed to face the guerrilla period. Sukarno was flown to a comfortable place of detention on Lake Toba, with Sjahrir and Agus Salim, while Hatta and other ministers were held on the island of Bangka. Sjafruddin Prawiranegara, the Minister of Prosperity, had flown to Bukittinggi in November, partly to ensure a government presence in Sumatra in the event of war. When he heard by radio about the arrest of the Jogjakarta leaders he proclaimed an emergency government on his own initiative. Only long afterwards he discovered that the cabinet had authorized the despatch of a mandate to the same effect, which he never received.[7] Mr Maramis, the finance minister, was named Foreign Minister in this government since he was safely overseas. The other members were senior officials in Bukittinggi, including two newly-appointed 'Government Commissioners' for Sumatra—Mr Lukman Hakim and Mr T. M. Hasan (the former Sumatran Governor). Armed with a powerful radio transmitter, the Sjafruddin government established contact with Singapore, and gradually also with some guerrilla centres in Java. Nevertheless it was ignored in subsequent negotiations with the Dutch, normally the role *par excellence* of central government. In the areas Sjafruddin and Colonel Hidajat were able to visit—West Sumatra, Tapanuli, and Aceh—it was able to play a co-ordinating as well as a symbolic role. The existance of large areas like Aceh which the Dutch did not penetrate allowed the civilian apparatus in Sumatra to retain some authority. Military government was proclaimed, but in each area it was the former civilian 'strong-man', who became military governor: Daud Beureu'eh in Aceh; Dr Ferdinand Lumbantobing in Tapanuli; Mr St. M. Rasjid in mid-Sumatra and Dr A. K. Gani in South Sumatra.

In Java, however, it was unquestionably the military who 'felt themselves to be "boss" within their respective areas'.[8] Five ministers had been outside the capital on 19 December, and attempted to form a government in Surakarta the following day. However the Dutch advance immediately forced them out of that town and into total reliance on guerrilla units. One of the ministers, Supeno (PSI), was shot by an indiscriminate Dutch patrol on 24 February; another, the ageing Dr Sukiman (MASJUMI), gave himself up in Jogjakarta. The remaining ministers, Mr Susanto Tirtoprodjo (PNI), Kasimo (Catholic), and K. H. Masjkur (MASJUMI), were appointed a commissariat of the emergency government for Java, when Sjafruddin eventually made contact with them in May 1949. In the meantime they acted as propagandists and occasionally advisers for the military, rather than as leaders.

More decisively even than the violent months of 1945–6, the guerrilla period placed power in the hands of those able to lead and inspire fighting units. Colonel Nasution, just thirty years old, established a headquarters in Prambanan, where on 22 December he decreed 'a military administration. . . for the whole of the island of Java' in his capacity as territorial commander for that region. Officers were sent off in various directions with detailed instructions for the conduct of this military government.[9] Military respect for civilian authority was gravely weakened during this period, with results that have been obvious ever since. That the army did not immediately seize power after independence was due in part to the influence of a few key officers with Dutch training and strong political ties, but primarily to its own lack of internal unity. In practice Nasution's headquarters was unable to co-ordinate activity even in Java, and initiative rested more than ever with the unit commander. The only military figure of sufficient status to rally and unite the army was General Sudirman, who was moved about in a litter in the Pacitan area east of Jogjakarta during the guerrilla resistance. But he was too ill with tuberculosis (which killed him in January 1950) to make any serious bid for national leadership.

In terms of the sense of identity between élite townspeople and the rural mass, the guerrilla period was a climax to the whole revolutionary process. Army officers, politicians, officials, and refugees of all sorts from the occupied cities were thrown on the hospitality of uneducated villagers. The contact was not always without friction, but its impact on both sides was profound. For many villagers the presence of these refugees and their cat-and-mouse encounters with Dutch patrols was the first real experience of revolution. Some of the townspeople organized schools and development projects in the villages, and even encouraged distribution of village or plantation land to poor peasants in order to encourage commitment to the Republican cause. For the townspeople themselves the guerrilla supremely symbolized the hardship, the comradeship, and the solidarity of the common struggle. Most powerfully affected were perhaps the Tentara Pelajar of Central and East Java, most of whom were still at school during the 1945–6 upheavals, but who by 1949 formed an enthusiastic and disciplined volunteer army of the young élite. The solidarity which the guerrilla period forged between these future leaders and young army officers, and the populist legitimacy it seemed to confer upon the leadership of both, were important elements in post-independence national life.

Tan Malaka and the Left
The only politicians adequately equipped and motivated to contest

leadership of the resistance with the Army were those of the Left. Both Tan Malaka and Amir Sjarifuddin had long championed their respective conceptions of total people's war, and both had substantial support in the TNI and various irregular units. After Madiun, however, co-operation between PKI/FDR remnants and the TNI officer corps was impossible in the affected parts of Java.[10] On the second day of the Dutch attack (20 December 1948) Amir Sjarifuddin, Maruto Darusman, Suripno, Sardjono, Major General Djokosujono, and more than fifty other prominent communist captives were shot, presumably on the orders of the local TNI commander Gatot Subroto.[11] The military and political leadership of the Left was decimated. Although thousands of less important communist captives were released to join the guerrilla resistance, it would have taken years for them to rebuild party organization and a strong military base in Java. The Sumatra party had lost neither as a result of Madiun, and a number of TNI units were under its influence. The Sumatran PKI leader Xarim M.S. attached himself to the TNI units under his son's command in eastern Aceh, and Nathar Zainuddin to those of Bedjo in Tapanuli. Yet these men were ideologically closer to Tan Malaka than to Musso. Moreover they lacked the mass base of the PKI in Java. No serious challenge to the Republican leadership could arise from the Sumatran PKI.

For Tan Malaka the guerrilla period offered a wonderful opportunity. His uncompromising strategy of people's war appeared to be completely justified by the Dutch attack. His book *Gerpolek* (a syncronym of guerrilla, politics, and economics) was completed in prison in May 1949, in time to serve as a handbook of guerrilla warfare for many officers, not excluding Nasution.[12] With Sukarno, Hatta, and the PKI leadership out of the way by 20 December, Tan Malaka became the pre-eminent revolutionary leader in the Republic. On 21 December he was able to make a stirring call to total war over Radio Kediri, before that city fell to the Dutch. The utter bankruptcy of the diplomasi policy, he proclaimed, was now apparent to all. 'I shall lead the fight against the Dutch to the bitter end.'

Nevertheless Tan Malaka continued to suffer from his lack of immediate organizational backing. Had he been able to renew his former alliance with Sudirman in the Jogjakarta area, he might have succeeded in overthrowing the policy of negotiation. The guerrilla period found him, however, in East Java, where he obtained the support and protection of the TNI Sabaruddin battalion. In February 1948 this battalion was defeated in internecine battle with other TNI units. Tan Malaka was captured, and executed on the orders of Col Sungkono. Whether local warlordism or loyalty to the existing Republican leadership had the greater role in his killing remains obscure. In either case, the military had eliminated their last serious rival to effective leadership of the resistance. The ideas and to some extent the legend of Tan Malaka lived on in the 'People's Army' of Chaerul Saleh in South Banten, and in Sumatra, without providing any alternative for leadership of the Republic.

Darul Islam

Islamic dissenters were more numerous, if less organized, than those of the Left. In rural areas of traditional Muslim orientation, the religious teacher was the most powerful catalyst for involving the peasant mass in militant support for the freedom struggle. However, the appeal to a holy war and a glorious martyrdom could only be sustained in an atmosphere of crisis such as that which had prevailed at the end of 1945. This atmosphere was partially recaptured in the guerrilla period. The official Republic was no longer in a position to curb the 'holy war' mentality as it had in 1945.

The destruction of the traditional secular élite in Aceh during its 'social revolution', and the complete ascendancy of the ulama under Daud Beureu'eh, made that a unique area. During the first Dutch action of 1947 the central government had already appointed Daud Beureu'eh military governor of a 'special military region' of Aceh and Karoland in order to ensure the maximum mobilization of Aceh's well-known Islamic ardour in defence of the Republic. He was the only man with neither Dutch nor Japanese training to receive such a high appointment during the revolution. The second Dutch action strengthened his remarkable position still further. Sjafruddin's emergency government was in the position of guest rather than master of the military governor. It formalized the concentration of local power in his hands by abolishing the civilian North Sumatra government altogether on 16 May. The homogeneity and intensity of the Islamic revolution in Aceh gave the government no alternative.

In Java there was greater room for conflict between the TNI and guerrillas fighting on a traditional 'holy war' basis. The only substantial area where such Muslim forces held the advantage was Dutch-occupied West Java, which the Siliwangi Division had evacuated after Renville. This enabled the militant Islamic forces centred in the southeastern part of that province to emerge as an ideological as well as military challenge to the national leadership.

Leading this movement was S. M. Kartosuwirjo, a Dutch-educated politician whose militant pursuit of the Muslim State ideal had already brought about his resignation from the PSII (Sarekat Islam) in 1939. By 1947 Kartosuwirjo had a powerful following in the Garut-Tasikmalaya area, based partly on his prominence within the very loose structure of MASJUMI (whose first national secretary he had become in 1945) and partly on his *Institut Suffah* which had been training Muslim youths in military as well as spiritual matters since Japanese times. At the commencement of each of the Dutch offensives Kartosuwirjo proclaimed an uncompromising holy war. A fervent opponent of diplomasi, he resigned from MASJUMI in January 1948 in order to be free to continue fighting the Dutch despite the Republic's signature of the Renville agreement. His *Tentara Islam Indonesia* (Indonesian Islamic Army) came to control the rural areas in most of the eastern section of West Java/Pasundan after the departure of the Siliwangi Division. He now broke all contact with the Republic, and in May 1948 proclaimed himself *Imam* of a distinct *Negara Islam Indonesia* (Indonesian Islamic State), organized on what he held to be Koranic lines.

The TNI and Jogjakarta could afford initially to ignore this challenge. When the Rukman battalion returned to West Java in September 1948, however, it was surprised to find it had to dispute control of territory as much with Kartosuwirjo's forces, popularly known as the *Darul Islam*,[13] as with the Dutch. The fall of Jogjakarta and the return of the Siliwangi Division to West Java brought the conflict to a head. Kartosuwirjo did not mince his words:[14]

> The Republic has been wiped out and no longer has any authority or power. Therefore we must destroy all its authority and power, and in the first place its Armed Forces; give them no mercy any longer . . .

Despite its grandiose claims, the Darul Islam was in practice regionally based. During the guerrilla period it gained the upper hand against the TNI only in the 'Three Regions' (Tegal-Brebes) and Banyumas areas in addition to its original base in Garut and Tasikmalaya. On the national level its significance was in providing the first radical alternative to both the theory and the structure of the Republic—a potential pole of attraction for the whole santri community.

The Collapse of Dutch Strategy

The final Dutch onslaught against the Republic was an unmitigated disaster for the Netherlands. Dutch strategy had gambled on a sufficiently rapid movement from Republican to federalist ranks after the offensive to convince the United Nations that the Republic was no longer a meaningful party to negotiations. The failure of any prominent Republicans to defect, the liveliness of guerrilla resistance, and the immediate protest resignation of the NIT and Pasundan cabinets, demonstrated precisely the reverse. Moreover the distrust with which Dutch policies were regarded in the United Nations was exacerbated by a transparent uncertainty of direction within the

Dutch government. Particularly embarrassing was the discovery by the UN Good Offices Committee on 16 January that the conditions under which Republican leaders were confined in Bangka bore no relation whatever to the expansive statements being made on Holland's behalf in New York.

The Security Council Resolution of 28 January 1948 marked the defeat of Dutch plans and the turning point in the Republic's struggle for international recognition. The resolution demanded the restoration of Republican leaders to their state functions in Jogjakarta, followed by the formation of an interim USI government as envisaged by Linggajati and Renville before 15 March 1949. The UN itself was to supervise each step in the negotiations, up to an eventual transfer of full sovereignty not later than 1 July 1950.

The most crushing blow for Holland was that the leading sponsor of this resolution was the United States, the economic backbone of the postwar western world. US Marshall Aid to the Netherlands Indies had been suspended immediately following the Dutch offensive, while in February 1950 a resolution was tabled in the US Senate to suspend aid to the Netherlands itself. Negotiations were in progress for the establishment of NATO, making the American alliance the cornerstone of Dutch foreign policy. Much as both Right and Left in the Netherlands might complain about a humiliating capitulation to the American colossus, the Dutch government could not afford to stand firm.

Restoration of the Republic to Jogjakarta was rightly feared in The Hague, because it would symbolize for Indonesians the ultimate ineffectiveness of Dutch military superiority. To avert this prospect the 'Beel plan' was evolved whereby a round table conference of Indonesian (including Republican) and Dutch representatives would negotiate for the direct transfer of sovereignty to a USI by 1 May 1949. By eliminating the interim government they had previously insisted upon and accelerating the transfer of sovereignty, the Dutch leaders hoped to divert the demand for restoration of *de facto* Republican power.

The Security Council refused to budge on this central issue, although accepting other Dutch points. Under economic pressure from the United States and military pressure from guerrillas in Java and Sumatra, the Netherlands finally accepted this bitter cup in April 1949. The Republic would be restored to Jogjakarta, provided prior informal discussions with its captive leaders established a viable basis for the rapid formation of the USI as suggested in the Beel plan. In the so-called 'Van Royen—Roem' statements of 7 May, Sukarno and Hatta privately undertook to instruct a ceasefire on their return to Jogjakarta, while the Dutch accepted the principle of the Republic's participation as a functioning state in the round table conference. The Dutch would also refrain from forming any further federal states (thus ending the hopes of the federal movement in Tapanuli), and would accept the legitimacy of Republican government officials still active in former Republican territory.

Return to Jogjakarta

Because the Sultan of Jogjakarta was able to act as the Republic's representative from his impregnable base within the *kraton*, it was possible to overcome the practical problems of the Republic's resumption of authority by 6 July 1949. The return of Sukarno and Hatta to the city was celebrated with moving solemnity. This was the symbolic point of victory fore-ordained in the Security Council resolution of January. In Indonesia 6 July has continued to be celebrated as a national holiday, while the date of the formal transfer of sovereignty six months later is largely forgotten. The dramatic reconstitution of a Republican government responsible for its own armed forces left no-one in doubt who the final victors would be.

Nevertheless the return to Jogjakarta involved an immediate crisis for the Republican leadership. The gulf between diplomasi and perjuangan, between politicians and soldiers, had grown so deep during the guerrilla period that it was an open question whether it could ever be bridged. TNI spokesmen made no secret of their view that the politicians had betrayed the total guerrilla struggle, which they felt to be succeeding:

> Real attention must be given lest the guerrillas can be shaken, influenced by party ideologies or by political party members. What we want is only to be free, or to die . . . Free from all political currents, we must will this: *As long as the Dutch are here, guerrilla warfare will never end.*[15]

To this school of thought the Van Royen–Roem undertakings were anathema. They emanated from prisoners of the Dutch who had already given up the struggle. A week before they were announced, General Sudirman had warned his field commanders sharply against thinking thoughts of peace:

> Do not forget that the bitter suffering since 19 December 1948 has come about because a large proportion of our leaders, both civil and military, have forgotten that the Dutch are fully armed before our gates.

The army must fight on, trusting Sudirman himself to see that the politicians did not betray the spirit of freedom.[16]

After 6 July the General showed obvious reluctance to leave his guerrilla headquarters for a meeting with Sukarno. He consented only after the Sultan, Colonel Simatupang and Colonel Gatot Subroto had pleaded with him to avoid any premature and irreparable rupture. When on 1 August Sukarno and Hatta issued the 'cease-hostilities' order they had promised, Sudirman signed a letter of resignation. It was sorrow over the inconstancy of the national leadership, he declared, which had brought about both Urip Sumohardjo's premature death and his own grave illness.[17] The letter was withdrawn only after Sukarno in turn threatened to resign, throwing the Republic into certain chaos.

The guerrillas made their point by mounting their heaviest attack on 10 August, just before the cease-hostilities order had to take effect. For two days they took control of most of Surakarta, attacking Dutch troops in the streets. Clashes between Dutch troops and ex-guerrillas continued to be frequent during the last half of 1949, involving even the normally pro-government Tentara Pelajar. Groups like the Darul Islam, which insisted that the struggle continue, gained further adherents. Ending the revolution would be more difficult than beginning it.

Federal Indonesia

Since 1947 the older-established federal states had moved steadily to the Left. With the subsidence of the perceived threat from pemuda militants, federal politicians grew more impatient of the entrenched conservatism of old colonial hands, and more anxious to keep up with the pace set by the Republic. By the end of 1948 both the NIT and Pasundan had exchanged recognition and contacts with the Republic within the Renville framework. They needed the Republic's participation in negotiations, or at least its existence, as a balance to Dutch power. When Holland demonstrated on 19 December its determination to eliminate the Republic by force, the Cabinets of both these states resigned.

This was a devastating blow to Dutch attempts to build a 'co-operative' alternative to the Republic. In subsequent negotiations the Dutch could no longer expect automatic support from the federal states. Pasundan, which experienced to the full the pressure of Republican and Darul Islam guerrillas, had considerable difficulty even forming a new government acceptable both to its pro-Republican Parliament and to the Dutch. During the 1949 negotiations its position was very close to the Republic's.

Dutch setbacks in the United Nations and in the guerrilla struggle shifted federal opinion yet further. Even before the return to Jogjakarta it was apparent that the ideas symbolized by the Republic had prevailed over the military and technical superiority of the Dutch. The federalists would therefore have to come to terms directly with Jogjakarta. In the second half of July 1949 they did

just that, in an 'Inter-Indonesian Conference' in Jakarta and Jogjakarta without Dutch interference. The most significant bargain
struck was that no new armed forces would be formed by states
constituting the new federal Indonesia, leaving the existing TNI to
become its military core.

With this basis of agreement the two Indonesian delegations
to the round table conference in The Hague (August-November 1949)
were able to present a relatively united front. On the two hardest-
fought issues, the assumption by Indonesia of Netherlands Indian
debts, and Holland's refusal to allow West New Guinea to join the
new state, the federal delegation proved to be at least as tough
nationalists as their erstwhile rivals from the Republic.

On 27 December 1949 the Netherlands transferred full sovereignty
over former Netherlands India to a federal state known officially as
the Republik Indonesia Serikat (Federal Indonesian Republic) or
RIS. Only in West New Guinea did Holland retain control, its
status remaining unsettled. The carefully balanced constitution of
the RIS gave two-thirds of its legislature's seats to federal representatives. Nevertheless it had become increasingly clear that it was
Jogjakarta which had triumphed and its politicians who would
dominate the new state. A substantial minority of federal representatives had always considered themselves pro-Jogjakarta, and most
were prepared to acknowledge the political primacy of the battle-
hardened Republicans. No federal politicians could compare in
stature with Sukarno and Hatta, who were elected President and
Prime Minister respectively of the RIS before the transfer of
sovereignty. Only five of Hatta's fifteen RIS ministers were from
non-Republican areas, and only the former NIT premier Anak Agung
held a key portfolio (the Interior).

The Destruction of Federalism

The whole federal structure which Dutch, Indonesian, and United
Nations negotiators had battled to erect ever since 1946 disappeared
within eight months of its inauguration. For many convinced
Republicans the RIS was only tolerable as a stepping stone to the
true aim of the revolution, the unitary Republic proclaimed in 1945.
Whether or not Anderson is right in stressing 'the sense that one-ness
is power and multiplicity is diffusion and weakness' in the Javanese
mind,[18] four years fighting and propaganda against the federal
schemes of the Dutch had established this association. The RIS
settlement had been a compromise, the typical fruit of diplomasi,
which stood in the way of a complete and satisfying victory over the
Dutch.

Not only the Dutch, however, were aware of the cultural diversity
of Indonesia, which far exceeded that of any other post-colonial

state which has attempted a unitary structure. Prime Minister Hatta was among the Indonesian leaders who felt the need for great caution in demolishing federalism. It was the weakness of some of the federal states themselves which provided the initial impetus for the unitary tide. In Java and Sumatra the states erected by the Dutch had patently been defined by the ceasefire line rather than by natural geographic or cultural boundaries. They lacked the substance to provide any sort of balance to the Republic in those two islands. Federalists had belatedly attempted to stimulate a more broadly based 'Sumatran' regional identity, inviting even the militant and unconquered Acehnese to participate in a *Muktamar Sumatera* (Sumatra Congress) in March-April 1949. By then however the Dutch strategy was played out, and the Acehnese and other republicans did not attend. The federal states of East and South Sumatra were in reality based on purely local political antagonisms, not on fear of Javanese domination of the nation.

The NIT and the federal states in Borneo had a more realistic basis. They too, however, experienced the powerful pressures unleashed with the transfer of sovereignty on 27 December. Republican refugees returned to their homes in Dutch-occupied areas; Republican guerrillas came down from the hills; Republican prisoners were released from Dutch jails.[19] To all of these the federal states represented an intolerable denial of their victory. Others who had chosen to remain in the Dutch-occupied cities, often justifying their decision by the need to retain a Republican presence there, had now to prove their point. Movements arose in the capitals of all the states agitating for their dissolution. Parties and trade unions competed in showing their zeal. In Java particularly, a number of officials announced that they would follow instructions from Jogjakarta rather than the state they officially served.

Even if the state governments had had the will to resist this movement, they had not the power. Dutch soldiers could not be used for such a task. Only East Sumatra had its own military force, the *Barisan Pengawal*, but its officers too were Dutch. The backbone of the federal states had been a Dutch-led military and administrative machine and its removal left them flabby and lifeless.

The demise of the federal states was speeded by a desperate effort to save them on the part of Westerling, the already notorious counter-insurgency specialist from South Sulawesi. On 23 January 1950 he organized an abortive coup in Bandung and Jakarta with the apparent aim of shifting the military balance against the TNI in West Java and killing the most anti-federal members of the RIS Cabinet. The effect, however, was to reduce still further the possibility of KNIL or ex-KNIL forces playing a role in the maintenance of order, and to increase suspicion of Pasundan, whence the coup had been mobilized. By the end of March most of the state assemblies had acted to dissolve their states into the unitary Republic of Jogjakarta. In Java, in South Sumatra, and in South and East Borneo, there was no serious resistance to this movement. In West Borneo Abdul Hamid II, Sultan of Pontianak and a RIS minister, had genuine support. His arrest on 5 April for complicity in the Westerling affair, however, brought about the collapse of that state.

Only the NST (East Sumatra) and the NIT stood against the current. The unitary movement was unusually strong in Medan, the NST capital. The ethnic bitterness arising from the 'social revolution' of 1946, however, steeled the state government against any voluntary surrender of power. In the eyes of the Malay and Simelungun aristocrats who led the NST, unitarism would mean certain domination by 'alien' ethnic groups and possibly a repetition of bloodshed. For NIT politicians, on the other hand, their state was simply a fact. There was no republican structure there to rival its legitimacy; there had been little militant opposition except in South Sulawesi and Bali; and a remarkably thorough election by the standards of the day had been carried through late in 1949.

The downfall of the NIT, and with it of the whole federal structure, required pressure from three sides: from without, in the TNI-based RIS army, backed by Sukarno and the Sultan of Jogjakarta as Defence Minister; from within, in the threat of lawlessness in South Sulawesi and Bali in particular; and from another Westerling-style incident. The incident arose in a climate of suspicion between the predominantly Ambonese KNIL units in Makassar and elements of the TNI sent there to organize the formation of a RIS army in the region. On 5 April Captain Andi Abdul Aziz, commander of an ex-KNIL unit which had nominally joined the RIS army, led a coup which imprisoned the TNI officers already in Makassar and prevented the expected landing of TNI reinforcements from Java. Although Aziz was quickly obliged to climb down, his move did much to discredit the NIT government, especially its conservative Ambonese Justice Minister, Dr Soumokil. A crisis quickly developed leading to the formation of a new NIT 'liquidation cabinet' on 9 May. Dr Soumokil, a bitter opponent of the Republic, fled to Ambon where he led his people to proclaim the independence of the 'Republic of the South Moluccas' on 25 April.

This was the first serious regional revolt to emerge from the independence settlement, and the only one to arise from former federal ranks. Loyally pro-Dutch Ambonese representatives had with difficulty been induced even to accept a role within the NIT in 1946. The prospect of losing their federal autonomy, their special position in the KNIL, and their links with Holland all at once was too much to bear. Jakarta only established its control over Ceram and Amboina after a tough military campaign from July to November 1950. The TNI expeditionary force made very slow headway against resolute and locally popular Ambonese units, even though outnumbering them about eight to one.[20] Nevertheless the national leadership made sure of final victory, serving notice that challenges to the new unity of the nation would not be taken lightly.

The NIT and with it inevitably the small NST were finally dissolved only on the fifth anniversary of the original Republic, 17 August 1950. The two states refused simply to merge into the Jogjakarta Republic as other states had done. On 17 August they surrendered their powers to a new unitary Republic of Indonesia. In its parliamentary constitution the new state was closely akin to the RIS, but in its popular imagery it was a linear continuation of the 1945 Republic.

In the meantime parts of eastern Indonesia were experiencing some of the revolutionary pressures which they had been spared in 1945-6. In Bali and in South Sulawesi militant pemuda groups appeared again, identifying with the remnant of guerrilla forces which had held out in the hills of both regions. They attacked the local organs of NIT government, particularly those rajas and chiefs regarded as Dutch collaborators, such as the puppet ruler with whom the Dutch had replaced the Raja of Bone in 1946. The complex structure of local government, which in these two areas relied heavily on the traditional monarchies, appeared to be dissolving by June 1950 in a wave of terror and lawlessness. A new NIT law was rushed through on 15 June, transferring effective powers to representative assemblies at the level of both the region (*daerah*) and the petty kingdom (*kerajaan* or *swapraja*), in a manner which at least superficially resembled Jogjakarta's Law 22 of 1948. The power of the rajas was dramatically undermined. Because they shared in the discredit now attaching to the whole Dutch-created federal fabric, kingdoms were falling which had seemed unshakeable even in 1945. The institution of raja, now formally powerless despite its undoubted strength in the peasant mind, endured only until 1952 in South Sulawesi and a few years later in Bali and the Lesser Sunda Islands.

Stopping the Revolution

> *National Revolution stimulates and embraces elements who cannot distinguish means from ends, reality from an ideal, who believe that every change has to be by revolution.*
>
> Hatta, 5 October 1951[21]

The destruction of the old order had been remarkably complete, largely because Dutch attempts to bolster it had had the opposite effect. Only Ambon had provided serious opposition to the revolutionary settlement of 1950 from the Right. Much more challenging were the unsatisfied demands of various mutually irreconcilable elements within the revolutionary movement, for which the movement to destroy the Dutch-made federal system was only a temporary focus.

Workers naturally sought to obtain both the material and emotional rewards of independence from Dutch employers who had begun to operate under the shelter of Dutch arms and federal laws. 1950 was the worst year for strikes in Indonesian history. In East Sumatra, Indonesia's most important centre of export production, estates were hampered in addition by 'illegal' occupation of land. Former plantation labourers and immigrants from land-hungry Tapanuli took land for rice cultivation as their *hadiah revolusi* (prize of the revolution) from seasonally idle plantation land. This breaking up of plantation land had been occurring since Japanese times (when it had been officially encouraged to bolster food production), but the collapse of the East Sumatran State gave it a new dimension. The State had been portrayed by both its supporters and opponents as a dam against the irruption into wealthy East Sumatra of the dynamic Toba Batak people from their poverty-stricken homeland. The 'bursting' of this dam, together with the shift of Republican government personnel from Sibolga (in Tapanuli) to Medan, drew hundreds of thousands of Tobas into East Sumatra in the 1950s. Many of them occupied plantation land from which it was politically impossible to remove them.

To disarm guerrillas and return them to productive civilian life was a problem of still greater urgency. The TNI was forced to accept far more of them on its permanent payroll than the nation could afford. Others rejected demobilization for a life outside the law, whether or not they assumed the label of one of the movements rejecting government authority on ideological grounds. The largest of the latter was the Darul Islam, which held much of rural West Java to ransom in the early 1950s. Most of the smaller groups in Java, like the Tan Malaka-inclined People's Army in South Banten, the leftist 'Merapi-Merbabu Complex' groups near Surakarta, and the rural-Islamic *Angkatan Umat Islam* in Kebumen, were crushed militarily during 1950. In South Sulawesi and Bali banditry continued long after the fall of the NIT.

Any knowledgeable observer in 1945 would have agreed with Van Mook's calculation that the weakness of the Republic would lie in the centrifugal force of its divergent regions and peoples. The revolution had brought about a truly remarkable transformation. In practice each region had been on its own in the struggle to establish a republican state apparatus and resist the Dutch. The brunt of the struggle, however, had been borne by Java. Far from experiencing

Javanese domination, pemuda revolutionaries looked longingly to that island for inspiration and assistance, and accepted what little guidance came from the capital more enthusiastically than that which came from their own older leaders. The emphasis placed by the Dutch on ethnic fears, moreover, had associated the profession of such fears with treason against the independence struggle.

The weaknesses of the republican movement outside Java in 1945-6 became sources of strength for post-1950 unity. History had, indeed, been unkind to the established politicians of eastern Indonesia and Borneo. Conditions there had been so different from Java in 1945 that the natural path to independence had seemed to lie in co-operation with Dutch designs. Yet the sweeping away of these regional politicians in 1950 opened the way to younger men who had spent the revolution in Java, in the hills, or in Dutch jails, and who were fervently imbued with the ideals of Jogjakarta. Even in Sumatra few local leaders of permanent stature had arisen in the revolution, so intense had been the factionalism between ethnic groups, *pasukans*, and generations.

This explains the apparent paradox that the strongest regional challenges to the central government in the 1950s came from just those elements who had fought most tenaciously and successfully for the Republic during the revolution. The pemudas of South Sulawesi had been in a sense 'more Republican than Jogjakarta' in their determination to fight the Dutch-backed NIT. Many of these same pemudas took part in a drawn-out resistance to government authority during the 1950s, led by Kahar Muzakkar, a fiery Muhammadiah-educated Bugis from Luwu who had co-ordinated guerrilla training in Java for Sulawesi pemudas. Although this revolt began in July 1950 over post-revolutionary problems of demobilization and military rank, it eventually associated itself with *Darul Islam*.

Similarly in Sumatra it was Aceh, a model of resistance to the Dutch, which provided the greatest challenge to central authority. The very completeness of Aceh's 'social revolution' had eliminated from local power the Dutch-educated élite which elsewhere assumed leadership without question. This set Aceh apart from even the Islamic politicians of the capital. When the Acehnese religious leader and erstwhile military governor, Daud Beureu'eh, made his demand in late 1949 for the Islamic state which had been put off for four years in the interests of revolutionary solidarity, it rang very ominously in Jogjakarta. The central government went ahead with the 1949 Jogjakarta programme of local government, giving autonomy to the three provinces of North, Central and South Sumatra rather than to the residencies which coincided better with ethnic and linguistic realities in Sumatra. Acehnese leaders argued that their role in the guerrilla period deserved better recompense than absorption into what they called a 'Batak-dominated' North Sumatran province. Although Aceh's full-scale revolt was not launched until 1953, it was already foreshadowed in a demand for provincial status passed by its assembly on 12 August 1950.

Insofar as the aim of the revolution was to establish a united, sovereign Indonesia led by secular nationalist intellectuals, it came to a successful conclusion on 17 August 1950. In contrast to five years of uncertainty and upheaval, the period which followed was relatively stable in terms of political structure. The social pressures released by revolution, however, were neither suppressed nor satisfied. Many had been caught up in the fervour, the passions, and the hopes of the revolution, but only a few appeared to be enjoying its fruits. Marxists argued that the revolution had been betrayed and aborted; Muslims that it had received a hollow secular expression; nationalists that its enemy was still entrenched in economic privilege. The romantic pemuda vision was increasingly revived in Sukarno's rhetoric of unity, struggle, and sacrifice. The spirit of the revolution continued to live in a dozen divergent but passionate forms, at least until the terrible crisis of 1965–6 drove them all out of sight.

References

1 Cited Kahin, p. 393.
2 *Siliwangi dari masa kemasa*, Jakarta, 1968, p. 287. Cf. *ibid.*, pp. 227–9 and Alers, pp. 203–4.
3 Smit, *De liquidatie van een imperium*, p. 137.
4 This critical decision, which led to an attempted resignation by the premier, is well described in *ibid.*, pp. 135–40.
5 Cited in *Siliwangi dari masa kemasa*, p. 279.
6 Simatupang, p. 17, reports that he persuaded Hatta to sign a brief statement that the struggle must go on, while Kahin, pp. 393–5, cites short speeches by Sukarno and Hatta, and a longer one by Natsir, which the leaders were said to have prepared but not broadcast.
7 Interview with Sjafruddin, 20-7-1972, and Simatupang, p. 219. Cf. Kahin. p. 382, and Nasution, *Sedjarah Perdjuangan Nasional dibidang Bersendjata*, Jakarta, 1966, p. 149n.
8 Iwa Kusuma Sumantri, *Sedjarah Revolusi Indonesia* Vol. II, p. 201n.
9 Nasution, *Fundamentals of Guerrilla Warfare*, pp. 119–28.
10 A 9 May 1949 appeal by Sudirman to the PKI/FDR and its enemies in the Ponorogo area to bury the past and unite is evidence both of this tension and of Sudirman's characteristic desire to overcome it; Feith and Castles, pp. 364–5. Nasution, *Fundamentals of Guerrilla Warfare*, p. 131, mentions several abortive communist attempts to kill him during guerrilla operations in the Solo area, as well as successful attacks on two of his officers.
11 Aidit was subsequently anxious to lay the blame for these killings at the feet of Hatta and MASJUMI, though not of course Sukarno; *Aidit Accuses. Madiun Affair*, Jakarta, 1955, passim. Mass executions, however, particularly of élite politicians, were not to the taste of either Sukarno or Hatta,

and it seems unlikely that they could have had either the opportunity or the heart for this before their capture on 19 December.

12 Nasution, *TNI* Vol. II, p.p. 216–26, quotes it extensively.

13 Literally 'The house of Islam'; i.e. that portion of the world under legitimate Islamic government.

14 Decree of the Indonesian Islamic State, n.d. translated in Nasution, *Fundamentals of Guerrilla Warfare*, p. 150.

15 Instruction of Lt Col Slamet Rijadi, 23 March 1949, translated in *ibid.*, p. 225.

16 Advice of Sudirman to all commanders, 1 May 1949, as cited in Simatupang, pp. 129–30. Later publications follow Nasution, *TNI* Vol. I, pp. 12–13, in omitting the section quoted. Feith and Castles, pp. 364–5, translate an even later appeal to struggle by Sudirman.

17 The letter is reproduced in Nasution, *TNI* Vol. I, pp. 18–20.

18 Benedict Anderson, 'The idea of power in Javanese culture', in Claire Holt, (ed.), *Culture and Politics in Indonesia*, Ithaca, 1972, pp. 22–3.

19 12,000 prisoners were released between 10 August and 27 December 1949. Herbert Feith, *The Decline of Constitutional Democracy in Indonesia*, Ithaca, 1962, p. 61n.

20 Nasution, *Fundamentals of Guerrilla Warfare*, pp. 27 and 78–9.

21 Mohammad Hatta, *Kumpulan Karangan* Vol. IV, Jakarta, 1954, p. 171.

CONCLUSION

The National Revolution in Indonesian History
The historical process described in these pages formed part, and a
crucial part, of the world-wide rejection of colonialism following the
Second World War. Indonesia's successful blend of force and
diplomacy was influential well beyond its borders. The mix had
proved no less potent for being largely fortuitous. Without pemuda
courage in confronting Western arms and raising the spectre of
anarchy, Republican diplomats would have been crying unheeded
in the wilderness. A comparison with Vietnam or Malaya, however,
where comparable courage was expended but freedom long denied,
illustrates the remarkable superiority of Indonesian diplomacy. It
was only in part a deliberate diplomatic calculation to keep leadership of the Indonesian independence movement in non-communist
hands, unlike the Vietnamese or Malayan. Yet this was a vital
diplomatic card, indispensible for the American support which made
victory possible in 1949.

In this book, however, it is the internal dimension of the revolution
which has been of primary concern. The revolution provided the
reference point and legitimation for all the major trends in Indonesian
political life, whether Sukarno's 'guided democracy', the army's role
in power, communist or Islamic pursuit of the just society, the
constitutional pattern of the nation, or the political style of the
élite. It released unsuspected new forces, evident as much in
Indonesian art and writing as in the intense demand for education
and modernization. For the generation aged below thirty in 1945, in
particular, the revolution was an intense personal liberation, shaking
conventional standards and restraints and making all things
possible.

170

The term 'revolution' has been officially discouraged in Indonesia recently as a description of the events 1945–50. Nevertheless a revolution it was. The process begun in August-September 1945 in Java and Sumatra was not simply the capture of an administrative machine by a few nationalist politicians, but the temporary destruction of that machine by widespread popular forces beyond any leader's control. Unlike most revolutions, however, this one moved slightly to the Right rather than the Left over the five year period. The key leaders rightly saw in such a move a quicker path to independence. They were able to bring it about because appeals to unity and loyalty were traditionally persuasive, and because the radicalizing forces were neither adequately organized nor sure of their direction.

What then was the fruit of the revolution? It destroyed a colonial polity controlled from the other side of the world, with its racial castes, its anachronistic, powerless rajas, its rigid social categories. It released tremendous energies and aspirations. It did not, however, succeed in dynamizing the peasant majority of Indonesia's population, or substantially improving their lot. Only a few Indonesians were able to take a larger role in the nation's commerce.

If the 'social revolution' proved elusive, so did Sjahrir's 'democratic revolution'. A parliamentary democratic system was erected in 1950, but it had little vigour. The thrust of the revolution had not been against the tyranny of the *ancien régime* (except to a limited extent in its harsher Japanese form), but against its racial exclusiveness. In the absence of a genuine Indonesian bourgeoisie, the Dutch-educated intelligentsia who led the independent government became, as a class, heavily dependent on the state. The status and strategic situation of the Republican government undermined the concern for self-reliance which had been a feature of the pre-war nationalist movement. By 1953, 2·8 million Indonesians were estimated to be employed by the central government, a more than fourfold increase over 1940. The aim of all the strongest elements within the revolution had been a central government at least as powerful as that of pre-war Netherlands India. Yet the revolution had destroyed the legitimacy of both the old legal structure and the bureaucracy which enforced it. The 1949–50 compromise with the Dutch had postponed any final reckoning between the new revolutionary forces—army, communists, Muslims, and Sukarno—any one of which might have created a new basis for state power. Drift and uncertainty therefore marked the immediate post-revolutionary decade.

Already in 1950, however, the most remarkable achievement of the revolution was apparent—the creation of a united nation. In 1945 similar revolutionary processes had begun independently and without central direction in a dozen scattered parts of Indonesia. Because of their relative weakness and isolation, the revolutionary forces in the outlying areas had voluntarily and enthusiastically accepted the leadership of 'national' politicians in Java. In a remarkable way the Japanese policy of isolating the outer islands from the political progress of Java, and the Dutch abortive attempt to exploit distrust of Java, served the same ultimate purpose of driving Indonesia together. The only political leaders able to play an important role in post-revolutionary Indonesia were those who shared the vital, compelling bond of struggle in the cause of the Republic. Regional problems were by no means resolved in 1950, but a powerful Indonesian identity had been forged, which ensured that all such problems would find their solution in the context of one nation.

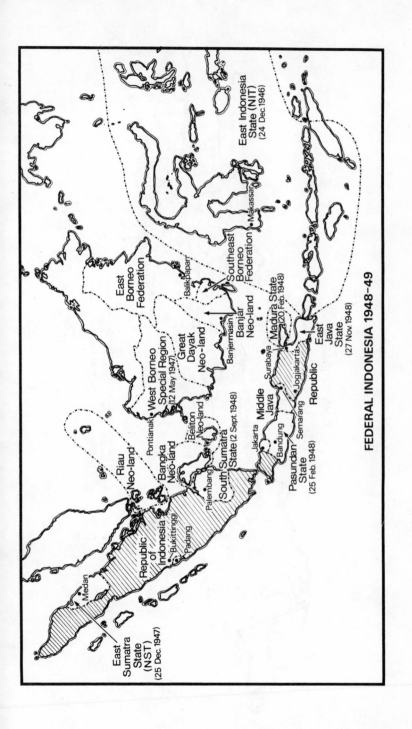

FEDERAL INDONESIA 1948–49

Medan

East Sumatra
State (NST)
(25 Dec.1947)

Bukittinggi
Padang

Republic
of
Indonesia

Riau
Neo·land

Bangka
Neo·land

Beliton
Neo·land

Pontianak·West Borneo
Special Region
(12 May 1947)

Palembang

South Sumatra
State (2 Sept.1948)

Great
Dayak
Neo·land

East
Borneo
Federation

Balikpapan

Banjermasin
Banjar
Neo·land

Southeast
Borneo
Federation

Makassar

East Indonesia
State (NIT)
(24 Dec.1946)

Jakarta Middle
Java

Bandung

Pasundan
State
(25 Feb.1948)

Semarang

Surabaya

Madura State
(20 Feb.1948)

Jogjakarta·

Republic

East
Java
State
(27 Nov.1948)

JAVA IN 1948-49

PROVINCE OR RESIDENCY
CAPITALS   ■

OTHER TOWNS   •

MAIN ROADS

MOUNTAINOUS AREAS   ﹀﹀﹀

AREA OF NOMINAL DUTCH CONTROL (Renville Line)   ••••••

AREA PRINCIPALLY AFFECTED BY MADIUN REVOLT   ‒ ‒ ‒

AREA PRINCIPALLY AFFECTED BY DARUL ISLAM
AND RELATED MOVEMENTS, 1949-50   ·······

BANTEN
Serang
Jakarta
Bogor
Sukabumi
Bandung
Garut
Cirebon
Linggajati
Tasikmalaya
SLAMET
Tegal
Pekalongan
Purwokerto
Banjumas
Kebumen
Wonogiri
Magelang
Semarang
Purwodadi
Pati
Blora
Cepu
Bojonegoro
MERBABU
MERAPI
Delanggu
Jogjakarta
Klaten
Surakarta
Magetan
LAWU
Sukoharjo
Wonogiri
Madiun
Nganjuk
Pacitan
GUNUNG KIDUL MTS
WILIS
Kediri
Blitar
BROMO
Malang
Bondowoso
MADURA
Surabaya

A REVIEW OF LITERATURE ON THE REVOLUTION

Published documentary sources
Relatively little such material has appeared from the Republican side. *Naskah-Persiapan Undang-undang Dasar 1945*, ed. Muhammad Yamin (Jakarta, Siguntang, 1959), Vol. I, gives the texts of the 1945 Constitution and the 'Jakarta Charter', as well as the constitutional debates over these documents from May to July 1945, and on 18–19 August 1945. The major laws passed by the Republican Government are collected in a series edited by Koesnodiprodjo, *Himpunan undang2, peraturan2, penetapan2, pemerintah Republik Indonesia*, with one volume for each of the years 1945–9 (reprinted Jakarta, S. K. Seno, 1951).

A generous selection of official Netherlands documents on the period is now being edited by S.L. van der Wal under the general title *Officiële Bescheiden Betreffende de Nederlands-Indonesische Betrekkingen 1945–1950*. The first two volumes, covering the period 10 August–31 December 1945, have appeared ('s-Gravenhage, Martinus Nijhoff, 1971–2). Another rich source for 1945 is the proceedings of a government commission: *Enqueetecommissie Regeringsbeleid 1940–1945. Verslag houdende de uitkomsten van het onderzoek*. Deel 8, A & B, *Militair Beleid 1940–1945. Terugkeer naar Nederlandsch-Indië* ('s-Gravenhage, Staatsdrukkerij- en Uitgeverijbedrijf, 1956). A parliamentary enquiry into Dutch military excesses is reported in *Nota betreffende het Archiefonderzoek naar gegevens omtrent excessen in Indonesie begaan door Nederlandse Militairen in de periode 1945–1950* (Document 10.008 of 1968–9 session of the Tweede Kamer der Staten-Generaal). The development of Dutch policies in 1946–7 is most fully revealed in a semi-official diary:

175

Het Dagboek van Schermerhorn. Geheim verslag van prof. dr. ir. W. Schermerhorn als voorzitter der commissie-generaal voor Nederlands-Indië, 20 september 1946–7 oktober 1947, ed. C. Smit (Groningen, Wolters-Noordhoff, 1970).

Among the many documents of the United Nations Security Council concerning Indonesia in the period 1946–9, the most informative about internal affairs are the 14 October 1947 report of the Consular Commission at Batavia, and the 4 August 1949 report of the United Nations Commission for Indonesia, appearing in the *Official Records* as Special Supplement no. 4 of 1947, and no. 5 of 1949, respectively.

H. J. Benda, J. K. Irikura, and K. Kishi (eds), *Japanese Military Administration in Indonesia: Selected Documents* (New Haven, Yale University Southeast Asia Studies, 1965) is indispensable for the Japanese period.

Indonesian Accounts
The importance of the revolution as a symbol of Indonesian identity and freedom has made it a difficult, perhaps increasingly difficult, subject for Indonesians to write about with candour. To the best of my knowledge only two serious attempts have been made to describe the revolutionary process as a whole, including its internal dynamics. Muhammad Dimyati, *Sedjarah Perdjuangan Indonesia* (Jakarta, Widjaya, 1951) is the earliest and best such account, dealing frankly with internal developments at the national level from a viewpoint sympathetic to Tan Malaka. The second volume of Iwa Kusuma Sumantri, *Sedjarah Revolusi Indonesia* (Jakarta, Grafica, n.d. [1965?]), is a partial account by one of the leading 3 July detainees, but it does give some attention to the 'social revolutions' and to events outside Java. Two slighter general accounts, Susanto Tirtoprodjo, *Sedjarah Revolusi Nasional Indonesia* (Jakarta, Pembangunan, 1962), and Samawi, *25 Tahun Merdeka* (Jogjakarta, Kedaulatan Rakjat, 1970), stress the international aspect.

The symbolic importance of the independence proclamation and the controversy surrounding it have provided the events of August–September 1945 with an exceptional wealth of accounts from different viewpoints. The pemuda view is given in Adam Malik [pro-Tan Malaka], *Riwajat dan Perdjuangan sekitar Proklamasi Kemerdekaan Indonesia 17 Agustus 1945* (Jakarta, Widjaya, 1950, revised ed. 1970); Oemar Bahsan, *PETA dan Peristiwa Rengasdengklok* (Bandung, 'Melati Bandung', 1955); Sidik Kertapati [PKI], *Sekitar Proklamasi 17 Agustus 1945* (Jakarta, Pembaruan, 1961); and Soebekti, *Sketsa Revolusi Indonesia 1940–1945* (Surabaya, Grip, 1966). The older leadership replied in Mohammad Hatta, 'Legende dan Realitet sekitar Proklamasi 17 Agustus', first published 1951, reprinted in *Kumpulan Karangan* IV (Jakarta, 1954), pp. 279–86 and in Raliby, pp. 655–9; Mohammad Hatta, *Sekitar Proklamasi 17 Agustus 1945* (Jakarta, Tintamas, 1970); Ahmad Subardjo, 'An Inside Story', in *Jakarta Times* 1 July–18 August, 1970.

Among the most important personal memoires embracing the revolutionary period are: Tan Malaka, *Dari Pendjara ke Pendjara* Vol. III (Jakarta, Widjaya, n.d.)—a very rare work; Soetan Sjahrir, *Out of Exile* (New York, John Day, 1949)—for the period to December 1945; *Sukarno, An Autobiography, as told to Cindy Adams* (Hong Kong, Gunung Agung, 1966); Abu Hanifah, *Tales of a Revolution,* ed. C. L. M. Penders (Sydney, Angus & Robertson, 1972); HAMKA [H.A.M.K. Amrullah—Sumatran Muhammadiah leader], *Kenang-Kenangan Hidup* (2nd ed. Kuala Lumpur, 1966); Margono Djojohadikusumo [director of Republican central bank], *Herinneringen uit 3 Tijdperken* (Jakarta, Indira, 1969); Sewaka [high official in West Java], *Tjorat-Tjaret dari djamen ke djaman* (n.p., n.d. [1955]).

The most detailed description of events in each province is provided by the Kementerian Penerangan (Ministry of Information) series of 1952–5, with one large volume for each of the then twelve provinces of Indonesia. The volumes are not numbered, and identified only by the title *Republik Indonesia* followed by the name of the province. The three volumes on Sumatra are particularly useful, while the volumes on Jogjakarta and Sulawesi cover national-level events from the respective capitals of the Republic and the NIT.

Of the various histories of particular institutions and parties during the revolution, the most useful are those of the army. A. H. Nasution, *Tentara Nasional Indonesia* Vol. I (Jakarta, Pustaka Militer, 1956), Vol. II (Jakarta, Seruling Masa, 1968). A. H. Nasution, *Fundamentals of Guerrilla Warfare* (Singapore, Donald Moore, 1965). Staf Angkatan Bersendjata, *Sedjarah Singkat Perdjuangan Bersendjata Bangsa Indonesia* (Jakarta, 1964). T. B. Simatupang, *Laporan Dari Banaran. Kisah pengalaman seorang pradjurit selama perang kemerdekaan* (Jakarta, Pembangunan, 1960), translated by Benedict Anderson and Elizabeth Graves as *Report from Banaran: Experiences During the Peoples' War* (Ithaca, Cornell Modern Indonesia Project, 1972), deals with events after the second Dutch action; and the same author's more general *Pelopor dalam Perang, Pelopor dalam Damai* (Jakarta, Pustaka Militer, 1954). Hassan Basry, *Kisah Gerila Kalimantan* (Banjermasin, Lambung Mangkurat, 1961)— concerning resistance in Borneo in 1945–6. Official histories of the three Army Divisions of Java have recently appeared: Kodam VI, *Siliwangi Dari Masa ke Masa* (Jakarta, Fakta Mahjuma, n.d. [1968]); Kodam VII Diponegoro, *Sirnaning Jakso Katon Gapuraning Ratu* (2 vols, Semarang, Semdam VII, 1970–71); Kodam VIII

Brawidjaja, *Sam Karya Bhirawa Anoraga* (Malang, Semdam VIII, 1968).

Useful material on particular aspects of the revolution can be found in Pinardi, *Peristiwa Coup Berdarah P.K.I. September 1948 di Madium* (Jakarta, Inkopak-Hazera, 1967); Djamal Marsudi, *Menjingkap Pemberontakan PKI dalam Peristiwa Madiun* (Jakarta, Merdeka Press, 1966); D. N. Aidit, *Aidit Accuses. Madiun Affair* (Jakarta, Pembaruan, 1955), and *Lahirnja PKI dan Perkembangannja (1920–1955)* (Jakarta, Pembaruan, 1955)—both included in Aidit's *Pilihan Tulisan* Vol. I (Peking, 1965); Hardjito, *Risalah Gerakan Pemuda* (Jakarta, Pustaka Antara, 1952); Tjantrik Mataram, *Peranan Ramalan Djojobojo dalam Revolusi Kita* (Bandung, 'Masa Baru', n.d.); and a Hatta *festschrift*, *Bung Hatta, mengabdi pada tjita-tjita perdjuangan bangsa* (Jakarta, 1972).

Much of the most convincing Indonesian writing about the revolution comes from the novels and short stories of the early 1950s. Particularly evocative of the conflicts brought to Indonesian families and villages by the revolution are the writings of Pramoedya Ananta Toer: *Keluarga Gerilja* (Jakarta, Pembangunan, 1950—Malaysian edition Kuala Lumpur, 1970); *Ditepi Kali Bekasi* (Jakarta, Balai Pustaka, 1957); and *Tjerita Dari Blora* (Jakarta, Balai Pustaka, 1952). The compassionate novel of Mochtar Lubis, *Djalan Tak Ada Udjung* (Jakarta, Balai Pustaka, 1952) has been translated by A. H. Johns as *A Road with no End* (London, Hutchinson, 1968). A graphic and bitter impression of the Surabaya fighting is Idrus' short story 'Surabaja', which has been translated by S. U. Nababan and Benedict Anderson in *Indonesia* 5 (April 1968), pp. 1–28.

Although professional historians are unrepresented in the above publications, an encouraging beginning at a scholarly approach to the revolution has been made by the history departments of the University of Indonesia and Gajah Mada University since 1967. Of the several unpublished MA theses on the subject the best is by the late Soe Hok Gie: 'Simpang Kiri dari Sebuah Djalan (Kisah Pemberontakan Madiun September 1948)' (UI, Jakarta, 1969). Also of interest are Ariwiadi, 'Perdjuangan Rakjat Daerah Bogor Selama Perang Kemerdekaan II (1948–1949)' (UI, Jakarta, 1969); Marsudi, 'Tentera Peladjar di Djawa-Tengah (Dalam Sedjarah Revolusi Indonesia, 1945–1951)' (UGM, Jogjakarta, 1970); J. Jahmin, 'Kekuatan Sosial Kiri dan Persetudjuan Renville' (UGM, Jogjakarta, 1971). The military historian Nugroho Notosusanto is the principal Indonesian scholar concerned with this period, though his publications have related mainly to the PETA in the Japanese period.

Foreign Writing

i The landmarks:

Four major foreign interpretations of the Indonesian revolution deserve broader discussion: G. McT. Kahin, *Nationalism and Revolution in Indonesia* (Ithaca, Cornell, 1952); J. H. Alers, *Om een rode of groene merdeka: 10 jaren binnenlandse politiek Indonesia, 1943–1953* (Eindhoven, Vulkaan, 1956); John R. W. Smail, *Bandung in the Early Revolution 1945–1946. A Study in the Social History of the Indonesian Revolution* (Ithaca, Cornell Southeast Asia Program Monograph, 1964); and Benedict R. O'G. Anderson, *Java in a Time of Revolution, Occupation and Resistance, 1944–1946* (Ithaca, Cornell, 1972).

Kahin was able to build upon an American tradition of sympathetic study of Indonesian nationalism, established by the US Vice-Consul in Batavia, Charles Wolf (*The Indonesian Story,* New York, 1948). He was, nevertheless, the first scholar to attempt a detailed study of Indonesian politics, on the basis of field work within both Republican and Federal territory in 1948–9. The momentous contribution of his *Nationalism and Revolution* is attested by the fact that it remains after twenty years the standard work on the subject. Without the benefit of any of the corpus of monographs which has since grown around the subject, Kahin was able to provide a picture which in scope, in detail, and in balance remains unrivalled.

He broke sharply with the Dutch scholarly tradition which had tended to stress the sociological exoticism of Indonesia. He tended to see the problem from the new perspective of the nationalist intellectuals themselves. Colonialism was an artificial constraint on the modernization or democratization of Indonesia, towards which the revolution was irresistibly heading. This perspective involved some sharing of the optimism of the nationalist leaders about their capacity to lead the new nation into modern democratic paths, and hence to play down the long-term significance of some of the challenges to the leadership which the revolution threw up. Only for the early years of the revolution, for which most of Kahin's sources appear to have been second-hand, does this tendency involve serious distortion. Such phenomena as communism, traditionalism, the military in politics, the 'social revolutions' and the appeal of Tan Malaka in this period are treated as dark peripheral challenges to the main theme of the revolution, rather than as part of its essence.

Subsequent challenges to Kahin's view have all given more attention to these phenomena, particularly as subsequent Indonesian developments demonstrated their relevance, while the work even of American sociologists devoted more attention to Indonesian cultural traditions. The first serious° attempt to revise Kahin's view of Indonesian internal history was, not surprisingly, by a Dutchman, Alers. Although without much personal experience in Indonesia, Alers was the first Dutch writer sufficiently detached from the heat of battle to try to see the events as revolution rather than as international conflict. Conscious of the cultural diversity of Indonesia as well as of the historical dynamic of revolutions in general, he attempted to explain how the authority of Sukarno-Hatta had been able to survive four strong and continuing challenges to its view of independence. Two of these challenges he described as 'red' (acquiring authority from below): Tan Malaka, and the FDR/Musso. The others were 'green' (authority from above): the Dutch 'counter-revolution' with its predominantly aristocratic supporters, and the more impatient Muslims. Alers is also the only serious writer on the revolution to have done partial justice to the area outside Java. His work is marred however by some carelessness with facts.

More limited and more profound was Smail's study of Bandung. He deliberately selected a region and period when the direct influence of both Dutch and Republican governments was limited, in order to be able to concentrate on the social changes which the revolution brought about within Indonesian society. His work remains the only adequate local study of the revolution. It relies heavily on oral information to ascertain the real power relationships existing during the turbulent early months. Thereby Smail brilliantly focused attention on the enormous spontaneous upheaval which followed the collapse of Japanese authority. His book is not yet social history in the sense of being able to define social and economic categories with any precision, or to describe the changing relationships between them. It may, however, long remain the closest that historians are able to get to it.

Benedict Anderson's *Java in a Time of Revolution, Occupation, and Resistance 1944–1946* is a more direct antithesis of Kahin. Anderson, like Kahin, is concerned with the centre-stage of Jakarta and Jogjakarta, but he concentrates on the period treated least adequately by Kahin, and uses meticulously the newspaper and pamphlet sources which Kahin appears to have ignored for that period. Whereas Kahin appeared to rely heavily on pro-Sjahrir informants for the internal conflicts of 1945–6, Anderson makes an eloquent case for the position of Tan Malaka. Above all, however, Anderson's book has emphatically lost the optimism of Kahin's. Focusing on some of the figures and forces which lost out in the internal power struggles, Anderson emphasizes what the revolution failed to become as much as what it became.

ii   Other important studies

In the following categories the first entries have been arranged in approximate order of importance for an understanding of the revolution. Theses for American universities have been included in this section even though written by Indonesians. I have indicated the author's partisanship only in cases where the purpose is obviously propagandist rather than scholarly.

The Japanese Occupation

Anderson, Benedict R. O'G. 'Japan: "The Light of Asia"' in *Southeast Asia in World War Two: Four Essays*, ed. Josef Silverstein, New Haven, Yale University Southeast Asia Studies, 1966.

Benda, Harry J. *The Crescent and the Rising Sun. Indonesian Islam under the Japanese Occupation, 1942-1945*. The Hague/Bandung, Van Hoeve, 1958.

Kanahele, George S. 'The Japanese Occupation of Indonesia: Prelude to Independence', Unpublished Ph.D. thesis, Cornell University, 1967.

Piekaar, A. J. *Atjeh en de Oorlog met Japan*. The Hague/Bandung, Van Hoeve, 1949.

Nishijima, S., Kishi K., et. al. *Japanese Military Administration in Indonesia*, trans. Joint Publications Research Service, Washington, US Dept of Commerce, 1963.

Anderson, Benedict R. O'G. *Some Aspects of Indonesian Politics under the Japanese Occupation, 1944-1945*, Ithaca, Cornell Modern Indonesia Project, 1961.

Aziz, Muhammad Abdul, *Japan's Colonialism and Indonesia*, The Hague Martinus Nijhoff, 1955.

Nakamura, Mitsuo, 'General Imamura and the Early Period of the Japanese Occupation', *Indonesia* 10, 1970.

Allied Military Activities

Helfrich, Conrad E. L. [Netherlands supreme commander in the East] *Memoires*, Amsterdam, Elsevier, 1950, 2 vols.

Wehl, David *The Birth of Indonesia*, London, Allen & Unwin, 1948.

Donnison, F. S. V. *British Military Administration in the Far East, 1943-46*, History of the Second World War, London, HMSO, 1956.

Long, Gavin *The Final Campaigns: Australia in the War of 1939-1945*, Canberra, Australian War Memorial, 1963.

Doulton, A. J. F. *The Fighting Cock: Being the History of the Twenty-third Indian Division, 1942-1947*, Aldershot, Gale and Polden, 1951.

Singh, Rajendra *Post-War Occupation Forces: Japan and South-East Asia*, Official History of the Indian Armed Forces in the Second World War, Kanpur, Combined Inter-Services Historical Section, 1958.

Diplomatic Developments

Taylor, A. M. *Indonesian Independence and the United Nations*, London, Stevens & Sons, 1960.

Smit, C. *De Liquidatie van een Imperium: Nederland en Indonesië 1945-1962*, Amsterdam, De Arbeiderspers, 1962.

Smit, C. *De Indonesische quaestie. De wordingsgeschiedenis der sovereiniteits-overdracht*, Leiden, Brill, 1952.

Djajadinigrat, I. N. *The Beginnings of the Indonesian-Dutch Negotiations and the Hoge Veluwe Talks*, Ithaca, Cornell Modern Indonesia Project, 1958.

Alberts, A. *Het einde van een verhouding: Indonesië en Nederland tussen 1945 en 1963*, Alphen aan de Rijn, Samsom, 1968.
Palmier, Leslie H. *Indonesia and the Dutch*, London, Oxford University Press, 1962.
Wolf, Charles *The Indonesian Story: The Birth, Growth and Structure of the Indonesian Republic*, New York, John Day, 1948.
De Kadt, J. [Dutch Social Democrat] *De Indonesische Tragedie. Het Treurspel der Gemiste Kansen*, Amsterdam, Van Oorschot, 1949.
Van Mook, H. J. *The Stakes of Democracy in South-East Asia*, London, Allen & Unwin, 1950.
Gerbrandy, P. S. [Dutch Right] *Indonesia*, London, Hutchinson, 1950.

Political and Theoretical
Feith, Herbert *The Decline of Constitutional Democracy in Indonesia*, Ithaca, Cornell University Press, 1962.
Overdijkink, G. W. [Dutch semi-official] *Het Indonesische Probleem. De Feiten*, The Hague, Martinus Nijhoff, 1946.
Overdijkink, G. W. *Het Indonesische Probleem. Nieuwe Feiten*, Amsterdam, Keizerskroon, 1948.
McVey, Ruth T. (ed.) *Indonesia*, New Haven, Human Relations Area Files, 1963.
Wulfften Palthe, P. M. van *Psychological Aspects of the Indonesian Problem*, Leiden, E. J. Brill, 1949.
Dahm, Bernhard *History of Indonesia in the Twentieth Century*, trans. P. S. Falla, London, Pall Mall Press, 1971.
Van Der Kroef, J. M. *Indonesian Social Evolution. Some Psychological Considerations*, Amsterdam, Van der Peet, 1958.

Economic and Social
Sutter, John O. *Indonesianisasi. Politics in a Changing Economy, 1940-1955*, Ithaca, Cornell Southeast Asia Program, 1959. 4 volumes.
Jay, Robert R. *Religion and Politics in Rural Central Java*, New Haven, Yale University Southeast Asia Studies, 1963.
Selosoemardjan *Social Change in Jogjakarta*, Ithaca, Cornell University Press, 1962.
Wertheim, W. F. *Indonesian Society in Transition*, The Hague, Van Hoeve, 1964.

Communism
McVey, Ruth T. *The Soviet View of the Indonesian Revolution: A Study in the Russian Attitude towards Asian Nationalism*, Ithaca, Cornell Modern Indonesia Project, 1957.
McVey, Ruth T. *The Calcutta Conference and the Southeast Asian Uprisings*, Ithaca, Cornell Modern Indonesia Project, 1958.
Brackman, Arnold C. *Indonesian Communism. A History*, New York, Praeger, 1963.
Mintz, Jeanne S. *Mohammed, Marx and Marhaen, The Roots of Indonesian Socialism*, London, Pall Mall Press, 1965.
Lockwood, Rupert 'The Indonesian Exiles in Australia, 1942-47', *Indonesia* 10, 1970.

Islam and Christianity
Nieuwenhuijze, C. A. O. van *Aspects of Islam in Post-Colonial Indonesia. Five Essays*, The Hague, Van Hoeve, 1958.

Muskens, M. P. M. *Indonesië: Een strijd om nationale identiteit: nationalisten, islamieten, Katholieken*, Bussum, Paul Brand, 1969.
Boland, B. J. *The Struggle of Islam in Modern Indonesia*, Verhandelingen van het Koninklijk Instituut voor Taal-, Land-, en Volkenkunde, Vol. 59, The Hague, Martinus Nijhoff, 1971.

The Revolution Outside Java
(This continues to be a sadly neglected field.)
Schiller, A. A. *The Formation of Federal Indonesia*, The Hague, Van Hoeve, 1955.
Reid, Anthony 'The Birth of the Republic in Sumatra', *Indonesia* 12, 1971, pp. 21–46.
Nawawi, Mohammad A. 'Regionalism and Regional Conflicts in Indonesia'. Unpublished Ph.D. thesis, Princeton University, 1968.
Van Langenberg, Michael 'The establishment of the Republic of Indonesia in North Sumatra: Regional differences and political factionalism', *Review of Indonesian and Malayan Affairs* 6, no. 1 1972, pp. 1–44.
Goudoever, W. A. van *Malino maakt historie, Een overzichtelijke bewerking van notulen en tekstueele redevoeringen ter conferentie van Malino 15–25 juli 1946*, Batavia, Regeerings Voorlichtings Dienst, 1946 [Netherlands Indies official].
Goudoever, W. A. van *Denpasar bouwt een huis. Een overzichtilijke bewerking van notulen en tekstueele redevoeringen ter conferentie van Denpasar, 7–24 december 1947* [sic i.e. 1946]. Batavia, Regeerings Voorlichtings Dienst, [Netherlands Indies official].

Personal Memoirs
Coast, John *Recruit to Revolution: Adventure and Politics in Indonesia*, London, Christophers, 1952.
Westerling, Raymond Paul Pierre *Challenge to Terror*, London, William Kimber, 1952.
K'tut Tantri ['Surabaya Sue'] *Revolt in Paradise*, London, Heinemann, 1960.

ABBREVIATIONS

AMRI	Angkatan Muda Republik Indonesia (Young generation of the Republic of Indonesia)
API	Angkatan Pemuda Indonesia (Indonesian young generation)
BFO	Bijeenkomst voor Federale Overleg (Federal Consultative Assembly)
BKR	Badan Keamanan Rakyat (People's peace-keeping body)
BPKI	Badan penyelidik usaha-usaha Persiapan Kemerdekaan Indonesia (Body to investigate measures for the preparation of Indonesian independence)
BP-KNIP	Badan Pekerja KNIP (Working Committee of the KNIP)
BPRI	Barisan Pemberontakan Republik Indonesia (Insurgent Corps of the Republic of Indonesia)
BTI	Barisan Tani Indonesia (Indonesian Peasant Front)
BTN	Badan Tekstil Negara (State Textile Agency)
Dr	Doctor (academic title of the holder of a Dutch medical degree)
FDR	Front Demokrasi Rakyat (People's Democratic Front)
GERINDO	Gerakan Rakyat Indonesia (Indonesian People's Movement)
GRR	Gerakan Revolusi Rakyat (Movement of People's Revolution)
Ir	Ingenieur (academic title of the holder of a Dutch engineering degree)
KNI	Komite Nasional Indonesia (Indonesian National Committee)
KNIL	Koninklijk Nederlands Indisch Leger (Royal Netherlands Indies Army)
KNIP	Komite Nasional Indonesia Pusat (Central Indonesian National Committee)
KPM	Koninklijke Paketvaart Maatschappij (Royal Mail Company)
MASJUMI	Majlis Syuro Muslimin Indonesia (Consultative Council of Indonesian Muslims)
MIAI	Majlisul Islamil a'laa Indonesia (Great Islamic Council of Indonesia)
MIT	Majlis Islam Tinggi (High Islamic Council)
Mr	Meester (academic title of the holder of a Dutch law degree)
MULO	Meer Uitgebreid Lager Onderwijs (more extended lower education—i.e. an intermediate school)
NICA	Netherlands Indies Civil Administration

NIT	Negara Indonesia Timur (State of East Indonesia)
NST	Negara Sumatera Timur (State of East Sumatra)
PARAS	Partai Rakyat Sosialis (Socialist People's Party)
PARI	Partai Republik Indonesia (Party of the Indonesian Republic)
PARINDRA	Partai Indonesia Raya (Greater Indonesia Party)
PARTINDO	Partai Indonesia (Indonesia Party)
PESINDO	Pemuda Sosialis Indonesia (Indonesian Socialist Youth)
PETA	Pembela Tanah Air (Defenders of the Fatherland)
PKI	Partai Komunis Indonesia (Indonesian Communist Party)
PNI	Partai (initially Persatuan) Nasional Indonesia (Indonesian National Party)
PP	Persatuan Perjuangan (Struggle Union)
PPKI	Panitia Persiapan Kemerdekaan Indonesia (Committee for the Preparation of Indonesian Independence)
PRI	Pemuda Republik Indonesia (Youth of the Republic of Indonesia)
PS	Partai Sosialis (Socialist Party)
PSI	Partai Sosialis Indonesia (Indonesian Socialist Party)
PSII	Partai Sarekat Islam Indonesia (Indonesian Islamic Union Party)
PUSA	Persatuan Ulama-ulama Seluruh Aceh (All-Aceh Union of Islamic teachers)
PUTERA	Pusat Tenaga Rakyat (Centre of People's Strength)
RIS	Republik Indonesia Serikat (Federal Republic of Indonesia)
SARBUPRI	Sarekat Buruh Perkebunan Indonesia (Indonesian Estate Workers' Union)
SERINDO	Serikat Rakyat Indonesia (Union of the Indonesian People)
SOBSI	Sentral Organisasi Buruh Seluruh Indonesia (All-Indonesia Secretariat of Labour Organizations)
STII	Sarekat Tani Islam Indonesia (Indonesian Muslim Peasants' Union)
TKR	Tentara Keamanan Rakyat (People's peace-keeping Army), 5 October 1945—7 January 1946
	Tentara Keselamatan Rakyat (People's Security Army), 7–25 January 1946
TNI	Tentara Nasional Indonesia (Indonesian National Army), since 3 June 1947
TP	Tentara Pelajar (Student Army)
TRI	Tentara Republik Indonesia (Army of the Republic of Indonesia), 25 January 1946—3 June 1947
TRIP	Tentara Republic Indonesia Pelajar (Student Army of the Republic of Indonesia)
USI	United States of Indonesia

INDEX

Indonesians are listed after their last names. Following the names of prominent Indonesians are ethnic identity, birth, and death dates where known. Ethnic identity is abbreviated as follows: A—Acehnese, Am—Ambonese, B—Balinese, Bug—Buginese/Makassarese, C—Chinese, CB—Christian Batak, J—Javanese, Mad—Madurese, M—Malay, Men—Menadonese/Minahassan, Min—Minangkabau, MB—Muslim Batak, S—Sundanese.